TRIGGER POINTS

TRIGGER POINTS

INSIDE THE MISSION TO STOP
MASS SHOOTINGS IN AMERICA

MARK FOLLMAN

DEY ST.
An Imprint of WILLIAM MORROW

DEY ST.

HarperCollins books may be purchased for educational, business, or sales promotional use. For information, please email the Special Markets Department at SPsales@harpercollins.com.

FIRST EDITION

Designed by Angela Boutin

Library of Congress Cataloging-in-Publication Data

Names: Follman, Mark, author.
Title: Trigger points : inside the mission to stop mass
    shootings in America / Mark Follman
Description: First edition. | New York, NY : Dey St., an imprint
    of William Morrow, [2022] | Includes bibliographical references and
    index.
Identifiers: LCCN 2021055418 (print) | LCCN 2021055419 (ebook) |
    ISBN 9780062973535 (hardcover) | ISBN 9780062973573 (paperback) |
    ISBN 9780062973559 (ebook) | ISBN 9780063216181 | ISBN
    9780063216198
Subjects: LCSH: Mass shootings—United States—Prevention. |
    Criminal behavior, Prediction of—United States. | Violent crimes—
    United States—Prevention.
Classification: LCC HV6536.5 .F65 2022 (print) | LCC
    HV6536.5 (ebook) | DDC 364.152/340973—dc23/eng/20211227
LC record available at https://lccn.loc.gov/2021055418
LC ebook record available at https://lccn.loc.gov/2021055419

ISBN 978-0-06-297353-5

22 23 24 25 26 LSC 10 9 8 7 6 5 4 3 2 1

For Lisa, Charlie, and Eleanor
And for my parents, Joyce and Gary

CONTENTS

LIGHT IN THE DARK

Many people remember where they were when they first learned the news on December 14, 2012. I was on vacation and with family at City Museum, an adventure cornucopia for kids built inside a former shoe factory in my hometown of St. Louis. As my wife and I stood watching our nieces, ages four and six, scamper through tunnels and down slides, we also harbored the secret joy of having just learned that we would soon welcome our own first child into the world. My phone buzzed with news alerts and urgent messages. For the previous six months, my work as a journalist had been focused on investigating the recurring problem of mass shootings, but even that familiarity couldn't prepare me for the headline: GUNMAN KILLS 20 SCHOOLCHILDREN IN CONNECTICUT.

The attack at Sandy Hook Elementary School in Newtown, in which six adults also perished, felt like a catastrophic wound opening up in the world. If something like this could happen, nothing was sacred, nowhere safe. I absorbed the news for another moment and then looked around again for my nieces, who were now romping in a colorful ball pit full of other happy kids, most of them around the same age as those twenty first graders.

One incoming call was a request for me to join a rare live broadcast of National Public Radio's *All Things Considered*, to give some context from a mass-shootings database I'd been building in my work for *Mother Jones*. I was soon on the air with NPR's Robert Siegel, whose placid voice I'd known since I was just a kid myself, speaking to a mournful and outraged audience of millions. Though I'd summoned the resolve, it was hard that day to think about the unfolding event beyond how shattering it was for those Newtown families, a new depth to an endless problem quickly to be framed by the contentious national argument over gun control. Before long, however, I would start to learn of a very different way to look at the daunting phenomenon of mass shootings and what could be done to stop them.

First things first: Guns are not the focus of this book. But before going further, I'd like to respectfully offer a few brief words about them. Growing up in the Midwest, I loved the bold thrill and big responsibility of learning riflery and achieving marksmanship. As a professional journalist, I have reported extensively about the impact of gun violence on American society. Personally, I share the view held by a clear majority of Americans, as measured in public opinion polls over the past three decades, that the nation's gun regulations are inadequate and should be strengthened. Not all mass murderers use firearms, but the majority do—and more than three quarters of those killers acquire their guns legally. Extensive public health research and investigative journalism show that weak regulations correlate with a broad range of gun violence in the United States, from bullet-ridden city neighborhoods to accidental child deaths in suburban homes to suicides in rural towns. Those problems produce far more casualties than the indiscriminate school and workplace mass shootings that so dominate public attention. Study of disparate state laws has made clear that stricter gun regulations would help diminish an overall national toll of nearly 40,000 shooting deaths and 115,000 injuries annually.

Even so, the scope of the mass shootings problem is larger and more complex than its tool of destruction. With this book, my aim is to leave behind the battle over gun laws and instead tell the story of an additional solution to the affliction of mass shootings, one with powerful potential to reduce harm. Its focus is on the intricacy and possibilities of human behavior.

I first began to learn about the field of behavioral threat assessment in 2013, about a year after turning my attention to a spate of gun rampages and working with colleagues at *Mother Jones* to build a database we called "A Guide to Mass Shootings in America." After the July 2012 massacre at a movie theater in Aurora, Colorado, I'd been startled to find that virtually no data were available on this particular type of attack, whether from government agencies, academic researchers, policy groups, or news organizations. No one had put forth a comprehensive, detailed set of cases, let alone any in-depth analysis of the problem. The void was owed in no small part to a political chill dating from the mid-1990s, when the National Rifle Association and its allies in Congress orchestrated a de facto prohibition of federal funding for gun-violence research. An additional factor was likely the challenge of defining a "mass shooting," which, historically, was a matter of loose consensus among criminologists and FBI experts: an attack by a lone assailant in a public place, with an arbitrary baseline of four or more victims killed. Excluding attacks with conventional motives like robbery or gang violence, I worked with my team to assemble a first-of-its-kind online database detailing dozens of cases in the United States going back three decades. The frequency with which it required updating in the following months, and years, was sobering.

Beyond documenting the legal provenance of most mass shooters' guns, my initial analysis of cases revealed that more than half of the killers ended their attacks in suicide. I grew aware of another stark pattern. Details from news reports, court and police records, and my interviews with experts made clear that many of the perpetrators had acted in worrisome or disruptive ways prior to attacking, often for a long time. These had been potentially lifesaving warning signs, and yet the saturation of news coverage following mass shootings almost always told a different story, routinely quoting people who knew or had come in contact with the killers and expressed utter surprise in the aftermath: "I never imagined he'd do something like this" or "Nobody could have seen this coming." Evidence from dozens of cases suggested those perceptions were mistaken.

The theme of astonishment was further contradicted by a remarkable development: many attacks in the making were being stopped, according to the top law enforcement official in the United States. Ten months after Sandy Hook, in October 2013, Attorney General Eric Holder stated in a speech to the nation's police chiefs that the FBI had helped thwart more than one hundred "active shooters" since the beginning of that year. Now *that* was compelling news. I soon learned that a little-known threat assessment team within the FBI's elite Behavioral Analysis Unit had been ramping up outreach to state and local law enforcement agencies, public universities, and other institutions around the country to assist with threat cases at the request of local leaders.

Meanwhile, America's endless debate over guns bred apathy and surrender. Even as the nation was freshly grieving Sandy Hook, one widely cited criminologist published an article titled "Mass Shootings in America: Moving Beyond Newtown," in which he wrote: "Eliminating the risk of mass murder would involve extreme steps that we are unable or unwilling to take—abolishing the Second Amendment, achieving full employment, restoring our sense of community, and rounding up anyone who looks or acts at all suspicious. Mass murder just may be a price we must pay for living in a society where personal freedom is so highly valued."

I couldn't accept that way of thinking. Especially not as a father-to-be, who, like so many parents around the country, would soon have to contemplate school safety for his child. This was a complex problem that demanded an equivalent response, not complacency or glib pandering. Mass shootings had long been occurring far more frequently in the United States than any other place in the world that wasn't a war zone. But if this was inordinately an American problem, there also had to be the possibility of American ingenuity. Our society had eradicated diseases, dreamed up airplanes, put people on the moon, and invented the internet. Why couldn't we contend with this challenge?

Though mass shootings were on the rise, they remained a small fraction of America's overall gun violence, with the chances of being injured or killed in one infinitesimal. But from the early 2010s, they became everyone's problem due to their outsize psychological, financial, and cultural impact. It didn't matter where you lived or what your politics were; this was now the era with "active shooter" in the lexicon and schoolkids everywhere doing defensive drills just in case one came storming in. (Never mind that those drills could be harmful to children's well-being, fueling anxiety and depression.) In a range of public venues, particularly in the nation's schools, major resources have since been poured into physical fortifications, attack-response plans, and other "target hardening" measures. Those have included redesigning buildings, arming teachers and administrators, and installing additional locks, cameras, metal detectors, and security officers. Such measures were the focus after Sandy Hook in 2012, and again after the massacre in 2018 at Marjory Stoneman Douglas High School in Parkland, Florida.

"Unfortunately," wrote a group of leading researchers, "these responses are not likely to be effective in preventing planned attacks." The authors were threat assessment experts who reached that conclusion in a study published not long after another devastating gun rampage—the one at Columbine High School, back in 1999.

Nevertheless, in the two decades since then, school security had grown into a multibillion-dollar industry, with sales including everything from high-tech gunshot-detection systems installed in buildings to "bulletproof" ballistic-plated backpacks for kids and consultant-run training drills, whose participants were in some cases shot at with blanks or splattered with fake blood. Some schools went so far as to store miniature baseball bats or buckets of rocks in classrooms for fighting off a possible attacker. What wasn't available was any credible research showing that these kinds of measures had value beyond the salve of safety theatrics.

Disaster preparedness at a fundamental level makes sense, including for unpredictable, low-probability events. But there was something baffling about the picture of our societal response to mass shootings, especially if other ways existed to diminish the peril.

Between 2013 and 2020, I traveled to numerous cities and towns throughout the United States to look into details of mass shootings and learn about the work of professionals who investigated these attacks and prevented others. Every single case featured in this book involves a subject who showed a mix of warning behaviors—not fulfilling any checklist, as the public commonly expects per the notion of criminal profiling, but comprising a set of actions and conditions that revealed danger to threat-assessment experts. These warning behaviors fall into eight broad areas: entrenched grievances, patterns of aggression or violence, stalking behavior, threatening communications, emulation of previous attackers, personal deterioration, triggering events, and attack planning and preparation.

No single element from any of the eight areas forecasts violence; it is their variety and coalescence in each individual's unique case that threat assessors must evaluate and work with. Over time, I came to see how greater recognition of warning behaviors, both among trained professionals and everyday citizens, has vast potential for reducing mass shootings.

What if there existed a community-based model for intervening constructively with troubled people well before they armed themselves and went on a rampage? What if, instead of so much emphasis on shooter response, we put a lot more on shooter *prevention*?

The pages to come unfold the stories of various individuals who have focused on understanding the darker dimensions of human experience and who subscribe to a hard-won belief that good can, and frequently does, win the day. They include innovative mental health specialists, elite FBI agents, psychologists who became cops, an artist turned school security leader, and ordinary people who were harmed by mass shooters' bullets and responded with extraordinary courage. Collectively, their work debunks myths about mass shooters as inscrutable monsters and reveals a strategy whose twin goal is heading off violence while getting help to people in serious need of it. It is a story of constructive resolve against an excruciating problem, the hard work of community, and above all, hope.

A NOTE ON SOURCES

Trigger Points is based on reporting and research spanning eight years, including interviews I conducted with more than 150 mental health experts, law enforcement professionals, education leaders, security specialists, and survivors of mass shootings. It is also built on my examination of hundreds of pages of confidential case files from several different threat assessment programs and my firsthand observations of a leading threat assessment team working cases over the course of a year. The book further draws upon a broad range of scientific research, government reports, archival documents, and other public and private materials related to mass attacks and other violence.

In some accounts of threat cases and investigations, I have omitted or altered names and certain other details to protect the identities of the case subjects and some practitioners who agreed to share sensitive private information. I approached this anonymization with the utmost care and deliberation, relying in part on my numerous conversations with experts directly involved in these cases and other leaders in the field. The goal was to maintain the integrity of the narratives and how they illustrate the threat assessment process while safeguarding the privacy and legal rights of the subjects involved. Every specific detail I use in these narratives that is not publicly available is drawn directly from case files and my interviews with threat assessment professionals. Where possible, I have expanded on sourcing or case material of interest in the endnotes.

Throughout the book, I focus to a varying degree on the killers. This is integral to understanding the problem of mass shootings and reflects how the field of behavioral threat assessment itself operates and develops research, including its use of reporting from journalists. However, such focus requires a careful balancing act, weighing the benefits of reporting in the public interest with the importance of avoiding sensationalism and excessive attention on these perpetrators, many of whom seek notoriety through their actions. I include their names and focus on their lives only to the extent that doing so serves to illuminate the prevention of future violence.

PART I

chapter one

IT'S A SMALL WORLD

On a sun-soaked afternoon in August 2015, the Downtown Disney district in Anaheim, California, bustled with families crowding storybook shops and cafés, the promise of funnel cakes sweet on the air. A short walk beyond the main plaza led to the central courtyard of the Disneyland Hotel resort, with its tiki bar and swimming pools ensconced in tropical foliage. Weary parents lounged with cocktails in hand as kids flung themselves down pool waterslides and others frolicked to pop tunes from a DJ. Summer vacation season was peaking just as it should in the Happiest Place on Earth.

Once the late afternoon sun descended and families departed for dinner, the deepening quiet revealed a faint jingle of classic theme music from speakers tucked into the courtyard scenery: *It's a world of laughter, a world of tears, it's a world of hopes and a world of fears* . . . Behind the scenes, a very different kind of activity was also beginning.

By dark, hundreds of forensic psychologists, plainclothes cops, FBI agents, and other mental health and security experts traveling from around the country would finish arriving on the hotel grounds. They were about to spend the next four days sequestered in the conference center's chilly, windowless ballrooms, training and trading tips on how to head off psychopaths, rapists, and mass murderers. While families meandered through Downtown Disney enjoying ice cream cones and played in the nearby theme parks, these specialists would be treated to sessions such as "20 Years of Workplace Shootings," "Homicidal Cyberstalking," and "Evil Thoughts, Wicked Deeds."

The gathering here was no accident. Disney had played host to the annual summit of the Association of Threat Assessment Professionals ever since the group's establishment in the early 1990s, owing in part to ATAP's roots in the Los Angeles Police Department. More than two decades later, professional interest in the emerging field of behavioral threat assessment was rising alongside an ever-expanding list of places marred by gun rampages: Aurora, Newtown, the Washington Navy Yard, Fort Hood, Isla Vista, Charleston. As mass shootings in the United States increased both in frequency and lethality during the 2010s—soon further to include Roseburg, San Bernardino, Orlando, the Las Vegas Strip, and Parkland—the blast and quick fade of the national gun debate became ritual. But beyond all the "thoughts and prayers" and polarizing vitriol, something else was happening across the country, albeit mostly out of view: threat assessment teams were cropping up. These collaborative groups were based in suburban school districts, university police departments, corporate headquarters, and theme parks, meeting regularly to evaluate and manage cases of concerning behavior. In 2008, Virginia had become the first state to require threat assessment teams at its public colleges and universi-

ties, a policy that began to trail high-profile gun massacres throughout the US, with Illinois, Connecticut, and other states soon to
follow. The experts trained in this vaguely ominous-sounding work
were striving to thwart America's next rampage killers, handling eye-
opening cases that were unknown to the public simply due to the
fact that disasters had been averted.

The twelve hundred or so members of ATAP, a small but flag-
ship organization for the field, convened each year in Disneyland
to focus on the developing science, and also the art, of preventing
violent tragedies. There was perhaps no more prolific research expert among them than Reid Meloy, a forensic psychologist based at
the University of California–San Diego, who, sporting a charcoal
suit, bright tie, and his signature white hair and goatee, gave the
keynote address that first morning. Any lingering air of family fun
from beyond the walls of the low-lit main ballroom dissipated with
an image on the big screen showing a 430,000-year-old skull exca-
vated in northern Spain. Researchers had recently concluded that
the two gaping cracks in the skull's forehead region resulted from
"interpersonal" blunt-force trauma, the earliest known anatomical
evidence of a homicide.

"Our recognition of patterns is an evolved skill that helps us sur-
vive threats," commented Meloy, a longtime consultant on threat
cases for the FBI. His presentation cruised between primal human
history and modern Hollywood as he peppered the forensics with
some gallows humor on psychopaths. A few short video clips illustrated the point that these dangerous specimens came in various
kinds: There was Kathy Bates's chillingly polite, sledgehammer-
wielding kidnapper in *Misery*, and then Bryan Cranston's cancer-
surviving, homicidal meth maker from *Breaking Bad*. With further
discussion of the evolutionary traits of such killers came images of
Anthony Hopkins's FBI nemesis from *The Silence of the Lambs* and

a wild-eyed Jack Nicholson "playing himself" in *The Shining*. "I've been getting mileage out of that line for thirty years," said Meloy, grinning amid the burst of chuckles.

Reviewing some underlying science for the newer practitioners in the crowd, Meloy displayed an image of a pet kitten recoiling with a hiss, its eyes aflame and teeth bared. This was what the imminent threat of reactive violence looked like—defensive, exploding from instinctive fear and rage. Mass shootings, however, were not impulsive crimes, he explained. Case evidence had long shown that virtually every attack was planned, thought out over a period of days, weeks, or months. The more apt image, Meloy suggested, was the subsequent one showing a mountain lion on the hunt, its body lowered and taut. This was the imminent threat of predatory violence—offensive, calculating, and targeted. The animal's stare didn't burn with danger; it was focused and icy blank. Research dating from the 1940s showed that violence in mammals, humans included, evolved with two distinctive modes of aggression, each important to survival and activating differently in the brain. But the pair of cats depicted more than that behavioral contrast. They showed the potential for stopping a predatory attack. Watchfulness, preparation, the stretch of time before the pounce—these were the terrain of prevention work.

The field of behavioral threat assessment was conceived in the 1980s and forged in the crucible of America's rising gun massacres, yet the work had long remained an obscure professional niche, virtually unknown to the general public. Its leaders could seem aloof, with their clinical jargon and elusive professional koans, like "The map is not the territory" and "Follow the rules, but think outside the box." The field's growing body of case research made clear how little the public understood about the behaviors and conditions that led to mass shootings, the rise of which had defied a steady decline in America's overall murder rate since the early 1990s. "Personally and professionally that trend is a big concern, especially as violent crime has decreased," Meloy later told me, further describing the ideal of the mission. "With a lot of these cases, you peel back the curtain and there are good social and mental health interventions that are diverting the person onto a better course."

Threat assessment cases are closely held for a variety of legal, ethical, and strategic reasons, and between the confidentiality of mental health treatment and the tight-lipped culture of law enforcement, it was easy to see why the field remained inaccessible. Until now, a journalist like me had never been allowed inside the training summit. On the first morning, I was met by an emissary, Russell Palarea, ATAP's sergeant-at-arms and soon-to-be president. A genial forensic psychologist in his mid-forties with a close-shaved head, Palarea was known among colleagues for his indefatigable pace, working cases and traveling nonstop to conduct trainings and help build threat assessment programs. He was optimistic but also notably frank when we talked in between sessions. "We'll never be able to stop every attack," he said, referring to his work with private companies and the federal government. "But we can stop a lot of them, and we have."

His claim sounded inspiring, but what evidence was there to support it? Details of two cases soon shared with me confidentially by sources elsewhere began to reveal how threat assessment teams had intervened at stages of heightened concern and helped people who appeared headed for terrible acts. There was a sixteen-year-old student in suburban Wisconsin who commented indirectly but repeatedly about the possibility of a shooting at his high school. School leaders soon learned that he carried around a notebook containing a list of "top enemies" he wanted to "eliminate." He'd been bragging to a friend about plans to steal a handgun from his uncle's truck, telling the friend to make sure to be around for an upcoming school assembly because "something big" was going to go down. Another case involved a twenty-nine-year-old military veteran in Arizona who had recently lost his job and girlfriend. He posted a picture of himself on Facebook posing at a gun range along with the comment: "I'm not putting up with any of the bullshit anymore." In another post, he indicated he planned to show up at his former place of employment, where his ex-girlfriend still worked. "Wait till they see these beauties," he commented, displaying two recently purchased handguns.

Investigations into each individual revealed prior incidents and volatile behavior that, taken together with the above circumstances, spelled serious danger in the view of threat assessment professionals working the cases. Yet, how these two cases were handled as their subjects spiraled into deeper states of agitation looked at first to be counterintuitive—there was no rush to expel the student, or to take legal action against the military veteran, who had since been involved in a drunken bar scuffle and could have been arrested and charged. In the Wisconsin student's case, school officials worked closely with the local police department, also consulting behind the scenes with a threat assessment liaison in a FBI field office, to put together an intervention and management plan. In Arizona, the veteran was approached by law enforcement members of a threat assessment team, who made clear that they had eyes on him but emphasized their interest in steering him toward help. In each case, periods of mutually agreed upon mental health counseling, along with support for accessing educational and work opportunities, led to more stable circumstances for both individuals. While some quiet monitoring of the student continued, neither of the cases remained an active concern by the time I learned about them.

Nonetheless, there existed fundamental reasons to be wary of behavioral threat assessment as a prevention method, including the risk to civil liberties. Reckless comments from kids are a given, typical youth behavior only compounded by the disinhibiting effects of social media. Countless adults have coping problems or anger-management issues but don't act criminally or plan violent attacks. Was this field and its close monitoring of individuals not a slippery slope to Orwellian thought-policing or the "precrime" dystopia imagined in Steven Spielberg's 2002 film *Minority Report*? Even presuming a thorough, lawful process in the hands of seasoned experts, was it fair to turn an investigative spotlight on someone over a few dark comments or an online display of armed bravado? And with threats communicated ever more frequently via digital platforms, wouldn't there be temptation to use data mining or other broad surveillance tactics, with vanishing regard for personal privacy?

These were important questions with complex answers, and yet I couldn't stop thinking about a different equation that haunts the American public whenever mass shooters' troubling backstories surface in media reports. If we could have done more to detect and resolve the danger before it was too late, wouldn't we have done it? The affirmative answer to that question hinges on proving a negative: in threat assessment cases, the absence of a violent outcome is evidence of success. But how could you really know you prevented an attack if one didn't occur?

Meloy favored an analogy to fighting heart disease. Cardiologists, he suggested, couldn't determine how many of their patients never had heart attacks because of the care and treatment they provided. But they could do a lot to mitigate risk: "You try to lower the probability."

Meloy, Palarea, and other threat assessment leaders acknowledged that it was far easier after the fact to see why certain behaviors or circumstances were telltale. But with the expanding capabilities of the field came a compelling possibility: so many tragedies—at schools, office buildings, movie theaters, festivals—never should have happened. And the next ones could be stopped.

———

The work of threat assessment professionals is a process of identifying, evaluating, and intervening. Many in the field use the term threat assessment to refer to the entire process, though the intervention phase is also widely known as threat management and involves longer-term monitoring and care for people who act in ways indicating danger.

Cases often begin with an ordinary person having a gut feeling that something is off. That pang of worry or fear, itself a sensation connected to evolved survival instincts, can prompt the person to seek help. A teacher notices something disturbing about a student's comments or notebook marginalia, for example, and alerts a principal. Or an office worker gets freaked out by a colleague's odd or vaguely menacing behavior and tells a supervisor. Or a family member or friend senses an unsettling change in a teen, perhaps accompanied by a conspicuous interest in weapons, and reaches out for assistance. Behavior that provokes instinctive discomfort in bystanders along these lines often hints at a broader mix of warning signs, which could range from aggrieved or threatening communications to an aberrant focus on graphic violence or signs of suicidality.

When a case comes to the attention of a threat assessment team, the group moves quickly to gauge whether there is any immediate risk of violence. They will talk with family, friends, teachers, or coworkers to gather context and gain insight into the alleged or observed behavior. They will also talk directly with the case subject and investigate any relevant lawfully available records. The imperative is to determine whether the person has the intent, the means, and possibly a plan to kill.

Forensic psychologist Mario Scalora, a longtime trainer for ATAP members in Disneyland, recounted a case from the threat assessment program he oversees at the University of Nebraska–Lincoln. His campus team grew alarmed after receiving a tip about a twenty-something graduate student named Bob who reportedly was muttering to himself and making ominous comments. The team dispatched a pair of plainclothes women detectives to the young man's residence for a wellness check, where they expressed concern for Bob and asked to come in and talk. Hanging on one of the walls inside was a theater mask, its mouth sewn over with black string. Bob soon told the detectives that voices were commanding him to hurt people at the behest of God and that he was scared. The string, he said, was "the voices telling me to shut up about them." The detectives further gleaned that Bob had been following around potential victims at night.

Their empathetic approach from the moment they knocked on his door was key. They persuaded Bob to voluntarily check into a psychiatric ward immediately for evaluation. "This made him feel cared for and gave us a mechanism by which we could continue to manage him," Scalora said. "By building rapport with Bob, we're learning a lot about him and getting rich assessment data, and in the meantime he's not stalking people on our campus. It's a win-win." When the lead detective followed up with Bob during his hospital stay, he asked her, "Can you go to my room and get the mask and this big knife that's under my bed? I don't want them anymore."

Seasoned threat assessors know that a top priority is to find out whether a person of concern has access to weapons. This isn't limited to firearms, as Bob's story suggested. Mass attackers also use explosives, knives, poison, and motor vehicles. But guns have been the weapon of choice in more than half of all cases since the 1980s. "There are so many firearms out there, you just assume everybody has one," Scalora noted. "It's safer to assume that than the opposite."

A case like Bob's also exemplifies how effective threat management often goes against pressure in a community to rapidly expel or lock away a person thought to be dangerous. The university offered Bob a more dignified path: He could withdraw indefinitely and potentially reenroll later through a petitioning process. The threat assessment team also let Bob know he could stay in contact with the lead detective. He called her periodically as his condition improved and he eventually returned to the university, grateful for how his situation had been handled.

This approach to evaluating and managing potentially dangerous people requires a remarkable shift in thinking, especially for law enforcement. Ideally, arrest and prosecution are to be used only when necessary for stopping imminent danger. Defaulting to those tools can easily be counterproductive: history shows that troubled people eventually return to the picture, sometimes as dangerous as ever. Lesser punitive measures than criminal charges also carry this risk. A disruptive person might be booted out of school, fired from a job, or served with a restraining order, but those actions can create a false sense of resolution—in some cases even setting off unstable individuals and advancing their thoughts or plans for committing violence.

One possible example of this peril was the mass shooting that took place in January 2011 as US Representative Gabrielle Giffords held a meeting with constituents outside a Safeway store in Tucson, Arizona. Three and a half months before the attack, twenty-two-year-old Jared Loughner was barred from continuing to attend nearby Pima Community College. Campus administrators and law enforcement were aware of Loughner's behavioral and mental health problems, including several classroom outbursts and other disruptive incidents that had involved campus police. They also knew of a video recorded by Loughner while walking around campus, in which he appeared to ramble nonsensically and declared the school a "genocide college" and "illegal" under the US Constitution. As one Pima instructor rightly observed in an email to an associate a few days after the attack, Loughner "could just as easily have come back and shot up the school rather than Gabby's event."

There are piles of cases, from murders of women at home by intimate partners to public mass shootings, in which temporary restraining orders have triggered plans to kill. One high-profile instance took place in February 2016 in Hesston, Kansas, where a disgruntled thirty-eight-year-old employee went on a deadly rampage at a manufacturing plant after being served just hours earlier with a restraining order from a girlfriend. This particular strain of the problem goes back decades, including a notorious 1988 case in Sunnyvale, California, where an ex-employee opened fire at technology company ESL Incorporated, killing seven people and wounding four others. One of the victims, a twenty-six-year-old engineer named Laura Black, who survived wounds from a shotgun blast, had rejected assailant Richard Farley's romantic advances. After the thirty-nine-year-old military veteran and software engineer refused to stop pursuing her and turned abusive, the company fired him. He continued his relentless harassment and threats, and Black eventually obtained a restraining order against him. By then, Farley had also lost his house and owed back taxes. The day before a follow-up court hearing on whether the restraining order would be made permanent, he struck. Farley callously told investigators who later questioned him behind bars that once the company had fired him, "They lost control of me." He'd continued stalking Black for almost two years.

Yet what responsible company would possibly allow such a transgressive individual to continue his employment? What stalking victim wouldn't want and deserve court-ordered protection from him? Serious punitive actions could seem undeniable in response to menacing or abusive behavior, but possibly to a fault.

"This was a consciousness-raising incident," said court commissioner Lois Kittle the day after Farley's rampage, visibly shaken as she conducted the scheduled follow-up hearing to confirm the injunction while Black recovered in a nearby hospital. Restraining orders, she acknowledged, "do not stop bullets."

Black herself had strongly sensed the danger. "I have been afraid of what this man might do to me if I filed this action," she had told the court two weeks earlier when seeking the order. Reflecting on her ordeal years later, Black said she believed the order was the triggering event that "pushed him over the edge."

Threat assessment experts would come to understand the essential priority of contending with an individual's root grievances and pathologies. It was imperative to carefully manage a dangerous person like Farley, accounting for his compounding problems and thinking broadly with tools of mental health and legal intervention. Laws criminalizing stalking behavior did not yet exist in the United States in 1988, and behavioral threat assessment was a nascent discipline. But the ESL mass shooting was an early case study of inadequate response to an escalating danger, and many years later it would continue to be recounted in trainings by Russell Palarea and other leaders in the field.

———

One evening during the August summit, Palarea and I met up for some further mutual assessment at a New Orleans–themed eatery in Downtown Disney. At a private reception for conference goers in the upstairs bar, business casual was now mostly swapped out for Hawaiian prints or linen short sleeves and sandals. We stood on an ornate balcony meant to evoke the French Quarter, overlooking the crowds at the adjacent restaurants and souvenir shops. Soon the nightly Disney fireworks display would pop and sparkle overhead. How exactly did one end up in this line of work?

"I wanted to study murder," Palarea said. He'd felt the calling after he earned his undergraduate degree in psychology in the early 1990s but had little interest in pursuing traditional career paths. Forensics was the way forward. His sense of mission was traceable perhaps as far back as his youth in suburban Southern California, where, as an elementary school kid in the late 1970s, he was both riveted and indelibly horrified one night while watching television. He had snuck past his bedtime to finish a movie when the late local news came on. Another body had been discarded in Long Beach, this time in a trash dumpster at a gas station not far from Palarea's house. He went to sleep and dreamed a serial killer was coming for him and his family. "I woke up and got out of bed and threw up, I was so scared," he said. "I think for me that was the beginning of, 'Why do people do this?'"

A decade passed before the infamous serial killer Randy Kraft, one of several to torment California in that era, was captured and eventually put on death row at the close of the 1980s. A couple of years later, as Palarea worked on his undergraduate thesis at UCLA on serial murder and victim selection, he realized he was reading about the very case that had terrified him as a kid. Now he knew a whole lot more about what made a deadly psychopath tick. He also realized he didn't want a career providing expertise for criminal justice proceedings, a traditional purview of forensics. Instead, he wanted to use his study of murder to help stop it. He headed for a graduate degree at the University of Nebraska–Lincoln, where under Mario Scalora he delved into a niche area of "operational psychology," the work of consulting on law enforcement investigations. That led to a stint as a researcher with the Los Angeles Police Department and a decade on staff at the Naval Criminal Investigative Service, where he served as "a translator of mindset and behavior" for special agents investigating a wide range of violent crime and threat cases, a role that would even end up supplying a character for the popular TV action series *NCIS: Los Angeles*.

Like others in the field, Palarea was blunt about his skepticism of the news media. Public understanding of mass shooters and what could be done about them had long been poor. Whether during training sessions or after hours at the poolside tiki bar, more than one threat assessment professional could be heard criticizing journalists for sensationalizing cases and getting the fundamentals wrong.

One of the enduring myths about mass shooters is that they can be profiled. It is impossible to predict who will go on the next rampage by focusing on types of people. Threat assessment researchers and other violent crime experts have long sought but never found a reliable checklist or set of attributes. There exist some well-known contours of mass shooters: A great many are young or middle-aged white men. Many harbor rage, paranoia, and bitter grievances. In numerous cases, they are misogynists or domestic abusers. Some subscribe to extreme political ideology. Most have a heavy interest in weapons. And simply by definition of their acts, all mass shooters can in a basic sense be described as mentally unhealthy.

The problem is, such broad traits and conditions have no predictive value. Categorically, they offer little to help threat assessment professionals identify who might actually attack. That the overwhelming majority of mass shooters are male narrows it down to just under half of the US population. What if you start to build a checklist? Countless young white males partake in graphically violent entertainment, are interested in guns, get angry about problems with school, jobs, or personal relationships, and struggle with mental health challenges. But the number among them who might aspire to commit mass murder is exceedingly small.

Early efforts to anticipate who would try to kill top public figures or become the next school shooter pointed to the futility of predictive profiling. Six years after Lee Harvey Oswald was taken into custody for gunning down President John F. Kennedy in 1963, members of a national investigative commission stated they could forecast that, among other traits, "the next assassin would probably be short and slight of build, foreign born, and from a broken family," and that he would be unemployed and "would identify with a political or religious movement" directly motivating his mission. That hardly squared with the two women who later tried to shoot President Gerald Ford in separate incidents in 1975—one a mother and employed full-time as an accountant—or with the American-born man of average build whose attempt on President Ronald Reagan's life in 1981 was motivated ostensibly by a desire to win the heart of a Hollywood actress.

Almost two decades later, the FBI produced an "offender profile" shortly after two students carried out the suicidal mass shooting at Columbine High School in 1999. It focused solely on white male teens—overlooking the nearly two dozen young men of Asian, Black, Latino, Native American, and other backgrounds who had and would continue to attack from the 1980s on at middle schools, high schools, and colleges, from Massachusetts to Alaska.

There simply is no useful character profile for identifying mass shooters. But as Reid Meloy's talk had underscored, the promise of behavioral threat assessment is prevention, not prediction: As mass shooters plan and prepare, their attacks are preceded by a window of opportunity to intervene.

Two other entrenched misconceptions about mass shooters revolve around mental health, and are recycled continually by news media, public officials, and the general public. One takes the form of a question: "What made the guy snap?" This line of inquiry plays to the popular narrative that indiscriminate mass shootings burst forth from nowhere and are in no way rational. But mass shooters don't just suddenly snap. They decide. They develop violent ideas, arm and ready themselves, and then choose where and when to strike. They are the mountain lion on the hunt, not the recoiling house cat.

The other misconception, closely related, is that mass shooters are all insane. The idea that acute mental illness produces the carnage is marshaled after every major attack for emotional and political arguments. But although psychosis or personality disorders have been significant factors in some cases, there is no scientific evidence showing that mental illness can be blamed as the *sole cause* of mass shootings. Rarely is it the primary one or even among the major contributing factors. A deep investigation by FBI threat assessment researchers into sixty-three active shooters who struck between 2000 and 2013 confirmed that only a quarter of them were known to have been professionally diagnosed with a mental illness of any kind—a revelatory finding even when accounting for the possibility that some successfully suicidal attackers may have gone undiagnosed for conditions that were no longer discoverable. In only three cases, or 5 percent of the total examined in the FBI investigation, was the perpetrator known to have a psychotic disorder.

What the blame on mental illness does accomplish, if anything, is the spread of a damaging stigma for the millions of people who suffer from mental health afflictions, the vast majority of whom are not violent. Decades of research show that the link between mental illness and violent behavior is small and not useful for predicting violent acts; people with diagnosable conditions such as schizophrenia or bipolar disorder are in fact far more likely to be victims of violence than perpetrators of it.

Myths about snapping and insanity driving killers go back more than a century, to a suicidal school shooting. In April 1909, a twenty-eight-year-old Dartmouth College graduate shot his ex-fiancée in broad daylight on the campus of Smith College, then stood over her body and turned the revolver on himself. He had stalked her for days after she'd broken up with him and rejected further contact. "Sudden insanity caused by the young woman's refusal to accept his attentions is given as the cause of the double killing," stated one magazine article at the time. "A nervous breakdown is responsible for my son's act," the killer's mother told the *Chicago Tribune*, adding that after the breakup, "My son could not recover from the blow and brooded until it unbalanced his mind. He did not know what he was doing." The newspaper also quoted a cousin who further suggested that the killer had been overcome with madness: "He was a steady, cool-headed fellow. He was handsome and easily made and kept friends. I could not have suspected him capable of such a thing."

Fast-forward to the early days of the mass shootings era, which began stirring in the mid-1960s and gained steam two decades later. After a 1983 attack at a middle school in suburban St. Louis, where a fourteen-year-old student fatally shot one classmate, injured another, and killed himself, the principal suggested at an emergency school assembly that insanity was to blame in the broadest sense. "Nobody knows why this happened," he said, emphasizing that the attack had come out of nowhere and couldn't have been prevented by anyone. Yet the deceased shooter had not suddenly snapped. A note he left behind had described his plan to "eliminate some exceptionally bad people" and commit suicide.

Over the next three decades of intermittent mass shootings, these themes of snapping and insanity became culturally ingrained, the presumed explanation for attacks as the problem scaled up in the 2010s. Their marquee emphasis was inevitable in October 2017, when a sixty-four-year-old man named Stephen Paddock rained down automatic gunfire from a hotel suite on a crowd of concertgoers on the Las Vegas Strip and then committed suicide. In a poignant monologue the following evening, late-night TV host Jimmy Kimmel channeled what millions of Americans were no doubt thinking about the unprecedented calamity in Kimmel's hometown, where fifty-eight victims died and hundreds of others were wounded and injured. Kimmel spoke of an inexplicable act by "a very sick person" with an "insane voice in his head." "We wonder why," he said, choking up, "even though there's probably no way to know why a human being would do something like this." Elsewhere in the aftermath, the mayor of Las Vegas called Paddock "a crazed lunatic full of hate." A gun store manager who encountered Paddock frequently as a customer was mystified: "He was upbeat, happy, a normal guy," the manager told a reporter. "It just wasn't there, man. At some point, he snapped. What made him snap? I don't know."

After many high-profile mass shootings, the public is left craving a clear explanation, a way to make sense of "senseless" tragedy. But motive is often complex and in some cases possibly unknowable, as the Las Vegas Metropolitan Police Department concluded about Paddock, announcing after a ten-month investigation that it could not "definitively answer" the question of why he attacked.

That did not mean, however, that there were no warning signs from Paddock, as his personal life deteriorated and he amassed an arsenal over many months.

Herein also lies the promise of behavioral threat assessment: Determining precisely *why* people commit mass shootings doesn't necessarily matter as much as knowing *how* they reach the point of attacking. A perpetrator's mind-set figures fundamentally into actions leading up to the violence and is a key barometer—but ultimately, seeing the totality of behaviors and circumstances that give rise to a case is more important to the science and strategy of preventing future attacks. It's one thing to know an express reason that a person feels anger and threatens violence, but another to grasp the broader context and recognize what that person is doing to signal intent, plan, and prepare.

Social barriers are what keep most people from deciding to kill, remarked psychologist Lisa Warren, an expert on stalking and threatening communications who leads a threat management firm in Australia, when we spoke at the training summit. "We all have this in our nature," she said. "The question is, when do those barriers get crossed and how do we get in the way of that?"

This perspective, shared widely among threat assessment professionals, echoed a theme found in *The Better Angels of Our Nature*, scholar Steven Pinker's 2011 treatise on the decline of violence in modern civilization: "The alternative to the myth of pure evil is that most of the harm that people visit on one another comes from motives that are found in every normal person." In other words, while it is both morally reassuring and perfectly reasonable to see nothing of ourselves in mass killers—to keep them at a distance as unfathomable lunatics who snapped—the uncomfortable truth is that many of them are more like us in their struggles, life circumstances, and human capacity to act violently than we wish to acknowledge. But that truth is also hopeful, because the closer we look at how they act and under what circumstances, the better the chances for stopping them.

In the long-term study of cases both tragic and thwarted—the heart of the field's emerging scientific research—there lies a road map to a less violent world. Its contours were first discovered long before mental health experts and law enforcement agents started coming together to train in Disneyland.

———

chapter two

BEYOND THE MAGIC MEDICINE

Early on a mild day in September 1976, Robert Fein drove forty miles south from his home in Boston, parked his old light-blue Saab in a barren lot, and walked a short footpath toward the entrance to the Bridgewater State Hospital for the Criminally Insane. Dressed in a suit and tie, his side-parted hair neatly trimmed and his briefcase in hand, the twenty-nine-year-old paused for a moment in the cool air to collect himself before going in. Between him and a series of low-slung concrete-and-brick buildings loomed two layers of tall metal fencing topped with razor wire. Just beyond those barriers awaited the most disturbed and brutally violent men in the state of Massachusetts.

Fein had just completed a new Harvard University program designed to put clinical psychology to broader use, its goal to train graduates to be therapists and to take on problems of public health and safety. He had studied under Dr. Shervert Frazier, the renowned chief psychiatrist at Boston's McLean Hospital and one of the country's foremost experts on violent behavior. Following a clinical internship at McLean, Fein had thought of focusing on struggling youth or the elderly, and he sought Frazier's advice about launching his career.

"I think it would be good for you to go work with dangerous men," Frazier had told him.

"That stopped me in my tracks," Fein recalled, during one of our series of conversations beginning in 2017. "I had no idea what he was talking about."

A year before Fein arrived at Bridgewater, in the fall of 1975, his mentor Frazier had begun ramping up a new initiative with the Massachusetts Department of Correction for improving the maximum security institution under its jurisdiction, which was notorious for misdiagnoses and harsh treatment of its incarcerated patients. Bridgewater's dark history included unsanitary conditions, overmedication, forced feeding, beatings, and sometimes even fatal abuses. That same fall, the Hollywood adaptation of *One Flew Over the Cuckoo's Nest* was becoming a cultural sensation, with Jack Nicholson starring as the rabble-rousing convict from Ken Kesey's 1962 novel who feigned insanity to avoid serving a prison sentence. *Cuckoo's Nest* was set at a bleak state mental hospital in Salem, Oregon. Bridgewater was an even more prison-like version of such a place. Rather than being lorded over by the likes of the tyrannical Nurse Ratched, it was run by stern correctional officers, some of whom did their jobs with reason and skill, and others who operated with indifference and cruelty. Bridgewater itself had in fact been the subject of a film—a controversial 1967 work of "direct cinema" called *Titicut Follies*, whose revelatory footage of disturbing inmate treatment was banned by Massachusetts from viewing by the general public for more than two decades, after the state cited privacy concerns on behalf of inmates. Named for a talent show put on by the institutionalized men, the obscure documentary was eventually unshackled for public audiences by a court ruling and later was credited with helping provoke reform of the system.

Fein had arrived during a transitional time. The era of nation-wide deinstitutionalization of the mentally ill—however poorly diagnosed or understood they were in many cases—was well under way, with legal challenges mounting against the indefinite commitment of patients. The Bridgewater facility had been rebuilt in 1974, and new clinical expertise from McLean promised to improve evaluation and treatment for those deemed "the most psychotic and violent men" in state custody. Fein's training as a psychology intern had included some observation inside hospital psych wards, but he had almost no experience talking directly with patients who had acted violently, and none beyond a conventional therapy setting. "You can read all you want about violent behavior," Frazier had told him, "but if you sit with these guys and listen and learn from them, you develop a kind of moral authority about violence that you cannot get otherwise." Fein had agreed to come to Bridgewater so long as Frazier promised to keep supervising him.

Inside at the mantrap entrance, Fein slid his ID through a slot beneath a thick glass window as the stone-faced security officer on the other side eyed him. A loud buzzer sounded and the steel door to Fein's left clanked open. Beyond a second steel door and out the main front building, he was escorted across an open yard, where lower-risk patients meandered under the watch of patrolling correctional officers, toward a building known as Max 1. This was one of two structures housing the more volatile inmates. Just beyond stood a medical building containing F ward, also known as the seclusion ward. Its twenty narrow cells were bounded by thick concrete walls and locked metal doors, and each contained little more than a thin bed. This was where Bridgewater put the men who still exploded into fits of rage.

Men were sent to Bridgewater for a simple reason: they were considered too dangerous to be handled anywhere else. It sunk in for Fein that his new place of work was a hospital in name only; in reality, he was the new clinical director for a maximum-security facility. The pressure of coming face-to-face with extreme violent offenders was compounded by his mandate to make a range of consequential decisions, from assessing their capacity for court proceedings to determining their treatment protocols or their further placement in the health or prison systems. Much to his relief, in the early days he was able to watch a seasoned psychiatrist navigate this environment, as Dr. Harold Morgan, who had come from South Carolina for a fellowship at Harvard Medical School, took the lead on some patient interviews. Whereas the correctional officers typically commanded the inmates by their first names or sometimes in cruder terms to assert control, Morgan addressed interviewees respectfully by their surnames. "Please do tell me a little more about that, Mr. Jones," he would say in his tranquil Southern drawl.

"I mimicked a lot of what he did," Fein recalled about his own early patient interviews, which he conducted with a Morgan-like twang. A colleague later noted wryly to Fein that he didn't lose his newly acquired Southern accent for about the first six months.

The work in Max 1 included regular group meetings with roughly two dozen men inside a sparse dayroom, where exterior windows reinforced with wire mesh allowed in a little sunlight and correctional officers on the hall kept a watchful eye. The dayroom sessions were intended both as therapy to foster more normal social interaction among the men and as a means for Fein and the attending social workers to learn more about their experiences. Fein would have the group vote on topics to discuss. Some of the men stewed, while others sat in silence, but soon Fein began to gain insights into their thinking. Some, it turned out, were skilled manipulators. One morning the room was noticeably tense, with a few of the men murmuring to each other after the group was called together. Among them was an individual who was well known to the Boston police department for a history of calling in bomb threats from pay phones, projecting stress and sounds of background chaos so realistically that in one instance he'd sent police scrambling over a nonexistent attack. Fein soon discovered that the bomb hoaxer had quietly convinced others in the room that three of their fellow inmates had been secretly put to death the night before in the seclusion unit.

On another day, a short, conspicuously quiet new patient named Steve made a strong impression on Fein, during a discussion of how the men had ended up at Bridgewater. A couple members of the group prodded Steve about not speaking, but he stared straight ahead and said nothing. The discussion moved on. Eventually, Steve raised his hand. "I'm the only guy here without a criminal record," he muttered. Fein understood the dejection he was conveying. Many in the room had committed vicious acts. But despite the attention that Steve had drawn at several hospital psych wards for his uncontrollably assaultive behavior, in here he was essentially a nobody. That feeling of inadequacy bothered him deeply—he needed to be a somebody, even in this place.

Fein noticed from early on that violent conflict within Bridgewater's confines was relatively infrequent. One morning, as he went through the mantrap entrance and back onto the grounds, he was struck by a basic fact that he hadn't yet consciously considered: Bridgewater had no back doors. Any other health institution—a treatment center or an actual hospital—would have multiple ways to get out or to discharge someone acting disruptively. Here, there was only one way in and out, and that meant all behaviors had to be managed inside the place, not only in volatile moments but over the longer term.

He grew more aware that he was investigating the obliterated humanity of these men, however obscured by their awful deeds. Many offenders had gone from being victims early in their lives to becoming violent aggressors. And then they had become victims again, this time locked away in obscurity by the system, in some cases for life. Some were diagnosable as acutely mentally ill, while others were not. Yet in virtually all of these men, Fein found himself examining the grip of humiliation, and the nature of entrenched grievances and smoldering rage. He found that many of the offenders had never been in normal circumstances or had even a basic language for dealing with their problems. They had thus relied on brute force. One man who was serving a long prison sentence for rape had been sent to Bridgewater after surviving a self-castration attempt. At one point, he declared to Fein that instead of continuing to rape women once he got out of prison, he would use a rifle to shoot them from a distance. Though he was psychotic, it was a deep-seated misogyny that seemed the key to his intent for future violence.

Within a couple of years, Fein began treating two murderers individually on a longer-term basis. One young man, who repeatedly engaged in self-mutilation, had been treated and rejected by all the major teaching hospitals in Boston after he kept injuring himself. Fein worked with him for several years, examining a profoundly damaged life and confronting the limitations of his efforts as he was unable to help the man cease from self-harming. "It almost killed me emotionally, realizing that I couldn't help him," Fein said. "Eventually I had to quit treating him for my own sanity."

He took to calling the work extreme men's studies. "Obviously in the beginning I was pretty freaked out about spending time with people like that, and I had no idea how anxious it was making me. There's a reason why we have the word 'unspeakable.' Some of the things these guys had done, and that had been done to them, were unspeakable."

Yet Fein's intimate exploration into some of the darkest of human behaviors held the promise of progress. He came to see that nobody is born a killer. None of his patients' acts had been inevitable. "I listened to the humiliations they went through, from trying to get a job and being treated like a piece of dirt, to awful physical and psychological abuses—unimaginable things. Anyone who spends time with people like this ends up becoming committed to prevention. And that's not necessarily anything fancy: it's about offering more respect, more kindness, and more options."

————

In those early years, Fein underwent therapy himself with an esteemed Boston psychoanalyst, which proved fruitful beyond helping him process his exposure to so much gruesome subject matter. The sessions crystalized an idea he had begun discussing with Shervert Frazier. He wanted to help turn the tough and generally thankless work done by staff at Bridgewater into an opportunity more like one at a teaching hospital. In the late 1970s, it was still very much in vogue in elite mental health circles to explore the latent motives of patients who fantasized about killing their parents. Fein bantered with Frazier about putting together a different kind of program for top Boston therapists—the pitch, as they discussed only half jokingly, would be about the chance to meet with subjects who *actually had* murdered their parents. ("Come talk to some people who've really done it.")

Fein aspired to bridge a gulf in the profession. Theorizing on parricide in cosmopolitan private practice was a world apart from better comprehending the all-but-abandoned perpetrators of shocking violence who were locked away in Boston's own backyard. Systemic indifference for Bridgewater, as it turned out, had left Fein in a bizarre situation early on: the work he was doing was not legal. He was the first-ever psychologist to conduct court-ordered evaluations at Bridgewater, but state law required a psychiatrist (medical degree included) to perform the role. Fein had already handled scores of cases by the time a colleague realized the oversight, and Fein promptly informed Frazier and the Department of Correction that he needed to resign. He and Frazier agreed that Fein would continue only if the agency's commissioner worked expeditiously to get the rule changed, allowing evaluations by psychologists with specific training. Frazier then urged Fein to expand the staff, and continued to back the development of the program by his protégé.

Sherv, as Frazier was known among colleagues, was a towering Texan, a Navy veteran of World War II and a larger-than-life figure in the world of mental health. He had long examined the nature of violent behavior, particularly since a calamitous school massacre. On the morning of August 1, 1966, a highly intelligent and heavily armed ex-Marine sniper named Charles Whitman rode an elevator to the top of the Main Building clock tower at the University of Texas in Austin and spent the next hour and a half gunning down people in and around the building. The victims he targeted more than two hundred feet below with his magnifying rifle scope and marksman training included an unborn baby just a few weeks from delivery, whose mother, incredibly, survived. By the time police officers reached the twenty-five-year-old former architectural engineering student on the observation deck and fatally shot him, he had killed fourteen people on the campus and wounded thirty-two others. Such a ghastly attack in an everyday public space was so inconceivable at the time that two people who had walked past Whitman on their way down from the tower's observation deck reportedly thought he was carrying rifles with him to shoot pigeons. Whitman's politely smiling demeanor—"Hi, how are you?" was how he'd greeted the passersby—gave no clue that a few hours earlier he had killed his wife and mother at home.

At the time of the attack, Frazier was teaching psychiatry at Baylor College of Medicine in Houston and serving as the Texas commissioner on mental health. He immediately formed an investigative team of top medical and psychiatry experts reporting to Governor John Connally, who himself had been wounded by a sniper's bullet during the Kennedy assassination three years earlier and was adamant about getting to the bottom of Whitman's crimes. It turned out that Whitman had consulted a psychiatrist at the university's health center six months before the massacre about having recurrent "overwhelming" violent impulses, but he had never returned for further help. He visited the clock tower twice that spring and summer and may have envisioned his rampage as far back as five years, when he had stood on campus looking at the structure and commented to a friend: "You know, that would be a great place to go up with a rifle and shoot people." He typed a lengthy suicide letter justifying the deaths of his wife and mother as mercy killings that would prevent them from "suffering alone" after he was gone.

Frazier's investigative team scrutinized Whitman's background through personal records and extensive interviews with those who knew him. They found that mounting acrimony between his parents, his personal failures in school, and his strained finances had led him to withdraw into "increasing psychological isolation." Yet they also determined that he had good friendships, was "admired and respected by many" and had "strong loving ties to his wife." They allowed that a malignant brain tumor revealed by Whitman's autopsy might have affected his functioning, though they emphasized that its impact was unknowable. Interviews with Whitman's volatile and abusive father conducted by Frazier and two colleagues suggested that hereditary psychopathy was another possible factor in the case.

No clear answers existed, in other words, to the question of why. But with Frazier's years of research into causes of violent behavior, the atrocity could start to be seen from a different perspective. In his influential essay "Violence and Social Impact," published in 1975 as he was launching the Bridgewater program, Frazier in part reframed the puzzling over Whitman's and other killers' minds. His discussion was a prescient foil to the difficult questions of motive that would bedevil the coming age of mass attacks:

> *Murder may not be perceived as a violent action by the murderer himself. Often it fits so closely into a system of thinking that it becomes the only logical outcome because of the nature of the murderer's thinking and feeling. In the thoughts of the cornered, the only way to escape the feeling of being systematically cornered is to murder, an action which is an end in itself.*

"Murder is a process," Frazier further observed, "not an event, but a phasic development."

The study of violent offenders at Bridgewater deepened through the late 1970s, with Frazier helping Robert Fein to expand the research and train a growing team. Fein would pick up his mentor at McLean Hospital in Boston once a month, always bringing along Sherv's favorite deli tuna sandwich, and they would discuss craft during the drive. On one memorable ride, Frazier talked at length about how to coax access with especially hardened or mercurial patients, locating them in their experiences and drawing out details through delicately calibrated questioning. It was crucial, he explained, to be empathetic yet purely factual with lines of inquiry, and to convey clearly to patients that the purpose was to understand what their lives were really like.

One evening around eight p.m., after an intense run of teaching interviews, patient rounds, and staff debriefings, the two were about to leave the hospital grounds and head back to Boston when a correctional officer called. An inmate in Max 2 was acting highly agitated and complaining of physical pain. The officer asked if they could come help. When they got to Max 2, all the men were locked down in their rooms for the night. The pair of clinicians asked two correctional officers on the hall to stay with them as they went into the one room still open. A scrawny man lay on the bed, contorted and jabbering. Frazier, who had begun his career as an internist, told the man he was also a medical doctor. The man looked up at him, eyes ablaze, and blurted that he had a broken leg.

"I see," Frazier replied. "How about I take a look?" After examining him for a moment with his hands, he assured him the limb was fine.

"I think I've also got a broken jaw, Doc," the man said next, a little calmer. Frazier nodded, examining him again briefly. "Your jaw is OK." The exchange continued in a similar manner for another minute or two. "I think it's time to go to sleep now," Frazier said. "You're going to be just fine."

They were already late getting back home to their families and easily could have waved off the detour to Max 2. Fein would not forget how Frazier took the time to handle the agitated man, settling him down almost like a child at bedtime.

Any patient housed in the maximum-security buildings had the potential to lash out dangerously. That was a given. But the two clinicians hadn't asked the two officers on the hall to stick around and watch the encounter for safety purposes. Correctional officers at Bridgewater served much of the time as de facto primary caretakers, yet few built any rapport with the volatile men in their charge. When a patient became unruly, a common response among the officers was to call in the doctors with the "magic medicine"—shots and pills were believed to be the way to control the beast. Those could be vital tools in certain situations, but rarely if ever did medication solve root problems or fix deficiencies in the basic skills of human interaction. Instead, Fein and Frazier wanted to show the officers their team's approach, with the goal of instilling greater collaboration and some new ways of thinking in the whole institution. They intended to broaden the regime for managing and preventing dangerous behavior, even in a place whose inhabitants remained culturally out of sight and out of mind. Soon enough, there would be reason for their germinating strategy to reach beyond Bridgewater's walls.

————

chapter three

ON THE TRAIL OF ASSASSINS

The memorial gatherings spanned from New York and Chicago to London and Liverpool and many other cities around the world. Among the multitudes who defied winter weather and came together in public spaces throughout America, younger and older generations alike wept and embraced. Many clutched flowers or candles, or held up hand-drawn signs that read: IMAGINE NO MORE HANDGUNS, GIVE PEACE A CHANCE, or just WHY? In Central Park on that Sunday, against a backdrop of leafless trees and a gray sky auguring snow, the tens of thousands who gathered stood still for an impossibly heavy ten minutes of silence, the vast hush of their mourning disrupted only by a helicopter circling overhead and the ambient murmur of the city carried on the wind.

It was mid-December 1980, and John Lennon was dead.

When Dr. Shervert Frazier arrived at Bridgewater State Hospital at the start of that next week, he knew the music icon's devastating murder was about to resonate even more for Robert Fein and his team. Questions had been swirling in the media about Mark Chapman, the twenty-five-year-old assailant who for several days had waited around the Dakota building at the corner of Seventy-Second Street and Central Park West. Late in the day on Monday, December 8, as Lennon had departed the posh residential building and paused to greet some fans out front, a grinning Chapman finally got an autograph from him on a copy of Lennon's newly released album *Double Fantasy*. Then Chapman continued to linger. It was almost eleven p.m. when Lennon and his wife and co-artist, Yoko Ono, returned from a recording session, stepping out of a limousine in front of the building. As the couple walked into the stately entryway, Chapman, wearing a black trench coat and fur cap, emerged from the shadows and reportedly called out, "Mr. Lennon." He then took a "combat stance," as a New York City chief of detectives described it, and fired four hollow-point bullets from a .38 caliber revolver into Lennon's back. Lennon was rushed in a police car to Roosevelt Hospital, where doctors were unable to resuscitate him. Amid the shock and global outpouring of grief, Chapman was being described by various news media and public officials as "an obsessed fan," "deranged," "a kook," and "a wacko."

Frazier had just returned from a trip to Washington, DC, where he was serving on a committee for the Institute of Medicine at the National Academy of Sciences. He asked Fein to gather the Bridgewater team, which by then had expanded to sixteen psychologists, psychiatrists, and social workers. The timing was now a little uncanny for the news Frazier shared with them: His IOM committee had been talking in recent months with the US Secret Service about developing behavioral science research to enhance capabilities for thwarting assassins. One in every four presidents since the founding of the country had been the target of an assassin's bullet, and the contemporary era was even more fraught with danger for top political figures. Following the traumatic slayings in the 1960s of President John F. Kennedy, the Reverend Martin Luther King Jr., and Senator Robert Kennedy, targets included Richard Nixon, Gerald Ford, and Jimmy Carter. Those three had gone unscathed, but there were two close calls involving President Ford, and a perpetrator who wanted to kill Nixon had gone on to gravely wound Alabama governor and presidential candidate George Wallace. Secret Service leaders were intent on improving the agency's knowledge and tactics. To that end, Frazier told the assembled group that he'd made an ambitious promise. The Bridgewater team, he told them, was about to produce the definitive study on mentally ill assassins.

The team was taken aback by the unexpected mission, but the conversation quickly focused on the fresh tragedy in New York City, including Chapman's notably bizarre behavior after he pulled the trigger. "I'd go away if I were you," he'd said to a woman who approached him just moments after the gunfire to ask what happened. Chapman was not interested in escaping. He had dropped his weapon and had hung around nearby on the sidewalk, where he pulled out a copy of *The Catcher in the Rye* and thumbed through it briefly until police swooped in. He apparently wanted to convey that he embodied Holden Caulfield, the landmark novel's embittered young protagonist. Chapman had grown up devoutly religious during some of his youth in Georgia and had deemed Lennon to be among the "phonies" of the world, resentment he may have rationalized in part over Lennon's famous assertion in a 1966 interview that Christianity would decline and the Beatles were "more popular than Jesus." Chapman's performance at the crime scene, however, was more than a jarring example of an assassin's pathological identification, in this case with a fictional figure.

Unbeknownst to Chapman, he had just created a new version of a "cultural script"—a kind of narrative template for future killers to mimic.

Assassins and mass murderers sometimes looked to notorious predecessors for inspiration, picking up on their appearances and actions in what would come to be called copycat or contagion behavior. A related historical phenomenon was known to behavioral science experts: the "Werther effect," referring to a spate of suicides in eighteenth-century Europe that followed the literary success of Goethe's *The Sorrows of Young Werther*, some of whose readers dressed in imitation of the novel's romantically despondent protagonist and shot themselves, sometimes even with a copy of the book in hand. Chapman would gain certain disaffected admirers, a harbinger of the emulation behavior that would animate rampage shooters in the decades ahead and draw the attention of threat assessment experts.

The Bridgewater team knew that potentially dangerous vitriol focused on celebrities and politicians went beyond the shocking attacks known to the public. The facility housed some men who had made threats about high-profile figures, including the Boston bomb hoaxer, who'd talked of killing a US president. "Let's start with what more we can learn here," Frazier said to Fein and his colleagues, urging that they examine such behavior additionally by talking directly with the Secret Service. Frazier had further promised that the new research would be ready for an elite gathering of mental health and law enforcement leaders he was helping organize for three months later in Washington.

Fein and several colleagues pored through Bridgewater case files, reviewed their interactions with violent offenders who'd talked of assassination, and met with Secret Service agents from Boston and Washington. In early March 1981, Frazier, Fein, and their research colleague Sara Eddy traveled to the nation's capital to meet behind closed doors with Secret Service leaders and a handful of luminaries from research institutions around the country. A primary goal of the confidential gathering was to establish active working ties between special agents and top experts on behavioral science, mental health, and the law.

But were federal agents really going to start working hand in hand with psychologists to thwart murder plots? The role of law enforcement was to investigate crimes, not to prevent them. Even with the unique protective mission of the Secret Service, which relied on arresting suspects under what was known as the federal "threat statute," the concept was unlikely. The vanilla title of the new report delivered by the McLean clinicians hardly exuded lofty ambition for collaboration: "Problems in Assessing and Managing Dangerous Behavior." Yet, the report's opening section held the contours of a new discipline, conveyed in a particular highlighted phrase:

> *Although the literature on "dangerousness" is substantial, the concept of dangerousness is still not adequately defined. Because anyone can be dangerous, the Secret Service is concerned only with persons whose specific aim is to harm those it protects. It works to <u>identify, assess, and manage</u> the small particular subset of people who might act on thoughts or impulses they have about injuring or killing government leaders and/or their families. Secret Service agents in Boston report that increasing numbers of mentally disordered individuals threaten the president primarily to get attention and care. These people might or might not be dangerous to a protected person and often need sophisticated assessment by mental health professionals.*

The McLean team observed that no scientifically valid method existed for determining "dangerousness" in people, and that trying to predict over the long term whether a person would commit an act of violence was likely futile. Yet, in individual cases, it might be possible to anticipate such behavior in a useful way. "Rather than think about dangerous people," the team wrote, "we prefer to think about dangerous situations—situations involving a specific subject, a victim, and an act under specific circumstances."

This was a striking leap forward from the traditional practice of violence risk assessment, which involved time-consuming clinical observation and analysis of a subject's personal history and mental health profile. Instead, the McLean team was suggesting how the Secret Service could tap psychological expertise in a much more immediate and pragmatic way. Agents sometimes encountered perplexing behaviors: an allegedly threatening individual who seemed essentially normal but joked repeatedly about hearing conspiratorial voices, or another who had a bizarre-looking homemade shrine to a top political figure in his garage. Rather than relying just on standardized interview questions and perhaps some specific case experience to gauge the possible danger, the agents should be able to ask for help interpreting the relevance of such behaviors on a case-by-case basis, as an investigation evolved in real time.

The McLean team laid out several sets of questions for conducting thorough but expeditious assessments of concerning people brought to the Secret Service's attention. These included rapidly getting a handle on their mental health histories, their relationships with others, any serious grievances they seemed to have, and whether they appeared capable of carrying out a violent attack. The McLean team also offered guidelines for eliciting such details in interviews, and further suggested setting up a national network of mental health practitioners experienced with violent offenders, proposing that these experts should be available as needed "around-the-clock" to consult with agents on evaluations and threat management plans.

The fact that the opaque and close-knit Secret Service still operated in old-school ways posed a challenge. The top federal protective agency was created within the Treasury Department in 1865 to combat rampant counterfeiting—after being authorized by President Abraham Lincoln, in an uncanny historical twist, on the very day he would be assassinated. Its mission eventually came to include presidential protection after the assassinations of James A. Garfield in 1881 and William McKinley in 1901. Now, the better part of a century later, certain rethinking of the agency's ingrained culture and methods, catalyzed by the March 1981 gathering of experts in Washington, would prove consequential both for the evolution of behavioral threat assessment and for Robert Fein's future.

The McLean team had learned that Secret Service agents sometimes relied significantly on ad hoc sharing of case experience or knowledge of individuals long on the agency's radar to help each other do assessments, an approach that had endured among a relatively small corps of agents. But now the ranks were starting to grow as the agency tracked hundreds of concerning people designated with QI status, referring to quarterly investigations in which agents would conduct follow-up interviews with subjects at least once every ninety days to determine if they should remain classified as dangerous. The McLean team also learned that, remarkably, the agency had never systematically analyzed its own case files. The team outlined how the Secret Service could build a more codified and strategic approach to collecting data and learning from the people they investigated. While the concepts were met with enthusiasm at the Washington gathering, Frazier and Fein knew that enacting them amid the fraught politics and budgets of the federal bureaucracy would be another matter.

Three weeks after they returned to Boston, fresh horror unfolded smack in the nation's capital. On the afternoon of March 30, 1981, as President Ronald Reagan departed from a speech to labor leaders at the Washington Hilton Hotel, a twenty-five-year-old man in a trench coat standing among the press corps in the light drizzle crouched slightly and raised a revolver. One ricocheting bullet from the six shots he fired pierced Reagan's torso, puncturing the president's left lung and stopping an inch shy of his heart. Other shots gravely wounded Reagan's press secretary, James Brady, leaving him paralyzed, and seriously injured police officer Thomas Delahanty and Secret Service agent Timothy McCarthy.

The assailant, John Hinckley Jr., had fixated for years on the teen actor Jodie Foster, watching her repeatedly in the 1976 film *Taxi Driver*, writing her letters, and stalking her at Yale University. He apparently came to believe he could win Foster's heart if he became famous. Like the paranoid and alienated young protagonist in *Taxi Driver*, he would attempt a high-profile political assassination.

Several threads twisted together in Hinckley's version of the cultural script. The screenplay for *Taxi Driver* had drawn inspiration from the diary of Arthur Bremer, the young man who had sought notoriety by targeting Nixon and later shooting Governor Wallace. Among the possessions federal agents found in Hinckley's DC hotel room was a copy of Bremer's diary. They also found another volume: *The Catcher in the Rye*. Hinckley had paid close attention to Chapman, further evidence showed. On audio tapes Hinckley had recorded shortly after John Lennon's recent murder, he'd talked of how Lennon and Foster were in his mind "binded" together: "John and Jodie, and now one of 'em's dead." The recordings also contained Hinckley strumming a rendition of Lennon's love song "Oh Yoko!" on a guitar, swapping in "Oh Jodie!" as he sang.

Stories about Hinckley flooded television and print media; his photo was featured on the front page of every major newspaper. By his criminal trial in spring 1982, an atmospheric portrait of him filled the cover of *Newsweek*, his visage staring into the distance against a backdrop of storm clouds with the cover line, "The Insanity Defense: Should It Be Abolished?" Among evidence considered by the jury that found Hinckley not guilty by reason of insanity was a poem he had written that included the line, "Inside this mind of mine, I commit front page murder, I think of words that could alter history."

Emulation behavior among would-be killers was little understood by experts at the time beyond its basic premise, but Hinckley's meteoric infamy had produced a copycat case telling both for its speed and specificity, and in how it suggested a danger from heavy media focus on assassins. Eight days after the shooting, federal agents arrested a twenty-two-year-old Pennsylvania man with sandy blond hair and a neatly trimmed beard who was armed with a revolver and headed to Washington. He was fresh from stalking Jodie Foster at a theater performance she was giving that week at Yale, telling authorities that after two nights in the audience, he had decided not to shoot her because she was "too pretty to kill." Tipped off by a cleaning employee, local police and the Secret Service had found several items in the man's New Haven hotel room: a letter professing his love for Foster, some .32-caliber bullets, a magazine photo of Reagan with an X scrawled across his face, and a separate letter about the president in which the suspect vowed "to bring to completion Hinckley's reality."

Neither Hinckley nor his own imitator were the first of their kind. Three months after the clock tower massacre in Texas in 1966, an eighteen-year-old high school student fatally shot five people inside a beauty school in Arizona and injured two others before surrendering to police. Clean-cut in appearance and described by schoolmates as a loner, the young man had been riveted by news reports about the carnage in Texas and another recent high-profile mass murder in Chicago. "I wanted to kill about forty people so I could make a name for myself," he said in custody, detailing his wish to be known "all over the world." A newspaper headline at the time captured the grim banality: HIGH SCHOOL SENIOR KILLS TO GAIN ATTENTION.

As the eminent social psychologist and scholar of violence Erich Fromm had written in the previous decade about the alienated individual, "His acts and their consequences have become his masters, whom he obeys, or whom he may even worship." In some respects for these perpetrators, the act of violence itself had become the goal.

———

As the cherry blossoms flowered again in Washington in late spring 1982, the Secret Service was set to nearly double in size to three thousand agents amid a federal reorganization and news reports of "Libyan-trained killers" possibly hunting President Reagan. Shervert Frazier worried that the agency was even more urgently in need of help.

Little had come of the March 1981 gathering. Frazier told Fein he was eager to connect with the new Secret Service director, John R. Simpson, an athletic, square-jawed fellow native of Boston who'd once aspired to play for the Red Sox before heading off to law school and later becoming a special agent. Simpson had served under every president since JFK, including as the head of Reagan's protective detail during his first campaign for the White House in 1968. Simpson had rushed to the hospital to help stand watch during the surgery that saved Reagan's life. Frazier called him down in Washington to ask how the Secret Service was coping with the rising tide of threats, and soon Frazier and Fein made a trip to the nation's capital to talk with Simpson and several other agency leaders. "If you think you might need it," Frazier told them, "Robert and I are prepared to help."

Simpson confirmed that the agency had been swamped with tips from the public ever since Hinckley shot the president. "What do you propose?" he asked the two mental-health experts.

Reagan's survival against the odds owed to the split-second valor of the agents who'd thrust him into the motorcade and raced him to George Washington University Hospital. The flip side to that story, of course, was a catastrophic security failure—and the Secret Service was under intense pressure behind the scenes to handle the surge of reportedly dangerous people being brought to their attention. Frazier suggested he would tap his McLean budget for him and Fein to start traveling to Washington. "Show us whatever cases you want and we'll help you sort through the mental health info you're getting on all these people." Simpson asked what resources they'd need. "Just give us a room," Frazier said dryly. "We'll bring our own pencils and paper."

As the thick heat of summer settled over the East Coast, the pair of clinicians caught an early flight each Wednesday from Boston to Washington and got to work in a secluded room inside Secret Service headquarters at 1800 G Street NW. A senior agent from the intelligence division plunked down stacks of case files for them to review. What they began to discover among them was startling, including a case involving a military veteran in Tennessee named

Carl who had served in Vietnam. Carl had been affixing photos of Reagan to sheep as they were grazing in a field, and would then walk back across the field, pick up a rifle, and blow the sheep away. He'd been taken to a Veterans Affairs facility for psychological evaluation. VA assessment notes in the file stated that Carl was not mentally ill, yet elsewhere in the file he was diagnosed as psychotic and prescribed medication. And while the VA had concluded that Carl the sheep killer was not dangerous, it urged that he be barred from possessing firearms.

This contradictory muddle was hardly unique among the Secret Service case files, the clinicians found, and Simpson soon arranged for Fein to continue longer term as a consulting adviser. "We were really concerned about the terrible information they were getting from mental health practitioners around the country," Fein recalled of the various incoherent diagnoses and claims about dangerousness. "What the hell were the agents supposed to do with it?"

Another stark problem surfaced with a case in Ohio. On an oppressively hot day in the summer of 1983, the Cleveland police department received a call with the urgent news that Reagan's life was in danger again. The young man on the line said he'd just learned of a direct threat to the president. The police notified the Secret Service, which dispatched a pair of agents from a regional field office to investigate, following protocols for rapidly vetting threats. The agents knocked on the young man's door later that night, up on the seventh floor of an apartment building. As they began interviewing him, they observed that a streetside window was open. "I heard two ladies walking down there on the sidewalk," the young man told them. "One of the ladies asked, 'Who is the president?' And the other one answered, 'Reagan. He ought to die.'"

It was quickly obvious who the actual concern might be. The

agents learned from the young man that he was currently getting mental health treatment, but he gave no indication that he intended to go after Reagan. He agreed to sign a release form, and the next day the agents went to interview his psychiatrist, with whom they ran through some standard investigative questions regarding the patient:

"Does he have a history of violence?"

"No," his psychiatrist said.

"Does he have an interest in weapons?"

"No."

"Has he made any threatening comments about the president?"

"No."

Following a few other similar responses, they asked: "In your opinion, doctor, is he a danger to the president?"

"Yes, he is quite possibly a danger to the president," the psychiatrist replied.

The agents pressed him as to why he held that view. He explained that Dr. John Hopper Jr., a psychiatrist who had treated John Hinckley for five months prior to his attempt on Reagan's life had just been sued for $14 million by other victims wounded in the attack, who alleged negligence and misdiagnosis by Hopper. During Hinckley's criminal trial, Hopper had testified about his conclusion prior to the shooting that Hinckley did not have any serious mental illness. Thus the Cleveland psychiatrist wasn't going to take any chances, whether on the president's behalf or his own. "I'd rather be safe than sorry," he told the agents.

Despite finding no compelling evidence of a threat, the agents had no choice but to document that the young man's doctor considered him dangerous to the president. Such a prognosis was listed explicitly in the Secret Service internal policy manual as a warning sign of "mental dysfunction" in a possible killer.

Fein was aghast at the situation this created, both for its potential to squander resources and to impose unwarranted intrusion on a subject. A call to local police involving a fantasy about Reagan's death, fraught though that topic was in the early 1980s, did not equate per se with sinister intent, let alone a capacity to act on it. The Secret Service was tracking a monthly average of about 350 people under QI status, the vast majority of whom had come into some form of contact with mental health practitioners. At that time in 1983, about a fifth of those people were confined in mental hospitals or prison psychiatric units, while the rest, including the young man in Cleveland, fell under the more complicated task of monitoring and intervening while respecting their rights as free citizens. Fein wrote an addendum stating that his review of the case file confirmed that the young man did not appear to pose a threat, though his QI status remained up to the agents.

Fein began advising agents on interviewing strategies and how to gauge bizarre or volatile behavior they encountered in the field. Secret Service agents were also coming to Bridgewater to train, observing and participating in staff interviews with patients. The McLean team's research had emphasized the importance of maintaining distinct roles for mental health and law enforcement professionals while acknowledging that, as a practical matter, agents often made referrals and helped steward the long-term care of troubled people. Criminal justice and therapeutic work were not synonymous and could come into conflict, but the knowledge that agents were gaining at Bridgewater could help them assess and manage cases.

One skill was how to better read disordered thinking, which could seem like phantasmagoric "crazy talk" but might well follow an internal logic for the subjects themselves. The concreteness of details elicited in an interview could also help to measure a person's conviction and wherewithal to pursue a violent idea. A conspicuous enthusiasm shown by someone for the notion of a president dying while in office might have different implications than, say, focus on purchasing a gun from a local pawnshop the week before the president was scheduled to come to town. Thoughts of self-harm were also important: the latest research at Bridgewater had shown that suicidal intentions frequently comingled with homicidal ones.

These collaborations in Washington and Massachusetts were the making of a new kind of prevention work. The mental health side was operational rather than clinical, tailored specifically to each case and focused first and foremost on how potentially dangerous people were behaving. The approach held promise, but it needed a stronger scientific foundation on which to build.

———

The advancement of complex endeavors occurs through investment and toil but also through the nudge of unpredictable developments. For the field of behavioral threat assessment, a mysterious incident involving a preeminent federal judge would generate such a fateful effect.

The sudden burst of glass came shortly before eleven p.m. on a Thursday in late February 1985. US Supreme Court justice Harry Blackmun had just stepped away from the living room in his third-floor apartment when he was jolted by the shattering sound and a scream from his wife, Dorothy. He rushed back into the room. His beloved Dottie, as he called her, had been sprinkled with shards where she sat. To his great relief, she was uninjured. The living room window had a jagged hole in it roughly the size of a baseball.

Police and FBI agents raced to the apartment building in Rosslyn, Virginia, just across the Potomac River from the Georgetown neighborhood of Washington, DC. They quickly found the 9 mm bullet, lodged in a living room chair.

Justice Blackmun was accustomed to being a target. The stoic seventy-six-year-old Nixon appointee had faced an endless barrage of harassment and threats ever since he had authored the 1973 majority opinion in *Roe v. Wade* legalizing abortion in the United States. Over the course of his judicial career, Blackmun received more than eighty thousand pieces of angry and menacing correspondence. As one of his former law clerks recounted many years later in an interview with National Public Radio, "There was a room upstairs at the Court that was filled with nothing but hate mail that he got. And he got it every day."

This scare at his home came at an especially tense time. Blackmun was under recently tightened security, as he was targeted by political extremists. They included the so-called Army of God, a militant far-right group that had mailed Blackmun a death threat a few months earlier and was thought to be behind a recent string of abortion clinic bombings in the Washington region. A few days before the bullet smashed through the apartment window, Blackmun had received an explicit threat by mail, whose unknown author vowed to "shoot his brains out" and revel at Blackmun's funeral.

The FBI urged local authorities to maintain a news blackout on details of the apartment shooting for four days while it investigated. Soon the FBI acknowledged publicly that it had done a ballistic analysis within hours of arriving on the scene and announced an eyebrow-raising determination: The gunshot appeared to be random in nature, most likely "accidental" in where it had struck. The steep descent of the bullet's trajectory from the window to the chair indicated that it was probably fired from a long distance, according to the FBI, possibly from across the river in Georgetown.

"We are fine and shall carry on as usual," Blackmun assured

close friends and confidants, who remained convinced that he and Dottie had barely escaped an assassin's bullet. The identity of who fired it was never discovered. But even if the near miss had been an extraordinary coincidence, Blackmun certainly would not forget it, and the shooting would later ricochet in an unforeseen way, when the esteemed justice became personally involved in launching a groundbreaking project aimed at thwarting assassins.

That project was to emerge from Robert Fein's continued work with the Secret Service in the late 1980s, alongside a newly installed senior agent overseeing threat cases. When Fein first met special agent Bryan Vossekuil, neither had an inkling of the journey the two were about to begin together. By appearance, at least, they made a pair molded as if from a Hollywood screenplay: Vossekuil, a mustachioed, undemonstrative cop, the taller and lankier of the two, and Fein, the shorter and more bookish psychologist. Vossekuil had begun his Secret Service career as a young veteran just out of the Marine Corps in 1976, the same year that a young professional Fein had first walked up to the entrance of Bridgewater State Hospital. After stints in anti-counterfeiting and protective intelligence, Vossekuil later traveled the globe guarding Reagan, assigned to the presidential security detail not long after Hinckley struck. That attack still loomed large in American political consciousness, but unknown to the public was the peril that followed later in the decade.

As Vossekuil was stepping into his new supervisory post in the intelligence division, the Secret Service faced four serious threat cases within a period of eighteen months, which remain little known to this day. Reagan was endangered again, twice. Other targets included Vice President George H. W. Bush and 1988 Democratic presidential candidate Michael Dukakis. All four perpetrators from these separate cases—including two assassins who were armed when they moved toward their targets in public locations—were prosecuted. Two were eventually incarcerated, and two others were committed to secure psychiatric facilities.

The cluster of cases gripped the attention of the Secret Service leadership, who wanted Vossekuil and Fein to examine them posthaste. What the pair found stirred even greater concern.

Unlike many subjects the agency focused on, none of the four men had directly threatened their targets in letters or other communications. They all appeared to be relatively well educated. There was scant history of violence among them, and only one had a criminal record. None of them fit the common notions of how an assassin looked and behaved—the glowering, slightly disheveled person lurking at the edge of a crowd, perhaps muttering to himself, perhaps wearing a conspicuously bulky coat on a warm summer day. "We didn't find demons or insane people," Vossekuil recalled. "It turned out to be a lot more banal than that." Also striking was that two of the four did not appear to be clinically diagnosable as mentally ill.

These findings provoked a troubling realization at the Secret Service: some of the most dangerous people out there might not even be on their radar. The scope of stalking and planning activity in one of the cases was especially sobering, Vossekuil said: "How could somebody travel around the country on and off for three years, armed with a weapon and looking for an opportunity to attack the president, and the Secret Service not know about it?"

In 1990, Secret Service leaders and behavioral science experts convened again in Washington, this time with a focus on stalking behavior, a problem drawing sensational media attention around entertainment figures. Every celebrity stalking case and high-profile assassination attempt in recent memory had prompted news coverage depicting the offenders as madmen, while use of the insanity defense in trials reinforced the popular belief that acute mental illness was always the culprit. Fein and Vossekuil pulled together an overview of the roughly thirty ongoing threat cases considered most serious at the Secret Service—including their observations of organized behavior and rational thinking among some of the perpetrators. Mental illness as a singular explanation looked increasingly unhelpful in the quest to better understand what led to attacks.

Their sense of mission sharpened further when Henry Steadman, an esteemed sociologist and criminal justice expert in attendance, commented that the Secret Service must be sitting on rich data. "You should look further into the population you already know about," he told the pair. Moreover, while the agency remained heavily focused on people who made explicit threats against the president, Fein and Vossekuil now also knew that some plotters did not engage in that activity. They resolved to dig deeper into what they began conceptualizing more broadly as "pre-attack thinking" and "attack-related behaviors."

With director John Simpson's strong support for their plans, Fein got to work back home in Boston, haunting the library stacks at Harvard for several months. He aimed to review everything written on assassination in the English language over the past couple hundred years. The compulsively large pile of scholarly material he gathered from historians, political scientists, sociologists, and psychologists soon began to astonish him—not for what it contained but for what it was missing. From the failed attempt by a pistol-wielding man to kill President Andrew Jackson in 1835 to the murders of the Kennedy brothers and Martin Luther King in the 1960s, there were thousands of articles and books on American history alone that explored assassination through the lens of social and political conditions or that analyzed the demographics and psychological traits of the killers. But there were two glaring gaps in the literature. First, Fein couldn't find anything on assassination from the operational perspective of any profession or agency with protective responsibilities, like the Secret Service. There simply was nothing delving into how to go about the work of preventing attacks.

Second, and perhaps even more crucially, there was zero information from the perspective of political assassins themselves. What led them to conceive of such attacks, and then why and how did they move toward carrying them out? Fein was astonished that no one had made any real effort to ask the convicted plotters and killers these questions directly.

The terrain to be explored was not only coming into view but also needed to be expanded, Fein and Vossekuil reasoned. As the research literature going back to the March 1981 summit on evaluating dangerous behavior had described, it was difficult to study a rare phenomenon like assassination due to a lack of data—the "low base rate" problem. They could address this in two ways. One was to add proxy cases—"near-lethal" attempts that didn't quite reach an actual attack but otherwise closely resembled cases that did. The other was to broaden the set of targeted victims to include celebrities, civil rights leaders, business moguls, and other high-profile public figures. This approach would get them beyond a small sample group and produce a first-ever look at the "known universe" of assassins in recent US history. In addition to the significant time and funding required to gather and review records— they would study eighty-three offenders going back to 1949—Fein and Vossekuil determined that deep access and rapport-building would be paramount, to learn what could not be found in case files. They needed to speak face-to-face with as many assassins as possible.

Vossekuil was soon invited to speak at an American Psychiatric Association meeting in New York City, where he described their ambitions to Dr. Ruth Westrick, a sunny, mild-mannered practitioner serving as the chief of psychiatry at the Federal Medical Center in Rochester, Minnesota. Her enthusiastic response was the stroke of good fortune they needed. Westrick urged that they enlist the help of none other than Supreme Court justice Harry Blackmun, whom she had known personally since his early legal career, when he worked as counsel for the Mayo Clinic in Rochester. Blackmun would surely be interested in helping their cause, Westrick advised, given his experience with the bullet through his window. The federal judiciary had also since been shaken by additional events. In December 1989, Circuit Court judge Robert S. Vance was targeted by an angry ex-convict who sent a mail bomb to his Alabama home, killing him and seriously injuring his wife. Vance was the second federal judge in less than two years to be assassinated, an otherwise extremely rare occurrence. "I'll talk to Judgy," Westrick told Vossekuil, using her affectionate pet name for Blackmun.

In December 1991, Fein, Vossekuil, and Simpson, along with Westrick, joined the heads of the National Institute of Justice (a key potential source of funds) and the Federal Bureau of Prisons (key to accessing convicted assassins) for a meeting at the Supreme Court. Instead of the regal dark-wood environs typical of the Court's chambers, Blackmun's more eclectic offices provided the backdrop, the light-blue walls filled with photos and memorabilia: a baseball bat from 1930s Hall of Famer Mel Ott, insignias from the Illinois town where Blackmun grew up, a dress sword from his father's service in the National Guard during World War II. There was also a newspaper cartoon on display. It depicted 1960s extremist rage against a legendary chief justice as quaint compared to the vicious death threats since leveled at Blackmun, one of its character declaring, "I remember when the lunatic fringe was satisfied with 'Impeach Earl Warren!'" No Supreme Court justice in the twentieth century officially had been attacked by an assassin, but Blackmun kept the cartoon as a reminder of that harrowing Thursday night in 1985.

As the Secret Service team described the research plan to the other agency leaders, who questioned its potential, Blackmun listened intently. Toward the end, he spoke up: "I want to thank you all for agreeing to work together and prioritizing this very important project," he said. The Secret Service group departed with pledges of support from the other agency heads, whose follow-through they knew would be guaranteed by Blackmun's imprimatur.

Fein and Vossekuil soon assembled a small team of Secret Service agents and research specialists and launched what they would call the Exceptional Case Study Project. A first of its kind, it would take more than five years to complete. Among the assassins they began to scrutinize in person was John Lennon's killer, who agreed to meet with them in 1992 in New York's Attica state prison. When they arrived, they told Mark Chapman they hoped to learn from him as they developed investigative tools and training that might help prevent future violence. They would find most of their subjects forthright and useful in their feedback, including Chapman, who was both articulate and greatly enamored of the attention. (Around the same period, Chapman cooperated with a journalist writing a book about him and went on host Larry King's CNN show from prison.)

Chapman's behaviors preceding the attack were instructive. In September 1980, on the first of two trips he made to New York late that year, he had called his wife back home in Hawaii and told her that he'd intended to kill Lennon but had decided against it. His wife, who said decades later that Chapman had violently abused her and lied about disposing of a gun, apparently never told anyone about that communication, even after Chapman left Hawaii again abruptly that December to return to New York. Chapman planned what he would wear on his follow-up mission, including shoes suited for lengthy periods of standing around. He cultivated a rapport with a doorman at the Dakota, and with fans lingering at the building, bringing along a copy of Lennon's new album on the final day to burnish an appearance of authenticity. The copy of *Catcher* he carried, purchased at a local shop that morning, also served a tactical purpose: Chapman had concealed his revolver in a front pocket of his trench coat but worried that a police officer could conceivably notice the bulge, so he slipped the pocket-size book in over the gun, planning to pull that out if anyone questioned him.

Fein and Vossekuil discovered that Chapman had considered attacking other major public figures, including the governor of Hawaii, Jacqueline Kennedy Onassis, and the newly elected President Reagan. He said he'd seen himself as a failure and "a nobody" and had deemed these other major figures also to be "phonies" for what he viewed as their moral transgressions. Chapman's transference of his sense of grievance among multiple potential targets would stand out to the investigators as their research grew, as similar behavior turned up in a third of the eighty-three perpetrators they eventually studied.

Chapman divulged another striking piece of information. At one point during their hours of conversations, he brought up the many letters he received in prison from people all over.

"Did you get any that made an impression?" Fein asked, sensing Chapman's eagerness to discuss them.

"Yeah," he replied, describing one from a person he thought

had "serious problems" and seemed "very deranged." The person wanted to know about Chapman's experience as a killer and his subsequent life there in Attica. Chapman hadn't mentioned the letter to anyone before but now spoke of it, he said, because it had left him feeling distressed. "I got a letter from Robert Bardo."

The pair of investigators knew the name well. They learned that Chapman had received the correspondence in the spring of 1989, just a couple of months before its author had taken a fateful trip to Los Angeles in pursuit of a young celebrity. Fein and Vossekuil planned to speak with Bardo, who had done more than just make their shortlist. His case had helped set off a whole separate enterprise focused on combating menacing and dangerous behavior.

chapter four

———

THE PATHWAY TO VIOLENCE

Beyond the confidential research and collaboration developing inside the Secret Service, early concepts of behavioral threat assessment arose independently in several other settings. The Federal Bureau of Investigation had done threat assessment work in a broader sense since the late 1970s, although the focus in the 1980s at the FBI's new National Center for the Analysis of Violent Crime was on retrospective criminal profiling aimed at identifying and capturing elusive serial killers. The US Capitol Police had a small team of detectives, dating from the early eighties, who first worked out of an old converted basement boiler room next to the Capitol Building, tracking troubled people who threatened members of Congress and compiling information about their patterns of behavior. In California, a handful of experts in private security focused on the lucrative work of protecting celebrities, and by the end of the decade, a new approach to heading off dangerous stalkers was stirring in Los Angeles.

Stalking was an age-old problem in a cultural metropolis legendarily abundant with ambition and deviance. But in early 1989, a rash of activity included women in four separate cases who contacted the Los Angeles Police Department, fearing for their safety. While the eighties boom in television and tabloid culture had fixed a spotlight on celebrities coping with disturbing episodes of harassment, these four victims were ordinary private citizens. Without any apparent crimes to investigate in their cases, however, the response from the LAPD essentially had amounted to, "There's nothing we can do."

In less than a two-month period, all four women who'd sought help were murdered. Stalking didn't afflict just famous people at the hands of odd or frightening strangers—spouses, ex-boyfriends, coworkers, and former employees also engaged in obsessive and threatening behavior that could turn perilous. But the problem was little understood, let alone prioritized in the world of law enforcement. As with the shootings of Lennon and Reagan at the start of the decade, a high-profile tragedy would be requisite for change.

The morning of July 18, 1989, had arrived with promise for luminous young actor Rebecca Schaeffer. Around ten a.m., the twenty-one-year-old with cascading brunette curls, fair skin, and dark brown eyes finished showering and began to get dressed inside her apartment on the edge of West Hollywood. She was preparing to meet with famed director Francis Ford Coppola about playing the part of Mary Corleone in the third installment of the Oscar-winning *Godfather* films. Schaeffer had gushed about the audition in recent conversations with friends and confidants: This movie could rocket her to the big time—a chance to act alongside Al Pacino and Diane Keaton, in a role beckoning the likes of Julia

Roberts and Winona Ryder. Schaeffer was expecting imminent delivery of the closely guarded script by courier when her apartment buzzer sounded. The intercom system in the two-story Tudor-style building on North Sweetzer Avenue wasn't working at the time, so she paused over her laid out clothes and went to check the front entry. Just beyond the exterior glass door stood a young man holding a bag—not a courier, but instead the same awkward-looking guy in the yellow button-down shirt, jeans, and sandals who'd dropped by earlier that morning.

Nineteen-year-old Robert Bardo had been trying to reach Schaeffer for more than two years, writing her cloying fan letters and traveling from his home in Tucson to look for her. He'd failed on more than one occasion to gain entry to the Warner Brothers lot in Burbank where Schaeffer filmed her costarring role in *My Sister Sam*, the TV sitcom that had lit her career. This was Bardo's fourth trip into town. Starting around seven a.m., he'd wandered the neighborhood waving a glossy fan photo of Schaeffer at several standoffish passersby, trying to confirm that he was in the right place. Soon he pressed the buzzer, and a moment later Schaeffer had emerged in the foyer and opened the front door. Bardo held out the signed photo and told her he was a devoted fan. Schaeffer, who was known in Hollywood to be unusually down to earth and open-hearted, had wished him well in the short exchange and gone back inside. Bardo then left and walked to a nearby diner, astonished that he'd just met Schaeffer face-to-face. He ordered onion rings and cheesecake, used the restroom and made a call on a nearby pay phone. Then he walked several blocks in the bright midmorning sun back toward the apartment building.

"I forgot to give you something," he said when Schaeffer opened the front door again around ten fifteen a.m., just out of the shower and wrapped in a blue kimono.

"Hurry up, you're wasting my time," she allegedly replied.

In the plastic shopping bag he was holding, Bardo had another letter he'd written to her and a compact disc with music from the band U2, but he reached for neither of those things. Neighbors close by were startled by a loud bang and a bloodcurdling scream from Schaeffer as Bardo fired a single shot from a .357 Magnum point-blank into her chest.

Bardo later claimed that he felt Schaeffer had turned "callous" toward him, describing details of the encounter to Dr. Park Dietz, a forensic psychiatrist and expert on public-figure stalking who evaluated Bardo shortly ahead of the murder trial that put him in prison for life. There is no way to know how reliable Bardo's account of the killing was, other than perhaps as a measure of his fixation on Schaeffer. Both before and after his murder conviction, he recounted contradictory details about that morning regarding where he loaded the gun and how he pulled it out to shoot Schaeffer.

Investigators, however, were finding a long trail of warning signs that were of growing interest to the field of behavioral threat assessment. In addition to stalking behavior, an early focus for the field, Bardo had made threats—not to Schaeffer directly, but about her, elsewhere. He had also studied infamous killers, looking to them both for inspiration and tactics. One notable fragment turned up as soon as police gathered evidence near Schaeffer's apartment. When Bardo fled the scene on foot, headed for the bus that would soon take him back to Tucson, he had ditched items in the surrounding neighborhood, including something else he was carrying that morning: a paperback copy of *The Catcher in the Rye*.

Stalking behavior was widely seen at the time as a murky mental-health problem beyond the purview of law enforcement. But Schaeffer's murder shocked Hollywood and the public and set off two watershed developments in California. The first was the creation of the Los Angeles Police Department's Threat Management Unit, the first local police team in the country devoted to thwarting stalkers. LAPD leaders were frustrated over the four recent stalking murders of non-famous women, according to John Lane, a former detective who ran the team shortly after its inception at the start of the 1990s, and that frustration was now compounded by pressure from a powerful constituency, as details from Bardo's background went public in news reports. "The entertainment community was up in arms," Lane recalled. The supervising detective who had launched the unit, Bob Martin, attended a meeting with Hollywood executives who voiced the industry's outrage: "Why did we have to wait for Rebecca Schaeffer to die before something is done?" they demanded. "Why can't law enforcement be proactive?"

Police simply didn't operate that way. Moreover, until the moment Bardo pulled the trigger, his behavior exemplified a uniquely slippery problem. As veteran LA prosecutor Rhonda Saunders later put it, "There really is no way you can make it a crime to do most of the stuff that stalkers usually do—the letters, the phone calls, the gifts." Nevertheless, with LAPD leadership ordering action, Lane and two fellow detectives on the initial team began pursuing new ways to confront the menace aggressively. With victims' cooperation, they investigated the longer-term records and activity of alleged suspects, seeking to corroborate patterns of threatening behavior. They would get a bead on stalkers' own routines and then aim to turn the tables on them by showing up at their homes or jobs and putting them on notice, a tactic known as a "knock and talk." It was intimidation veiled in firm professionalism, and it could be an effective deterrent, particularly if the individual wasn't accustomed to interacting with the police. The team also firmly advised women who came to them for help that they should seek restraining orders in court, in part because violations of those could make prosecution an option.

In an era when emphasis on victims' rights was an ascendant theme in law enforcement, there was opportunity for these elusive cases to be worked over a period of months or even years. "Essentially the idea became, if you have a legitimate threat and you're honest with us and follow our advice, we will make you a 'client' for as long as you need," Lane recalled.

The team would urge victims to help them thoroughly document unwanted behaviors, and they insisted that the victims end all contact with suspects. They had learned that if an exasperated victim finally answered the phone by the twentieth call to try to placate or dissuade her tormentor, that told him he would simply need thirty calls to get through the next time.

The unit's tactics were imperfect at best and could backfire, provoking behavior later clarified in threat assessment literature as "boundary probing." If suspected stalkers felt they were being bullied or threatened by detectives showing up at their door, they might escalate their activity. Restraining orders could set them off dangerously. Others might serve brief jail time and then go right back to the harassment.

The LAPD Threat Management Unit had few legal tools to work with, but another big change was imminent. Around the time of Rebecca Schaeffer's murder and the cluster of other fatal stalking cases in Los Angeles, several women in neighboring Orange County who had gotten restraining orders against exes also wound up dead. A state senator from the region, Ed Royce, soon put forward legislation criminalizing stalking behavior in California. As Royce later recounted, for too long the paradigm for law enforcement had been, "Once a victim is attacked physically, then we can act." As of January 1991, California made it a crime to repeatedly follow or harass a person and make a credible threat with intent to put that person in "reasonable fear" of serious physical harm. The law was the first of its kind in the nation, and was soon revised to cover victims also fearing for the safety of their immediate families.

The scope of the stalking problem was greater than anyone had understood, as the LAPD unit's caseload and a new wave of research began to make evident. Up till then, focus on stalking at the Secret Service, Capitol Police, and among private security professionals had been attuned to narrow agency missions and the eighties Zeitgeist. In addition to the attacks on Lennon and Reagan (and the targeting of Jodie Foster), there had been the near-fatal stabbing of actor Theresa Saldana in 1982 by an obsessed man who traveled from the United Kingdom to Hollywood. Olivia Newton-John, David Letterman, Michael J. Fox, Justine Bateman, and other celebrities faced chilling cases of harassment and menace, with American television and print media obliging a hefty public appetite for sensational coverage of the phenomenon. But the national narrative about stalking as a "celebrity crime" by deranged loners was misleading. That wasn't the majority of the problem, as Lane and his colleagues were learning firsthand.

As the LAPD team drew some publicity and a growing caseload, they welcomed assistance from mental health professionals, including forensic psychiatrist Michael Zona, who offered to consult and conduct research. The effort was later joined by a young California native trained in forensic psychology at the University of Nebraska, Russell Palarea (who two decades later would usher me into the world of threat assessment at Disneyland). Their analysis drawing from nearly 350 cases handled by the LAPD Threat Management Unit through the first half of the 1990s showed that stalkers victimized ordinary people in more than three times as many cases as they did celebrities. Even that contrast was likely

understated, with the LAPD unit's caseload skewed by their working at the epicenter of the entertainment industry.

The research further revealed that the vast majority of stalkers
in non-celebrity cases had some form of connection or relationship with their victims, whether personal, job-related, or otherwise.
And while many of the strangers who hunted famous figures had
major mental illnesses, most stalkers from the much larger pool of
those actually connected to their victims did not. These generally
weren't offenders with schizophrenia, psychosis, or acute personality disorders. Much more commonly they nursed bitter grievances,
engaged in domestic violence and substance abuse, and sometimes
displayed signs of depression and suicidality. The cases with violent
outcomes confirmed that the most dangerous stalkers were the victims' own current or former intimate partners.

The potential duration and wider impact of stalking had also
become apparent with two traumatic non-celebrity cases in Northern California. In spring 1990, Kathleen Gallagher Baty was tied
up and nearly abducted at knifepoint from her home in Menlo Park
before police intervened at the last minute. The near-miss was part
of a twelve-year ordeal at the hands of a former high school classmate who eventually tried to follow Baty to her relocated home in
Florida. Another case had resulted in major collateral damage and
foretold how stalking behavior would be a significant factor in the
emerging phenomenon of mass shootings: the deadly 1988 workplace rampage at ESL in Santa Clara, where long-time harasser
Richard Farley had targeted his former coworker Laura Black.

Ten people were convicted and sentenced under the California
stalking law in its first year. As legal debate churned, both about its
constitutionality and whether it was hard-line enough to be effective against recalcitrance, emerging research suggested there were
an estimated two hundred thousand stalkers nationwide, with

roughly 15 percent of cases turning violent. (Research over the next two decades showed that to be a mere fraction of the problem: More than 3.3 million people were stalked in the United States each year, the majority of them women, but prosecutions under stalking statutes remained rare.) Lane and his colleagues realized that even after adding more detectives, it would be folly for the team to work this complex and sprawling issue alone. Reaching out to other agencies in law enforcement and mental health in the region, leaders of the LAPD unit convened a meeting at the police academy to discuss interagency collaboration, and they cultivated plans for a networked organization that would become known as the Association of Threat Assessment Professionals.

Lane also received a call about contributing to an effort under way with the National Institute of Justice to develop a model anti-stalking code, as legislation was beginning to spread in other states. He took a trip to Washington, DC, where, among others involved, he met Robert Fein and Bryan Vossekuil, whose ongoing research was on the brink of transforming the field. By 1996, all fifty states would have anti-stalking laws on the books and Congress would criminalize the behavior occurring across state lines. By then, Secret Service investigators were further learning that stalking was but one of multiple behaviors germane to the mission.

———

Fifty-five miles northeast of San Francisco, beyond the steel gates and down the bleak corridors of the California state prison in Vacaville, forensic psychologist Robert Fein and special agent Jim Lucey, another Secret Service agent working on the Exceptional Case Study Project, sat down face-to-face with Robert Bardo. By the mid-1990s, the Secret Service team was deep into a series of trips to interview nearly two dozen assassins and "near-lethal" plotters. Through multiple hours of conversations with each of the killers, some over several visits, they examined ideas, motivations, circumstances, and actions leading up to when the offenders attacked high-profile figures or were apprehended on the brink. They sought behavioral context that likely could only be discovered by talking at length with offenders, after their cases had been adjudicated. They cultivated rapport with Bardo as they had others: "You're one of the few experts in assassination," Fein said to him, explaining why they'd come to the prison. "We'd like to understand your perspective so that we can help prevent other tragedies."

Apart from a more recessive hairline, Bardo had the same awkwardly youthful appearance seen at his trial, with his dimpled chin and dark eyes beneath thick low-set brows. As the investigators would confirm, Bardo was the product of a broken background: the youngest child of seven from a dysfunctional family, an intelligent but failed student, and later a recluse who couldn't hold down a janitorial job at a fast-food restaurant and instead followed a warped and winding path to murder. Since his incarceration, he had been volunteering in the prison AIDS ward. "He was not some hard-bitten, awful, spitting-at-you kind of guy," Fein recalled. The team did encounter some hostile offenders as they traversed prisons and psychiatric facilities, but more were like Bardo than not: generally open and receptive to the idea of helping prevent future versions of what they'd done.

Bardo admitted that he had devastated Rebecca Schaeffer's family as well as ruined his own life. He saw his past self as hopeless and a loser: "The person you're trying to stop is actually very weak," he told the investigators. "Never think of him as strong." That person might dress in different ways, he noted, and would be thinking about how to outmaneuver security as he planned his attack. "People like me," he said, "can be deceptive."

Building on case records and information gathered by investigators for Bardo's trial, Fein and the Secret Service team were developing a detailed picture of Bardo's pre-attack thinking and activity—behaviors echoed in the accounts of many of their subjects. Bardo had a history of grievances and violent threats against schoolmates, teachers, and neighbors, and in the year before the murder had been arrested in Tucson, after which he took a plea deal to avoid conviction on charges of disorderly conduct and domestic violence.

He had become fixated on Schaeffer and made a series of oblique threats about her. By June 1989, he had apparently grown angry over Schaeffer's depiction of sexual intimacy with another actor in a newly released film satire, *Scenes from the Class Struggle in Beverly Hills*. Soon, Bardo gave a letter to an older sister, who was moving away from Tucson, informing her that he was going on a "mission" and that he hoped she could understand his emotional torment. "What I am about to do is cruel and negative and will shock you," he wrote. "I'm obsessed with something I can't have, so I'm going to make it so that something doesn't exist anymore."

Bardo's sister knew that her reclusive brother collected pictures of Schaeffer and liked to watch videotaped episodes of *My Sister Sam*. As she settled with her family in Tennessee, something clicked for her about his disconcerting missive. Her four-year-old daughter, whom Bardo had babysat back in Tucson, had mentioned Bardo talking about "putting a girl named Rebecca to sleep." But when Bardo's sister reached him by phone in Tucson on July 14, fearing he might be suicidal or perhaps even intending to hurt Schaeffer, he brushed aside her concerns about any such intentions.

Bardo reiterated his threat cryptically on the final morning.

During the pay-phone call from near the diner a little before nine a.m., he told his sister he was in LA. "You're going to hear something about me," he said. From her end of the line, he sounded calm and reasonable, essentially unemotional. What Bardo didn't say explicitly was that he was poised to fulfill a mission he'd written further about privately. He intended to stop Schaeffer from forsaking her youthful innocence and becoming a Hollywood "screen whore."

Numerous dangerous stalkers, whether a delusional stranger or a person connected to the victim, have harbored this type of vengeful grievance. Threat assessment experts came to know that it often marks a vision for murder-suicide. As a teen, Bardo had communicated homicidal and suicidal thoughts in writings to his schoolteachers, though after being hospitalized briefly at one point, his parents rebuffed school officials urging further psychiatric help. The police who captured Bardo in Tucson the day after the killing caught up with him on a freeway ramp where he appeared to be trying to get run over by oncoming cars. He apparently had lost his nerve in LA; he later stated that the moment after he shot Schaeffer, "I was fumbling around, thinking I should blow my head off and fall on her."

Bardo had undertaken extensive planning and preparations. He was organized and deliberate, researching where Schaeffer lived and initially taking an erroneous trip into the Hollywood Hills to a previous residence of hers. He contacted the talent agency representing her, first to suss out where she was working and again at a later date to find out when she would return from travel abroad in July 1989. He used an alias in his attempts to access the Warner Brothers lot. The escalation of his intent could be seen in what he carried on his travels to LA, beginning in June 1987: first, an oversize teddy bear and a bouquet of flowers he wanted to give to

Schaeffer. When he returned on a follow-up trip and was again turned away by studio security, he was carrying a concealed knife. Ahead of the final trip, he was rejected by a Tucson gun-shop owner who had picked up on his instability, but he soon persuaded an older brother to buy him a pistol, and he practiced shooting with it the day before he boarded his last Greyhound bus ride to LA.

Then there was Bardo's emulation of killers. He admired not only Mark Chapman, to whom he eventually wrote in Attica prison, but also John Hinckley and Arthur Jackson, the Scot who viciously stabbed Theresa Saldana in 1982. All three men's acts figured into Bardo's cultural script and influenced his stalking behavior, which wasn't limited to Schaeffer. As a young teen in 1984, Bardo had left home and traveled by bus to Maine looking for Samantha Smith, a charismatic young girl who'd become a media sensation after corresponding about peace with a Soviet leader at the height of the Cold War. Unable to find her, he was soon picked up by juvenile authorities and sent back home. In 1988, he went looking for pop singer Debbie Gibson in New York City, and while there paid a visit to the entry of the Dakota Building where Chapman gunned down John Lennon eight years prior. (Before shooting Reagan in early 1981, Hinckley had also visited the Dakota.) This specific type of emulation behavior, known as a "pilgrimage," would metastasize in particular around the Columbine High School tragedy a decade later. The Dakota visit was another way in which Bardo linked himself to his antiheroes before eventually heading to Los Angeles carrying his own copy of *The Catcher in the Rye*. His quoting of some of Lennon's lyrics in letters to Schaeffer may have also served that purpose.

Future threat-assessment research would articulate the increased danger posed by a subject who progressed from an interest in well-known killers to identification with them. At first Bardo admired these attackers; then he wanted to *be* them. He looked to them for tactics, deciding to use hollow-point bullets after reading about their lethality. And he found a strategic breakthrough in studying Arthur Jackson, who had pounced just outside of Saldana's own West Hollywood residence. Bardo had struggled to locate Schaeffer beyond the impenetrable Warner Brothers lot, but he'd eventually realized a way. Claiming he was trying to track down an old friend, he paid a fee to a private investigator, who tapped California motor vehicle records for Schaeffer's home address. Bardo later disclosed that he'd read an article in *People* magazine detailing Jackson's hunt for Saldana: "That's where I got the idea to hire a private investigator."

His focus on Jackson complicated the narrative that Schaeffer's suggestive bed scene in *Class Struggle* was what motivated Bardo to kill her—because he'd thought of doing the deed long before that movie came out. On a return visit to the studio lot back in summer 1987, this time carrying the concealed knife, Bardo grew enraged after he was again rejected by security. He later admitted that if he'd been able to get close to Schaeffer on that trip, "I'd have done to her what Arthur Jackson did to Theresa Saldana." From the perspective of threat assessment, Bardo's deluded reaction in June 1989 to Schaeffer's latest screen performance may have been a triggering event, but it was not an explanation of motive per se. Rather, his life was in a downward spiral, and he had now found a justification for pursuing a long-nurtured idea of violence.

The truth was that Bardo sought notoriety. In a fan letter to Schaeffer, he expressed longing for the life of a celebrity. He expanded on this in his diary, writing, "When I think about her, I feel that I want to become famous and impress her." In this way he echoed Hinckley, who wrote in a letter to Jodie Foster that he would attempt to kill President Reagan in the hopes of impressing her with a "historical deed, to gain your respect and love."

Bardo's case amounted to a deep aggregate of warning behaviors: the accumulation of grievances and threats, the burgeoning stalking activity, the personal deterioration and suicidality, a triggering event justifying his intent, the planning and preparations, and the emulation of killers, marked by an interest in multiple targets and a desire for fame.

The Secret Service research progressed well beyond just the thorny question of motive. What Fein, Vossekuil, and their team discovered through the scrutiny of various killers, including Bardo, was a distinct behavioral process. The patterns emerging from pre-attack behaviors and circumstances revealed how assassins moved from their initial violent ideas to eventual action. Fein and Vossekuil were zeroing in on what they called "the path to attack," a bedrock concept soon to be broadened and become widely known in the field as "the pathway to violence."

———

The foundational insights of behavioral threat assessment began circulating earlier than planned. On the morning of April 19, 1995, Fein and Vossekuil were working with an anti-stalking task force at the National Governors Association in Washington, DC, when breaking news sent them rushing back to Secret Service headquarters. A truck bomb detonated by an anti-government extremist had just pulverized much of the Alfred P. Murrah Federal Building in Oklahoma City.

Inside the Secret Service intelligence division's emergency command center, they stood among colleagues as details streamed in, the room palpable with worry. The domestic terrorist attack had killed 168 people and physically injured nearly 700 others. Nineteen children had perished, most of them inside a day-care center. Six Secret Service personnel working at the field office in the complex were among the dead.

The past several years had seen no shortage of jarring lethal attacks, including a string of gun rampages at health clinics in Boston, a law firm in San Francisco, a state unemployment office in Southern California, on a commuter train in New York, and on college campuses in Iowa and Massachusetts. American vernacular now included "going postal," with workplace grievances and stalking behavior marking recent attacks in New Jersey, Michigan, and Southern California, the latest in a trend of shootings at US Post Office branches dating from the mid-1980s. But the Oklahoma City bombing was a defining event, underlining at an excruciating scale the mission Fein and Vossekuil were pursuing.

Although their five-year systematic study of assassins was still two years from completion, the key insights were already in view and had clear potential to be applied more broadly. The behavioral similarities among violent stalkers, assassins, and mass killers would be further observable in Oklahoma City perpetrator Timothy McVeigh. Before developing the truck-bombing plan, for example, McVeigh had considered trying to assassinate the US attorney general or an FBI sniper who was involved in the deadly standoffs pitting extremists against the federal government at Ruby Ridge and Waco in the early 1990s. With those events fueling his own anti-government grievance and hatred, McVeigh had detonated a cultural script for violent far-right extremists that would smolder for decades to come.

If sharing the unfinished work of the Exceptional Case Study Project might mean boosting chances at all for stopping a new traumatic event, Fein and Vossekuil felt compelled to get the word out. Working with Gwen Holden, a criminal justice expert spearheading the anti-stalking task force, they pulled together a National Institute of Justice report for law enforcement leaders in all levels of government. The July 1995 report described an approach to thwarting what they now called "targeted violence." This was not just about assassinations, they explained, but a wider range of planned attacks that stemmed from domestic violence, workplace strife, ideological extremism, and other factors that could presage acts of vengeance and destruction. They articulated an essential insight: Acts of targeted violence were "the end result of an understandable and often discernible process of thinking and behavior."

None of the eighty-three assassins they were studying had pursued acts of murder impulsively; their attacks and plots were "the culmination of long-developing, identifiable trails of problems, conflicts, disputes, and failures." What mattered most was not who these various individuals were—their demographics, traits, or clinical histories—but what they did. The focus was on how they behaved and why, as they cultivated and carried out plans to kill. This was a process that could be recognized and therefore potentially stopped.

With the completion of the research in 1997 came more clarity about these killers. First, there were no useful profiles of them based on demographic or psychological factors. Most of the eighty-three plotters and assassins were white males, but some were Black, Latino, and Middle Eastern, and a few were women. The full group ranged in age from sixteen to seventy-three. Half either were or had been married, and more than a third had children. Almost half had some college or graduate education, including perpetrators who'd gone to medical or law school, or had worked as college professors. And while many of the subjects were experienced with weapons, including some who had military backgrounds, only one in five had a violent criminal history. It was evident that these deeply troubled individuals were not leading exemplary work or family lives by the time they hatched plans to kill, but Fein and Vossekuil wrote that any temptation to dismiss them as "inadequate, unaccomplished losers" would be misguided and a poor benchmark for identifying dangerous people.

Nor were the assassins all "madmen," they explained. While most had significant mental health problems in a broad sense, including suicidal thoughts, those conditions weren't a cause of the majority of the attacks. Fewer than half were delusional at the time they moved to carry out their plans, and very few were driven by psychotic hallucinations. In fact, most of the perpetrators were organized in their thinking and "behaved quite rationally" in pursuit of their missions. They conducted surveillance, calculating optimal times and locations for approaching their targets. They dressed to look normal and blend in with a crowd. One near-lethal plotter, for example, had scoped out the site for an upcoming speech by the US president—the perpetrator from the late 1980s who had traveled the country for three years looking for his chance to strike. He had once been a promising medical student but had suffered a breakdown. Yet his thinking had remained organized enough to acquire a .38 caliber handgun, track the president over time, and successfully rob a series of banks to pay for his travel.

"I decided I was going to dress up like a law enforcement person," he told Fein and Vossekuil of his final plan, "so I bought a suit, the shoes, and a trench coat, and had a haircut. And then I went north . . . because I was looking for a location where I could test-fire the gun."

Another important discovery was that the vast majority of the eighty-three assassins never directly threatened their targets, but almost all of them had indeed made threats—communicating their violent intent to others around them, either explicitly or in a veiled manner. Some conveyed their plans in dialogue with coworkers, friends, or family (such as Chapman's explicit comments to his wife about killing Lennon). Some detailed or implied threats in diaries, letters, or other writings (such as Bardo's cryptic message to his sister about going on a "mission" to make the source of his torment no longer "exist"). In the years and decades ahead, these patterns would extend through a growing number of mass shooters.

The area of communicated threats, however, held additional complexity. As Secret Service case files showed, there were many attention-seeking individuals who made noise about killing high-profile figures or other people but never actually took any action toward attacking, like conducting research and surveillance or acquiring and rehearsing with a weapon. "Recognizing the difference between 'making' and 'posing' a threat is crucially important," Fein and Vossekuil emphasized. All verbal or written threats had to be taken seriously at the outset of evaluations, but the expression of those did not necessarily mean a person was making or advancing a plan to do physical harm. The threats could be just empty bluster, but behaviors toward a planned action were a more urgent problem—and in some cases those behaviors did not include any communicated threats at all. Fein and Vossekuil expressed these principles with a plainspoken rhetorical triad:

Some persons who make threats ultimately pose threats.
Many persons who make threats do not pose threats.
Some persons who pose threats never make threats.

These concepts were soon affirmed by separate work from elsewhere in the expanding field that had been instigated by the mail bombing assassination of Judge Robert Vance and was focused specifically on protecting the federal judiciary. Titled *Hunters and Howlers*, a 1998 study from a chief researcher with the US Marshals Service articulated the idea that the quieter, more subtle plotters could often be more dangerous than the louder, more explicit threateners.

Fein and Vossekuil were determined to make their research useful in part by demystifying the behaviors and life experiences of their case subjects. Virtually all of these people had histories of unresolved grievances and resentments, with many having engaged in harassment or other openly hostile behavior. Failures in school, work, or social relationships, often combined with rough living situations or sometimes experiences of domestic or child abuse, had left these plotters and killers feeling angry and desperate, backed into a corner. A great many of them came to see violence as the only viable solution to their problems, to gain revenge or "justice," or to escape suffering. That such ideas seemed irrational was less important to assessing the danger than determining whether subjects were committed to this kind of justification and had both the *ability* and the *means* to commit an attack.

The mission then was to discern how far along those individuals were on the escalating pathway to violence. Smoldering grievances or deepening desperation gave rise to ideas about killing, which led to research and planning, then to preparation and a decision to attack. Fein and Vossekuil soon developed a lengthy "protective intelligence" guide that would be distributed by the National Institute of Justice and the Secret Service to thousands of state and local law enforcement agencies, which included a series of investigative questions for evaluating reportedly threatening individuals. Investigators could learn a lot through interviews and other information-gathering techniques short of making an arrest: What level of concern or fear were these subjects stirring in people around them? Had they obtained or begun practicing with weapons? How well were they known to cope with stress, and what circumstances or events could they be facing—a poor job evaluation, a major financial loss, a divorce—that might trigger a plan for violence? Had they shown a willingness to test or cross boundaries, such as violating a court order? Had they expressed a willingness to go to jail, or to die?

Plans to kill could be driven by multiple and sometimes shifting ideas. Some assassins wanted to bring attention to a cause or perceived injustice. Others had idiosyncratic beliefs about establishing relationships with their targets. Some hoped to die in an attack, a phenomenon known as suicide by cop, which was drawing heightened focus in law enforcement in the 1990s. Political anger or ideology could provide powerful feelings of justification, and yet, through the five years' worth of research, politics rarely turned out to be a primary motivation for attacks.

Fein and Vossekuil were struck by how often a desire for notoriety kept turning up, a goal for more than two dozen of the offenders they scrutinized. Some they interviewed in prison offered deeper insight into how fame-seeking had specifically shaped their thinking and behavior, including a young man who had gone to a presidential campaign event in 1988 to shoot the Republican nominee, Vice President George H. W. Bush. As he described to Fein and Vossekuil, he'd harbored thoughts of "instant celebrity" and getting his name "permanently in history." He was a high school dropout, but intelligent. While developing plans, he had spent a year and a half researching American assassins, including a contemporaneous book categorizing them in sociological and historical terms. "I'm a type two," he told them. His acumen for the material was impressive, Fein recalled. He also told them he'd selected a Colt .45 for his mission because he admired the infamous Manson Family member Lynette "Squeaky" Fromme, who had carried that type of handgun when she came close to shooting President Gerald Ford in Sacramento's Capitol Park back in 1975. Like Chapman, Bardo, Bremer, and others, the young man had considered going after several different high-profile figures, including his home state's governor. While in some cases the target transference was likely in response to a lack of access to a heavily protected person, Fein and Vossekuil came to see that, for some offenders, the act itself of trying to kill a powerful figure was more meaningful than who that figure was specifically.

"There was nothing crazy in thinking that targeting a politician or a famous person would get a lot of attention," Fein reflected. "It *did* get them a lot of attention."

The young man further explained that he had focused on Bush because no one had ever killed a sitting vice president—making that a unique feat he believed could earn him his very own chapter in a book someday.

The aberrant narcissism Fein and Vossekuil encountered in their subjects proved useful for cultivating their participation and sometimes led to darkly amusing circumstances. One day in 1994, they rode across a desolate stretch of freeway in central California's San Joaquin Valley, not far behind a small convoy of Secret Service vehicles. Like the other agents ahead of them, the pair of investigators were on their way to the notoriously brutal Corcoran state prison. They were set to meet at the facility with Sirhan Sirhan, the diminutive Arab-Palestinian man who in 1968 had assassinated Senator Robert F. Kennedy during a presidential campaign event at the Ambassador Hotel in Los Angeles. The timing of their trip had aligned coincidentally with a separate mission: the other agents were investigating a threat, and were en route to interview prisoners connected with the homicidal cult leader Charles Manson, who was also housed in the prison's protective unit for high-profile inmates. That summer, after the celebrity and former football star O. J. Simpson had been charged with murdering his ex-wife and a friend of hers, Manson reportedly became irate over the deluge of media attention on Simpson, whose low-speed pursuit by police along Southern California freeways had been viewed on live television by upward of ninety-five million people. Manson's long-held racial animus apparently coincided with a desire to seize the spotlight once again for himself. He had thus made it known through prison associates that he had authorized a hit on President Bill Clinton.

Word of the arriving Secret Service contingent flew through the prison unit. By the time Fein and Vossekuil got into an interview room with Sirhan, he was notably animated. At a little over five feet tall, he seemed even smaller and slighter in person. "All these agents are here for me?" he asked anxiously. "Why do you need so many for me?"

They explained the purpose of their visit. He thought it over for a moment, then said he would agree to talk with them only on the condition that he would be freed in a prisoner swap involving the Palestinians. Fein and Vossekuil exchanged a glance, and Vossekuil smiled back at Sirhan. "That's way above our pay grade," he said.

"But you work for the president," Sirhan insisted. "You should be able to arrange this."

"Sorry, but we can't do it. There's just no way."

So began a long conversation with the assassin whose ugly deed had for more than two decades been swallowed in questions about a flawed investigation and a swirl of epic Kennedy-worthy conspiracy theories involving everything from the mafia and CIA to weaponized hypnosis, an elusive "girl in a polka dot dress" and an alleged second shooter. Although Sirhan had testified at his 1969 trial that he had killed RFK "with twenty years of malice aforethought," he had later recanted the confession, claiming that he didn't remember doing the actual shooting. From Fein and Vossekuil's perspective, even a case so politically and historically fraught underscored an emerging principle of threat assessment: motive invariably was complex, and in many cases could offer only a partial explanation for pre-attack behaviors. In the run-up to the assassination, Sirhan had been explicit that his intent sprang from defending the Palestinian people against what he considered to be Kennedy's abhorrent policy of supplying military jets to Israel. "RFK must die!" he'd written in a notebook, among other declarations about the coming assassination. Yet notably, Sirhan was another perpetrator who had considered multiple targets: He had also thought of going after President Lyndon Johnson or US Ambassador Arthur Goldberg, targets he also justified with his grievance about the Israeli-Palestinian conflict.

As the hours in the interview room went by, Sirhan eventually came around to describing to Fein and Vossekuil what he had done: "I was there, I had a gun, and I fired at Senator Kennedy," he said. "But I am told that the ballistic evidence was equivocal, and I cannot believe that I killed Robert Kennedy. It must have been somebody else."

"As I watched him talk," Fein recalled, "I remember thinking that the immensity of the assassination was simply too great for this small, limited man, that he just could not fully accept the consequences of it. But there was also a part of him that wasn't going to lie."

Sirhan had long since swapped out political grievance for a popular conspiracy theory, in part because he wanted to seek a retrial based on alleged new evidence. He eventually did, and failed, in 2011. The shift was one among several indications that political motive may have been secondary for him, a grandiose justification to which he had arrived. As a young man in the mid-1960s, Sirhan had failed out of Pasadena City College, was fired from several low-level service jobs, suffered a head injury while working at a horse ranch (he'd hoped to become a jockey), and had no social life to speak of. He had few employable skills and was deeply frustrated with his lot in life. He had begun to nurture the idea of shooting a national figure whom he deemed to be an enemy of the Palestinian people, and perhaps he convinced himself that he might even help change his people's plight in doing so. But there was considerable evidence, Fein and Vossekuil concluded, that Sirhan's foremost interest in assassinating RFK was to gain a level of attention and status he so desperately craved, further reflected in his notion that he was someone whom the US president might trade to the Palestinians.

In this respect, Sirhan's decision to target Kennedy may have stemmed from a different view he held of the charismatic senator, which he'd revealed five years before Fein and Vossekuil sat down with him, in a conversation with TV journalist David Frost: "He was my hero. He was the protector and the defender of the downtrodden and the disadvantaged, and I felt that I was one," Sirhan told Frost during a 1989 jailhouse interview. "All my hopes were focused on Robert Kennedy. I was his supporter." Frost noted in response that "hope" had been Kennedy's defining message. Sirhan nodded in agreement as he moved on to Kennedy's planned military aid to Israel, telling Frost with a flash of seething anger that he had considered that policy "a betrayal."

But beneath the political grievance Sirhan was still performing two decades later, he surely knew something else. His killing of Robert Kennedy had been the killing of hope for a great many people. And for that, he would most certainly be remembered.

———

Targeted violence of a more quotidian nature became a focus for the field from the mid-1990s. On a Wednesday morning in July 1995, a city electrician in Los Angeles who was angry over a poor performance review and feared losing his job carried a Glock pistol into the C. Erwin Piper Technical Center downtown and methodically shot four supervisors to death before being apprehended by police. Piper Tech soon became shorthand for law enforcement in the region confronting the rising problem of workplace attacks, and it heralded an expanding mission for the LAPD Threat Management Unit. By the following decade, the TMU would be handling upward of two hundred threat cases annually, about half of them workplace-related and many involving city employees.

At the FBI, the era of "going postal" had drawn attention to stalking and grievance-fueled workplace violence among a handful of agents specializing in behavioral analysis at Quantico. They included John Douglas, whose best-selling memoir *Mindhunter* later recounted the innovative approach to investigating gruesome crime scenes that he and his colleagues developed in the 1980s for identifying serial killers. Another was a next-generation agent working under Douglas, Eugene Rugala, who was among those focused on thwarting targeted violence, a mission distinct from the kind of retrospective criminal profiling that had put the elite FBI unit on the map and since captured popular imagination with the 1991 Hollywood film, *The Silence of the Lambs*. (That film had starred none other than Jodie Foster, once the young stalking victim of

John Hinckley, who won great critical acclaim for her performance as a fledgling FBI agent confronting the darkest depths of predatory violence.)

Rugala and his colleagues had been looking into the backgrounds of the postal shooters and other workplace killers, combing through police reports and other records to learn about observable pre-attack behaviors that might inform prevention strategies. Rugala's interest in the work had deepened after two FBI agents, friends of his, were murdered along with a local detective in a 1994 gun rampage at the Washington, DC, police headquarters building. Rugala met Fein and Vossekuil in Washington and compared notes with them on what proved to be similar sets of principles for evaluating potentially dangerous people. The FBI team had picked up on a pattern: often there was a conspicuous change in behavior that created a feeling of distress in coworkers. "If someone was acting in some unusual or unsettling way," Rugala said, "a lot of times we felt it was useful just to go ask them directly, 'Hey, what's going on? This isn't like you, and we're concerned. Is there a way that we can help?'"

Depending on the circumstances, that intervention could be handled by senior company managers, human resources personnel, or outside counselors, ideally with Rugala and his colleagues serving purely in an advisory role behind the scenes, as they had begun to do. The relatively few in law enforcement who did behavioral threat assessment work in the late nineties were thinking in this direction, Rugala recalled, amid growing recognition that early intervention and a less outwardly harsh response from companies could sometimes be wisest for dealing with disgruntled employees.

In one case during that era, an industrial company working with local law enforcement had contacted the FBI for help with an alarming situation. After word had gotten around at the company that business was in a downslide, an employee had shown up to work and told a manager: "I just bought an AK-47, and I'm not gonna be a victim of another layoff." The employee had a history of personal problems, including periodic hostile conflict with co-workers. Moreover, the company made rocket fuel, and any gunfire in the vicinity of hazardous materials could mean additional danger. The FBI team confirmed the legal purchase of the weapon by the employee, the recent timing of which was potentially a serious warning sign in light of his threatening comment.

Company leaders intended to fire him posthaste. The FBI team advised against it. Termination could certainly be legal and appropriate, but it would amount to kicking the problem out the door—and could become a triggering event. Rugala and his colleagues instead recommended offering him immediate help through an employee assistance program. The company put him on administrative leave, continuing to give him full pay and medical benefits, and pointed him toward outside counseling, which would also potentially be a path back to the workplace. He took them up on the plan and soon showed progress, with his demeanor improving dramatically.

The employee returned to his job and performed well, though the situation wasn't case closed. A few months after returning, he was implicated in an unrelated incident involving sexual harassment. He was considered a productive worker, but at that point company leaders were no longer willing to keep him. The FBI team made recommendations about how to end his employment quietly and out of view, affording him the chance to exit with a sense of dignity. In the art of threat management, Rugala recalled, this was known as setting up a "soft landing." The company told the employee they would pay him out for a short transition period and would not stand in the way of his collecting unemployment insurance, among other gestures. What followed was striking. "I know how I screwed up, and I regret it and take responsibility," the employee told the HR manager handling his departure. "You guys really stood by me through a dark time and I don't have any bad feelings for you." He left without incident, and the company didn't hear from him again. Neither did the public.

Of the estimated 1.7 million "violent victimizations" that occurred annually in American workplaces during the 1990s, lethal violence of any kind constituted just 1 percent. The vast majority of incidents were simple or aggravated assaults, and roughly 80 percent of all cases involved criminals not connected to the businesses (who typically engaged in robbery). But practitioners also knew that the benefits of behavioral threat assessment could extend well beyond the remote risk of targeted killings to lesser acts of workplace violence. Those arose from interpersonal conflicts or stalking and harassment among employees, or with encroachment of domestic violence from the outside, an issue in general that was becoming less culturally taboo and more frequently reported by victims.

Rugala and other experts observed at the time that intense media focus on cases of "going postal" and other high-profile workplace shootings could be giving the public a false sense of overall prevalence. Such attacks remained statistically rare. Yet averted cases, like that of the fuel company employee, were not publicly known, and there was optimism that greater awareness of workplace violence might at least set the stage for the evolving field to gain wider traction, perhaps a silver lining to the media hype. The workplace was now a prime area of focus for threat assessment professionals. Then came Columbine.

————————

chapter five

THE KIDS AREN'T ALRIGHT

As the first mass shooting ever to play out on live television, the catastrophe at Columbine High School was seared instantly into the national consciousness. Beginning just before noon Colorado time on April 20, 1999, footage from news helicopters circling the suburban Denver high school interrupted Americans' TV screens with surreal and gut-wrenching images. From an aerial view, the public saw swarms of police and other emergency responders gathering at the perimeter of the school before moving in cautiously. Then, the motionless body of a dead student on the ground. Then a line of classmates fleeing the building with their hands up, and rescuers working to extract a badly wounded student dangling from a second-story window. "Everyone around me got shot," sobbed one girl, uninjured but with someone else's blood flecked on her hand, as a TV reporter interviewed her.

Confusion enveloped the early hours of the event, at first

misunderstood by law enforcement as a prolonged hostage situation inside the school. There was little sense of who was attacking or why, but soon the country learned the grim facts: In the span of less than an hour, *two of the high school's own students* had shot to death twelve classmates and a teacher, and wounded twenty-three others, before committing suicide in the cafeteria.

"We don't know yet all the hows or whys of this tragedy," said a solemn-faced President Bill Clinton at a White House press conference late that day. "Perhaps we may never fully understand it." Clinton also suggested during his remarks that such an attack could happen anywhere, and that America might now "wake up to the dimensions of this challenge" and "prevent anything like this from happening again."

Gun rampages at schools were rare but not new, with a handful scattered through the 1970s and '80s, and then a cluster in the mid to late 1990s, primarily in rural settings. Now the more affluent suburban community of Littleton had been hit with the deadliest shooting on a school campus since the clock tower massacre at the University of Texas in 1966. Perpetrators Eric Harris and Dylan Klebold had planned the attack for months, acquiring and practicing with firearms, experimenting with explosives, and creating home videos intended to glorify school shootings. The two seniors had desired infamy and nurtured a grandiose goal of outdoing the carnage caused by Timothy McVeigh in Oklahoma City, though their plan to kill hundreds of their peers went unrealized when the homemade devices they'd planted in the crowded school cafeteria failed to detonate.

The dawning internet age would allow Harris and Klebold to advance a cultural script on a whole new level, though they couldn't possibly have imagined how the mythology that sprang up around their heinous act would further metastasize and circulate world-wide more than a decade later through social media. Rather, the pair had entertained literal thoughts of a script, reveling in Oliver Stone's controversially graphic 1994 movie *Natural Born Killers* and fantasizing about top Hollywood filmmakers Steven Spielberg and Quentin Tarantino competing for rights to their "story." National outcry and debate in the aftermath roiled with blame of violent entertainment. Scapegoats included the first-person shooter game *Doom* and the music of spectral shock rocker Marilyn Manson.

Payback for bullying also became a prime explanation of motive in news coverage, buttressed by tales of the two perpetrators' supposed membership in a fringe group called the Trench Coat Mafia. The truth would turn out to be different. For starters, Harris and Klebold were in no such group, and while they had been ostracized by some peers, they had histories themselves of harassing and instigating conflict with others. They were not socially isolated: they'd played team sports, held down jobs, and socialized with various groups of friends. Nor did they target anyone specifically for revenge; they had killed indiscriminately.

By summer 1999, discussion of mental health and violence-prevention strategies was eclipsed by the moralizing over pernicious cultural influences and an intense focus on physical security and tactical response. A storm of criticism about how police had set up a perimeter and delayed going into Columbine High for more than half an hour was already stirring a fundamental change in law enforcement training nationally. Instead of waiting for backup or a crisis negotiation team, protocols shifted to confronting shooters immediately. Communities large and small began fortifying buildings for the coming school year with metal detectors, security cameras, and cops euphemistically known as school resource officers, or SROs. The Clinton White House had begun in the immediate hours after the rampage to plan federal grants for more SROs, whose growing presence would exacerbate punitive "zero tolerance" policies and the school-to-prison pipeline that was especially harmful to students of color. Behavioral threat assessment programs, often with the participation of SROs, would later work to reverse those trends using constructive interventions.

Few in Washington were more preoccupied with the Columbine tragedy than Bill Modzeleski, director of the US Department of Education's Office of Safe and Drug-Free Schools. As he and Education Secretary Richard Riley navigated a torrent of pressure over policy responses, they received an offer for help that was at first a bit mystifying.

"We'd never had any dealings with the Secret Service," Modzeleski recalled two decades later on a warm spring day near his home in northern Virginia. "What did they know about school crime or shootings?"

The skepticism of the education leaders soon dissipated, however, when they met with Secret Service director Brian Stafford and Bryan Vossekuil, now the head of the new National Threat Assessment Center at the agency's relocated headquarters just around the corner from the historic Ford's Theater in Washington, where Lincoln was shot. Leaders throughout the American law enforcement community had long considered assassination of a public official to be atop the list of the gravest possible crimes, but now another low-probability yet devastating problem was at the forefront. Amid the recent spate of school shootings, the Secret Service had launched the NTAC in 1998 to extend the agency's threat assessment expertise more widely, building in part from Vossekuil's work with Robert Fein on the Exceptional Case Study Project. Little was yet understood about targeted attacks specifically in schools, and Columbine had made that void no longer acceptable. Vossekuil explained how the agency's groundbreaking research on assassins could be a basis for studying and thwarting school shooters. Riley accepted the offer to collaborate, with the caveat that Modzeleski serve as an equal partner in the analysis and project oversight, thus helping to ensure that the work wouldn't be a theoretical quest or excessively focused on law enforcement goals.

Modzeleski began working with a team including Vossekuil, Fein, and Marisa Randazzo, a next-generation research psychologist with the Secret Service who would go on to be another leader in the field. Whereas the Exceptional Case Study Project had taken five years to complete, the mission to better understand school shooters needed to move much faster. Educators, law enforcement, and the public at large were demanding solutions, and for prevention those were sorely lacking—or worse, misleading.

It was that September, five months after Columbine, when the FBI published its dubious offender profile for identifying school shooters. The profile was part of a broader FBI report to law enforcement agencies nationwide that described school shootings as a community problem. The report pointed to behavioral warning signs, including communicated threats, fixation on previous attackers, and perceptions among troubled youth that violence was an acceptable solution to grievances or despair. While those descriptions were accurate and useful, the FBI report was limited to analysis of six recent attacks committed by teens, and it was undermined by the offender profile's inclusion of supposed "mass or spree murderer traits," some of which were uselessly broad or plain cartoonish. According to this list of traits, school shooters not only "seemed to have trouble with their parents" and "had a propensity to dislike popular students," but were into "songs that promote violence" and were "influenced by satanic or cult-type belief systems or philosophical works."

The FBI report also contained clumsy prescriptive assertions.

Although emerging research showed that some mass shooters documented their thoughts about aspiring to kill or die, the FBI's analysis of the Columbine perpetrators took the notion of telltale writings into genuinely eyebrow-raising territory:

> *One method for discovering potentially violent students involves having students write about their lives as a window into their thoughts. This would have helped in some of the school shootings if the teachers had had the essays and then been able to interpret their content and style. For example, one of the shooters' work was influenced heavily by the 19th-century German philosopher Friedrich Nietzsche, who is best known for having proclaimed the death of God and for calling himself an "immoralist," one who opposes all morality. Another suspect's writing was inspired by the musician Marilyn Manson who reportedly based his song "Antichrist Superstar" on Nietzsche's book* The Antichrist, *a critique of Pauline Christianity. While these influences and writing styles may not uncover a potential school shooter, they do represent signs that educators and parents should take seriously and explore further.*

The FBI had focused its offender profile around maladjusted white males who were "average students" and had histories of aggression and mental health treatment. Just three months after the FBI report was published, none of those attributes described a thirteen-year-old student who arrived on the grounds of Fort Gibson Middle School in Oklahoma, pulled a semiautomatic pistol out of his backpack and shouted, "I'm crazy, I'm crazy!" as he wounded five classmates. He was Native American, an honors student, athletic, and considered friendly and kind by peers, and he had no history of mental health treatment.

Help for better detecting danger was on the horizon from the Secret Service and Department of Education, but in the meantime, the FBI produced its own corrective research from a group that had begun focusing on school shootings in 1998 at the National Center for the Analysis of Violent Crime. That work gained momentum three months after Columbine, when the FBI held a summit in Leesburg, Virginia, bringing together about 160 educators, mental health experts, law enforcement agents, and prosecutors, including participants directly connected locally to each of eighteen school attacks and thwarted plots that the FBI team was now reviewing. Led by supervisory special agent Mary Ellen O'Toole, the FBI published a "four-pronged" model in early 2000 that emphasized a fundamental shift away from prediction and urged focusing on a "totality of circumstances" in threat cases.

"This model is not a 'profile' of the school shooter or a checklist of danger signs pointing to the next adolescent who will bring lethal violence to a school," the FBI monograph explained. "Those things do not exist." Instead, it was essential to gain a deeper understanding of the process giving rise to the danger: "How did a particular student come to the point of feeling that shooting fellow students and teachers was in some way an answer to his problems or emotional needs? Were there signs along the way—not a catalogue of traits identifying him as a predicted killer, but clues that could have indicated a need for help? What was the influence of family, friends, and community?"

The FBI monograph catalogued a robust list of personal struggles and warning signs increasingly familiar to threat assessors, from low self-esteem and a lack of resiliency to aberrant narcissism, anger, manipulativeness, and a focus on graphic or sensational violence. Two behavioral entries stood out.

The first was "leakage," whereby individuals reveal clues to their thoughts and feelings about committing violent acts. These indicators can be subtle, taking the form of innuendo, bragging, blame, or predictions. Beyond the verbal, they can be conveyed through writings, drawings, tattoos, or other forms of personal expression. The application of the leakage concept to school shooters was in fact a bridge forward from the FBI's legacy of criminal profiling. The term had been coined in the 1980s by former Behavioral Science Unit chief Roger Depue to describe a revealing deterioration or loss of control that could be seen in ruthless predators like Ted Bundy and other infamous serial killers the FBI hunted. The idea was that a killer's beliefs, fantasies, and urges would eventually seep out, no matter how hard he tried to conceal them—detectable through his expressions, his way of talking or acting, or perhaps in material he sought out to feed his inner life. In the context of school shootings, the FBI was now suggesting that leakage could reveal inner turmoil and rage or cries for help from those who had never committed a serious act of violence. Although the FBI flirted with overstating leakage as "one of the most important clues" to a potential school shooting, the term established a memorable framework for further detecting and understanding threatening communications.

The other notable entry on the list was "injustice collector," a categorization apt for describing the various entrenched grievances that mark many cases. Injustice collectors are individuals whose words or actions indicate they are driven chronically by bitter resentments, whether those are based on real or perceived maltreatment. "No matter how much time has passed," the FBI explained, "the injustice collector will not forget or forgive those wrongs or the people he or she believes are responsible." Some individuals displaying this behavior are known to voice blame or hostile comments repeatedly about their intended victims, or to make hit lists naming them.

While the FBI monograph advanced the evaluation of threatening behavior, its further utility was less clear. The FBI recommended establishing multidisciplinary threat assessment programs in schools but did not provide any explicit guidance on how to do so, let alone on how to manage cases. All of that would need to be figured out at the local level.

As had been the case with early efforts to thwart political assassins and celebrity stalkers, some crucial insight was also missing. What on earth really led up to *teens committing mass murder*? The suicidal shooters who had brought devastation to their Colorado high school were gone. But other shooters had lived to tell. And the field needed to hear from them.

———

In the fall of 1999, the Secret Service team had begun digging into evidence from thirty-seven school shootings dating from the mid-1970s and crisscrossing the country to interview more than a quarter of the offenders. Their work would produce a landmark study called the Safe School Initiative. It was a sprint that lasted a year and a half. "We felt we needed to get some quality information out there as quickly as we could that people could actually use," said Marisa Randazzo, who was with the Secret Service for a decade and later built a threat assessment consultancy focused on schools and corporations. The danger of retrospectively categorizing shooters as a tool for prediction wasn't just that individuals could be wrongly identified or unfairly stigmatized; there was also the risk of missing the actual peril. "The bigger concern about profiling," Randazzo said, "is that it can easily distract from behaviors that should be looked into and investigated, and then they aren't because the person doesn't match the characteristics."

White males would remain the most common perpetrators, but over the next two decades, more than two dozen targeted school shootings in the United States would be carried out by Asian, Black, Latino, and Native American assailants. Female shooters would remain rare but not unheard of, the tally dating from the 1970s rising to half a dozen, including two fourteen-year-old girls and a college professor.

The Secret Service team met with a total of ten incarcerated young men, some of whom had spoken little if at all about what led them to commit lethal attacks. The team was dispassionate by trade, yet there was an undeniable poignancy to the interviews; some of their subjects were pimple-faced kids in prison jumpsuits, downcast and laconic and from deeply traumatized backgrounds. In appealing to the interviewees as "experts" on their own cases and keepers of the truth about what had driven them to kill, what the team learned was in some ways even more fruitful and revelatory than with the assassins interrogated years prior by Fein and Vossekuil. The work affirmed major themes emerging in the field: the complex personal struggles, the attack planning, the easy access to weapons, the sense of alarm provoked in others, the lack of any useful profile.

The deeper research and face-to-face investigations also produced a particularly startling result: in almost all thirty-seven cases, the shooters had told other kids about what they intended to do.

In the case of sixteen-year-old Evan Ramsey, a whole crowd of students had gotten an indication of what was coming. On a cold, crepuscular morning in February 1997, Ramsey used his baggy jeans to conceal a shotgun as he walked into his high school in Bethel, Alaska, a town of about five thousand on the state's remote western tundra. He shot and killed fifteen-year-old classmate Josh Palacios and school principal Ron Edwards, and wounded two other students. Then he put the muzzle under his own chin but couldn't bring himself to pull the trigger. He surrendered after a brief standoff with police. When the Secret Service team interviewed him in prison three years later, he recounted the fateful final weeks.

"I told everyone what I was going to do," he said. "I'd called three people and asked them to go up to the library."

Ramsey wanted those peers to be watching from the balcony on the second-floor mezzanine when he opened fire in the commons area below. He had already revealed his intentions to two other friends, who'd egged him on. Initially, his plan had been to brandish the shotgun at school to scare off some students who were harassing him. One friend showed him how to load and fire the weapon, suggesting to Ramsey that he would need to pull the trigger if he wanted to send an effective message. The other friend encouraged Ramsey to expand his hit list to include multiple other classmates and the principal. The two friends later talked of Ramsey's plan with a sister of one of the boys, who spread the news further. The nature of what was to come was clearer to some peers than others, but by the morning of the shooting, upward of two dozen teens gathered on the mezzanine, typically all but empty before classes started, in anticipation of something big happening. One girl in the crowd said to another, "You're not supposed to be up here. You're on the list." Another student had brought a camera but got so worked up once the violence began that he didn't remember to take any pictures.

Not one of the students had spoken out to an authority figure.

The Secret Service team asked Ramsey what he would have done if the principal had caught wind of his plan and reached out to him.

"I would have told him the truth," Ramsey said.

While revenge for bullying had been wildly overstated in the media as the motive for the Columbine massacre, the bullying that Ramsey had faced was significant, and the issue came up, whether real or perceived, among more than two thirds of the school shooters the Secret Service team investigated. Given that countless kids experienced the dynamics of bullying in the nation's schools, it was a basic statistical truth that very few who struggled with harsh social rejection (and who sometimes also did bullying themselves) would ever pose a serious risk for committing lethal targeted violence. But what the team found was that in cases like Ramsey's, the bullying had translated as acute torment—a dangerous compounding factor atop other serious problems.

Ramsey had endured a brutal childhood. His father was a convicted violent felon, and his mother was an alcoholic who took up with abusive partners. Ramsey had been moved among a series of foster homes, including one where he was sexually abused. He experienced bouts of rage and suicidal depression. He never escaped the grip of profound trauma, but he had shown no indications of psychopathy or psychosis.

As the team explored Ramsey's pre-attack thinking, they pressed him about what help school authorities had given him.

"For a while they would go and talk to the person and tell them to leave me alone," he said. "But after a while, they just started telling me to ignore them." A fury had risen in him as he made his final preparations on the morning of the attack. "It was kind of an avalanche. You know, an avalanche starts with something small and builds up."

Ramsey had also left behind two notes, one of which suggested that he'd once had hope. He wrote about the school superintendent as "the nicest person I've ever met." She had been "like a mother" to him and one of his brothers, taking them in at a previous time when their home life was coming apart. In the other note, he raged about the school principal, whom he vowed would soon be dead.

"Why the school?" the team asked of his chosen attack location.

"That's where most of my pain and suffering was."

Ramsey also spoke of an enduring regret: "I wish I hadn't done it."

His case and others revealed another flaw in the FBI's post-Columbine offender profile: It had indicated that school shooters "exhibited no remorse after their killings." In many cases, the Secret Service team was finding the opposite. Moreover, by definition, remorse could exist only *after* a shooting, and in that respect its inclusion in an FBI analysis focused on prediction had little apparent value. However, the expressions of remorse encountered by the Secret Service team were meaningful in a different way. They suggested that some school shooters would have been receptive to constructive interventions.

"It's real hard to live with the things I've done," Luke Woodham told the team, describing what led him in October 1997 to carry a rifle into his high school in Pearl, Mississippi, where he murdered his ex-girlfriend and another female student, and wounded seven others. Woodham, then sixteen, had also stabbed his mother to death at home before the rampage. He too had experienced harsh bullying. Inside the grim confines of Mississippi's Parchman penitentiary, his feedback elucidated a mix of suicidal depression and rage increasingly familiar to the team, and it was telling in another way: "I just didn't really have anybody to talk to about all the things that I was going through. I kept a lot of hurt inside of me. I just felt like nobody cared."

It wasn't only that there were no reliable adult figures in his world, Woodham made clear. "I couldn't find a reason not to do it," he said.

Extreme as his case was, his perspective pointed up another
bedrock concept developing in the field: the necessity of cultivating
"positive inhibitors"—pro-social opportunities and relationships
that could steer troubled youth away from the idea of violence as a
remedy for suffering and rage. If a kid got involved in an activity
or youth group he liked, or connected with a mentor, he would be
less likely to head down the pathway to violence.

The story of fourteen-year-old Barry Loukaitis underscored how
widely case circumstances could vary, and why predictive profiling
based on a set of shooter characteristics had been doomed to fail.
After Loukaitis opened fire in February 1996 at his middle school
in Moses Lake, Washington, killing two classmates and a teacher, a
psychiatrist who examined him concluded, "His behavior did not
appear obviously different from that of other early adolescents until he walked into his junior high school classroom and shot four
people." Loukaitis was an A student in the algebra class where he
struck. The teacher he killed, forty-nine-year-old Leona Caires, had
written on his report card that he was "a pleasure to have in class."
Like Loukaitis, upward of 40 percent of the shooters scrutinized by
the Secret Service team were good students; some had even repeatedly made the honor roll. Only two were found to have been failing
in school. Nearly half, moreover, had what the team concluded were
"mainstream" social lives. Most had little or no disciplinary record.
Few had histories of substance abuse or diagnosed mental illness,
though many had shown signs of depression and suicidality.

Still, there were warning signs from Loukaitis. He had com-
plained to teachers about being teased, and he'd composed poetry
filled with images of death. The macabre writing alone wasn't unusual from an immature adolescent, but in the updated parlance of
the FBI, Loukaitis had started leaking like a sieve. He had enlisted
his mother on a mission to help him purchase the perfect overcoat,

visiting seven stores with her while never letting on that its purpose would be to shroud a weapon. Over a period of months, he
spoke repeatedly of his intentions to at least eight friends, including
showing off a sawed-off shotgun. He also asked his friends about
acquiring ammunition. As one later recounted, "He said that it'd
be cool to kill people. He said he could probably get away with it."

There would soon be more cases astonishing for their lack
of anyone sounding an alarm, including an attack at a Southern
California high school in March 2001, where the fifteen-year-old
shooter's threats were known to multiple other students. Though
bleak on its face, this "bystander problem," as it was becoming
known in the field, also represented an enormous untapped opportunity for intervention. The way forward would be to figure
out what kept bystanders from speaking up, then to build greater
community awareness and messaging akin to "see something, say
something," the mantra that would soon spread nationally after
the terrorist attacks of September 11, 2001.

Bill Modzeleski, reflecting on his decades as an education
leader in the federal government, observed that bullying and other
familiar deviance among adolescents were always met with a certain degree of tolerance among parents and communities. They
were considered behaviors that warranted interdiction and consequences, but that often were seen as an inevitable part of growing up. School shootings, of course, were another matter. "We can
say over and over again that these are rare events," Modzeleski remarked, "but no parents should ever have to accept their kid going
to school and coming home in a box." Improving physical building
security could be important, he said, especially for schools with students numbering in the thousands. But his experience with school
systems around the country had long ago made clear to him that
a robust prevention strategy was crucial. "You've got to do both."

In summer 2000, as Modzeleski and his Secret Service partners were preparing to draft a report publicizing the key research
findings of the Safe School Initiative, they huddled for a long session in a conference room at Secret Service headquarters. Glancing
around at his colleagues on the project, Modzeleski realized that
he had never fully let go of a concern lingering at the back of his
mind, that their work might ultimately put too much emphasis on
the role of law enforcement, building fortifications, and the like.
He felt relieved as the consensus in the room became clear: the top
theme would be connection. The more that schools could link up
concerning kids with prevention-minded adults, they all agreed,
the better off any given situation would be for dealing with a threat
of targeted violence.

As the team began a series of training sessions for education
leaders in various parts of the country—including showing them excerpts of their videotaped prison interviews with school shooters—
they argued that this approach would do more to stop attacks than
any additional metal detectors, security cameras, or cops ever could.
They sought also to demystify the problem: school shooters don't
come out of nowhere, they emphasized, any more than assassins or
workplace attackers do. "Believing that kids snap is comforting,"
was how Vossekuil put it as they rolled out the findings, because "if
kids snap, it lets us off the hook."

Educators and other community leaders instead needed to be
proactive about what was so often a detectable danger. With additional help from consulting psychologists Randy Borum and William Pollack, the team now had a lengthy guide under development
for setting up behavioral threat assessment programs in schools,
detailing everything from warning signs and a set of evaluative
questions to the importance of information sharing, legal and privacy considerations, and proper investigative documentation. The

team also emphasized how to cultivate a climate of school safety—including, crucially, improving on the bystander problem by working to change school cultures where a "code of silence" prevailed. Rather than "snitching" or "ratting," kids needed to view speaking up about an alarming situation as good citizenship, even as a potentially heroic act. (Years later, suggested use of the term "upstander" would aim to help this cause.) The team also articulated a goal for all students to have a positive relationship with at least one authority figure whom they saw as trustworthy and approachable for help.

"Connection through human relationships is a central component of a culture of safety and respect," the published guide stated. "The findings of the Safe School Initiative suggest that silence is far from golden. In fact, study findings indicate that silence may be downright dangerous."

Modzeleski remembered being struck with the end results born of the unlikely partnership with the Secret Service. "This is one of the premier law enforcement agencies in the country," he said, "and yet at the top of their list was connecting kids and educators."

Soon a nascent program on the other side of the country would take that strategy to heart, its leaders determined to head off the next Columbine. They would navigate the tough terrain of systemic change and some unforeseen tragedy as they built what would become a model, two decades later, for community-based violence prevention.

PART II

chapter six

─────

THE PROGRAM

The moist Pacific Northwest air grows milder as the nebulous skies of the Willamette Valley winter lift, the sunlight stretching a bit longer each day. In and around the city of Salem, Oregon, the abundant lawns and clusters of maples, cherries, and Doug-firs are thick with a dozen shades of green. Nothing brings vibrancy to the season, though, quite as the kids do. Springtime is when the majority of the forty-two thousand students in the Salem-Keizer school system are most animated, with the end to classes in sight and summer break calling.

Supporting the growth and safety of all those kids is the fundamental mission for security director John Van Dreal, lead school psychologist Courtenay McCarthy, and their dozen-plus colleagues serving on the Mid-Valley Student Threat Assessment Team. Much of the STAT's work in the district's sixty-five school buildings is about steering a struggling or wayward student in a good direction, sometimes helping to resolve problems with classroom disruption, bullying, or other garden-variety unwanted behaviors, which tend to be amplified by the pent-up energy loosed from March to June. The STAT experts also know that each spring will bring a few concerns of a more serious nature. Over the two decades following Columbine, a growth in threat cases included the emergence of what became known unofficially among leaders in the field as "school shootings season." The rare yet recurrent tragedies could and did happen any time of year. But by the late 2010s, in Oregon's second largest public K–12 system and in various other school districts around the country, the volume of threats and copycat behavior reliably increased with the restiveness of the school year's end.

From the first of several trips I took beginning in 2015 to the annual threat-assessment summit in Disneyland, I'd heard about the Salem-Keizer program, respected by leaders from the FBI to the US Department of Education and beyond. Among the first of its kind in the country, the program was launched in the aftermath of Columbine in 1999, though it had begun stirring the prior year after a school shooting took place about an hour's drive south of Salem. In Disneyland, I'd gotten to know Van Dreal, an easygoing school psychologist–turned–seasoned security leader, whose hipster attire and swashbuckling vibe at first made him seem an unlikely presence at the training conference. He wrote poetry, played keyboard in a bar band, and was an accomplished classical oil painter with a collector's market for his work. He also happened to be a founder and pioneer of Salem-Keizer's behavioral threat assessment system, a role he'd fallen into two decades earlier. Van Dreal introduced me to McCarthy, who succeeded him as the program's lead psychologist when he later rose to director of safety and risk management for the district, and eventually the two took me up on my entreaties to shadow them in Salem during the spring and fall of 2019.

An education setting had struck me as ideal for an immersion in the process of behavioral threat assessment. Efforts to guide a troubled person onto a better life path were likely to hold the greatest promise among youth. With their program rooted in the Safe School Initiative and expanded innovatively over time, Van Dreal and McCarthy were next-generation leaders in the field, building local institutional knowledge and ensuring its fidelity through perpetual training, creative problem solving, and some healthy doses of stoicism and wry humor. A deep examination of several long-term threat cases—including two I observed unfolding in real time, and one high-stakes case from the early years of the program—would illuminate the way their team worked together to prevent tragic outcomes.

The program extended to every corner of the sprawling district, with the centralized Student Threat Assessment Team its hub. Salem-Keizer's roughly 240 administrators and 100 counselors were trained by Van Dreal, McCarthy, and their colleagues on the fundamentals and led smaller teams within their own school buildings. The building teams used streamlined protocols designed by the STAT leaders to conduct Level 1 investigations—responding to an alleged or observed threat by using a brief series of questions to gather context on the incident and gauge the risk for violence. Often the building teams were dealing with reactive aggression (impulsive rather than predatory behavior) and responded with conventional measures: interfacing with parents and offering special-education assistance, counseling, and individual education plans. They could seek help at any time from the STAT when threatening behavior appeared serious but was unclear in nature or scope.

The STAT members, drawn from within the district as well as local and state agencies, brought diverse expertise in education, mental health, social services, juvenile justice, and law enforcement.

The team served as a highly specialized consultancy, conducting deeper information gathering and threat evaluations, then offering strategy recommendations to the building teams, which remained in charge of their cases.

Inside a quiet brick-and-glass administrative building, the STAT leaders' offices ringed a small operations center, where a bank of screens along one wall fed in surveillance footage and other security-related information from around the district. On a Thursday morning in mid-May, Van Dreal explained that the program was designed to be efficient and user-friendly for overworked educators on the front lines. "It's a pretty simple process: When a case comes up, you work together to figure out more specifically what's worrying you, and you make a plan to intervene. Then, you meet again and follow up on the plan." It wasn't a matter of whether a troubled student theoretically was capable of serious violence or becoming a school shooter, he noted. "Fundamentally speaking, the answer is yes. But what you're doing is getting in the way of a situation and stopping it from getting worse, before those possibilities approach."

"There's nothing esoteric here," he continued. "As an adult in the world, you know when the hair stands up on the back of your neck, so you pay attention to that. Now, here are ten questions to ask, and if the answers worry you as a team, then here are eight more to ask. If those answers are OK, then jump over to this plan for basic safety and supervision. You can get through the process in a half hour or less with this approach. And otherwise, if it's going in a bad direction with someone, we're here to help with what's next."

After McCarthy joined to talk over several cases on the day's agenda, the three of us headed downtown, to a neighborhood near the state capitol. The weekly two-hour gathering started promptly at 12:30 p.m. each Thursday inside a light-industrial building housing district operations, where the Student Threat Assessment

Team convened in an unadorned meeting room at conference tables arranged in a square. Fifteen members were in attendance, including several who had served on the team for a decade or longer. McCarthy, a skilled psychologist in her early forties with shoulder-length curly brown hair and a serene voice, called the group into session. Coffee cups and case files hit the tables and laptops flipped open. The atmosphere felt collegial and even relaxed, though neither McCarthy, in her fifth year of leading the team, nor Van Dreal, responding to all manner of daily brush fires around the district, were ever far from the next pressing email, text, or call.

The Salem-Keizer district saw about 250 new cases opened at the building level each school year. Upward of 55 cases each year, either new or ongoing, were elevated to the STAT experts for assistance. Among those, a handful proved particularly serious, rated by the team as moderate or occasionally high risk for targeted violence. The meeting agenda this afternoon included three new cases opened in the previous week, and five ongoing ones, either scheduled for further review or heating up with new developments.

For part of the session, the team focused on a longer-term case involving a seventeen-year-old Northeast High School junior named Brandon, who had taken a troubling turn. On Wednesday of the prior week, a student had told a Northeast faculty member that she felt "creeped out" after she overheard Brandon talking to a classmate while waiting for the bus home. "Don't come to school this Friday," she heard him say. "I'm coming back here with my dad's semiautomatic and shooting up the place." Another student who overheard the exchange reported that Brandon had bragged about having obtained the code to his father's gun safe.

The principal at Northeast contacted McCarthy as the building team worked immediately to determine whether Brandon posed any imminent danger. By that evening, a school resource officer visited Brandon's home, where he spoke with Brandon and his mother. As a member of the STAT, the officer was versed in rapport building and how to look for signs of personal deterioration, violent ideation, and attack planning. He found Brandon's mom both eager to engage and distraught. She denied that Brandon had access to firearms in the home or elsewhere. Sitting with them in the living room, Brandon himself said very little. He admitted that he'd made the comments at the bus stop but insisted he'd been joking. There was something else notable about his demeanor. While most students interviewed at home by law enforcement cry or react with embarrassment, Brandon's affect was flat. He appeared unmoved by the officer's visit. After getting consent from both Brandon and his mom, the officer briefly searched Brandon's room for evidence of weapons or any indications he was trying to acquire them, finding none.

This was not the first time Brandon had made eyebrow-raising comments at school, McCarthy noted. Another student interviewed after the bus-stop incident reported that Brandon had riffed earlier in the year about "doing a school shooting." The student said he hadn't taken those comments seriously. McCarthy also reminded the team of an incident detailed in Brandon's case file from the prior spring of 2018. As Northeast students were organizing for a national March for Our Lives walkout in response to the gun massacre at Marjory Stoneman Douglas High School in Parkland, Florida, a teacher had asked Brandon if he planned to participate. "Nah," he'd replied with a whiff of mockery. "Maybe I'll just shoot up the school instead."

Brandon was a lanky kid with a mop of brown hair, acne-mottled skin, and bright eyes. He had a learning disability and a relatively poor academic record but was above average in intelligence. Since middle school, he'd had some minor involvement with bullying, both as a victim and an instigator. Although he often spoke of himself as an outcast, he had a small group of friends at Northeast, liked to skateboard, and participated in the drama club. Several school staff had noticed a shift recently in his demeanor. He'd stopped showing up to a couple of classes and had abruptly quit drama. During a recent rehearsal, he'd tripped onstage and knocked over part of the set, which left him feeling deeply humiliated. A few days later, a teacher had come across Brandon asleep on the floor in a rear hallway, his jacket rumpled. When she asked him how he was doing, he turned hostile, got up, and walked away. Another faculty member reported the impression that Brandon had been going through a romantic breakup.

Next, McCarthy ran down the initial response and supervision plan. The morning after the bus-stop incident, she and a colleague went to Northeast to begin a Level 2 investigation, including meeting with Brandon's mother. "I don't know what to do with him," the mom pleaded, noting that she also was juggling a toddler at home. Brandon struggled to get out of bed many mornings, she said, adding that his father, who worked long hours and wasn't around much, was hard on him but didn't know the extent of his school problems. McCarthy gave the mom a number for contacting the team directly, persuading her to follow several recommendations for immediately boosting supervision: First, she would keep an eye on Brandon's online activity, watching out for violent material and any indications he might be interested in harming himself or others. She would work with the building team to ensure that Brandon continued to have no access to weapons, helping to do checks of his belongings to and from school. She also agreed to meet with a district counselor within two weeks to arrange a mental health evaluation and potential counseling for Brandon through a local health care provider.

McCarthy reiterated to Brandon's mom the importance of securing the gun safe, and recommended that she reach out to parents of any friends whose homes Brandon spent time in. The mom had balked at the idea of broaching conversations of that kind, a challenge the team was used to navigating and prioritized, as many school shooters used guns obtained from their homes or those of other family members or friends. McCarthy explained to Brandon's mom the value of having those talks where possible and gave her a brief tip sheet for discussing safety while avoiding alarmism or getting into gun politics.

Brandon had returned to Northeast two days after the reported incident—the Friday he'd allegedly planned to come armed—and extra security was quietly in place to keep track of him as the investigation continued. An assistant principal, a member of the building team, sat down with Brandon for a one-on-one in her office and was struck to find him in decent spirits. She told him that the school had already arranged for him to complete some course work independently, with tutoring help, if he were amenable to the plan.

"Yeah, that sounds good," he said.

"Do you think you've been feeling depressed?" she asked him. He said that he did and agreed with her suggestion that talking to a school counselor could help.

"Did you really want to do that, to bring a gun to school and shoot people?" she asked.

"No," he said.

"Why would you say something like that?"

"I don't know, maybe to get friends," he said. "Was that really such a big deal?"

"Yes, it was," she replied, kindly but firmly.

"How big?"

"Well, on a scale of one to ten, it was probably an eight or a nine."

McCarthy added one other notable piece of information just picked up from staff at Northeast. A popular science teacher known to students as Mr. K reported that Brandon had asked him in class the day before the STAT meeting about making poison gas. Mr. K noted in his email to the inquiring STAT member that such questions were common among high school boys, who often also showed interest in explosives. Brandon had raised the question out of the blue, however, saying that the formula could be "good to know." "He asked about making chlorine gas with a mix of bleach and ammonia cleaners," Mr. K reported, "like the kind they used to kill in the trenches in World War I." In response, the STAT member reminded Mr. K to stay vigilant about supervising lab work and keeping chemicals locked up, and asked him to continue strongly encouraging Brandon's interest in science. Brandon had also told the assistant principal during their one-on-one that he liked Mr. K and intended to make up work he'd missed in that class.

For several team members around the tables pondering the case summary, the evolving picture looked ominous. High on the list was the fact that the latest in Brandon's pattern of talk about school shootings included details on when and how he thought of committing one. That kind of specificity was a glaring red flag, because it could indicate a progression from violent thinking in the abstract to a concrete plan. Moreover, Brandon was generating anxiety among various students and staff, a corroboration of perceived danger. "It always increases our level of concern when multiple people independent of each other say they're worried or feeling uneasy about a situation," McCarthy told me during a momentary break in the discussion.

"I'm really concerned about this young man's perceptions of how other people see him," commented Gail Winden, a veteran school counselor and STAT member. She pointed out that Brandon had experienced the stage tripping incident as a devastating personal failure, and that he'd talked of having "no friends" despite his various social relationships and activities. "I'll call mom to schedule a sit-down with the two of them as soon as possible," she said. "If we wait two weeks on the clinic at Kaiser for the emotional-disturbance evaluation, we're waiting too long."

"Gail, is your concern here more about aggression or suicide?" asked Clem Spenner, a former police officer on the team.

"Both," Winden said. She'd spoken with additional Northeast staffers earlier in the week and found them to be visibly uneasy about Brandon, a further corroboration of concern. "There's something wrong here," she said.

Her emphatic response had the group's attention, a slight air of push-pull now hanging in the room between a seasoned police investigator looking through a just-the-facts lens and a mental health veteran listening to her long-honed intuition.

"It does sound like he's a pretty depressed kid," Spenner said.

"He seems very depressed," agreed McCarthy. "Suicide risk is certainly something to focus on here."

"But would he do it by cop?" pressed Winden. "I wouldn't be surprised. I'm just not convinced that he isn't looking to do something hurtful to others, and then he'll be unable to handle the consequences of that and want to be taken out."

Winden was pointing to a scenario familiar to experienced teams, where a psychology of compounding grievance and desperation could combust with rage or attention-seeking. Spenner, nodding, raised the Menninger Triad, a psychological risk-assessment tool used to account for a subject's possible desires to die, to kill, or to be killed by others. The presence of all three is considered highly dangerous. Were there any such indications from Brandon? McCarthy glanced back through the case file. "There's nothing we know of that goes beyond the three times he made the comments about school shootings."

Crucially, McCarthy and the other STAT investigators directly working the case had found no evidence of attack planning, nor of any efforts by Brandon to obtain a firearm. Still, taken together, his recent personal deterioration, the alarm in people around him, and his specific talk about a shooting merited high vigilance. The full team concurred that he was a kid in crisis, struggling with acute low self-esteem, erratic moods, and limited parental support. His more upbeat return to school potentially masked the level of danger.

With close supervision now in place both at school and home, they assessed him to be a moderate risk for targeted violence, defined in the STAT protocols as an attempt to cause serious or lethal injury to others. Together with the Northeast building team, STAT members would continue working expeditiously to guide Brandon in a better direction, using their "wraparound" strategy: They would extend to him academic support, counseling, and opportunities for programs both inside and outside the school, including a youth program at a local church where he and his friends liked to skateboard in the parking lot. The team would also encourage Northeast leaders to foster closer relationships between Brandon and two teachers he liked—Mr. K and the drama club leader, who had already agreed to take Brandon on as a production aid and forgive some fees he owed. Those efforts by staff would likely help improve Brandon's mood while allowing the team to keep close tabs on him, a strategy they called check-and-connect.

The following morning, McCarthy sat down with Brandon at Northeast in a small private room adjacent to the principal's office. He was reticent but soon opened up, telling her that he was looking forward to finally getting his driver's license and planned to seek a summer job at a local pizza restaurant so he could save up to buy a used car. Articulation of such goals was a good sign. (Conversely, a conspicuous lack of future plans is another red flag for threat assessors.) Slouching in his chair, Brandon lamented that he didn't fit in with any social crowd and said he mostly wanted to be alone. He rebuffed her suggestion about potentially doing some therapy, insisting he could "just figure it out" and get over his feelings of depression on his own. That was a notable contradiction to his positive reply to the assistant principal the prior week about seeing a counselor.

"Do you ever think about hurting yourself or others?" McCarthy asked.

"No," he replied.

"Do you feel like you have anyone you could talk to if you ever did have those kinds of thoughts?" He processed the question for a long minute.

"Well, if I was thinking about killing myself I wouldn't tell anyone else," he said. "Why would I tell someone? I would just do it."

McCarthy told him that made her feel concerned about him. He thought for another moment, then said he could talk to his parents if he really needed to, though he didn't have "a strong bond" with them, especially not with his father, who pressured him about grades and wanted him to go straight into the family construction business after high school, which he didn't want to do.

McCarthy asked him about the comments made at the bus stop. Brandon said he was just "being dumb" at the end of a bad day. He had just blurted that out, he said, and didn't remember the moment very much. She pointed out that these had not been his first comments about a school shooting. Why, then, did he include the details about breaking into his father's gun safe and shooting up the school on a Friday?

"Well, I knew that the more descriptive I got, the more shocking it would be."

He also said he understood why his comments had stirred fear, "because school shootings happen all the time." He said he wasn't sure why he'd done it but that he regretted it.

As McCarthy was wrapping up their conversation a few minutes later, Brandon had turned inward again. Then he broke the lingering silence and asked her: "Am I ever going to talk to you anymore?"

Another good sign. McCarthy knew Gail Winden would be following up with Brandon and his mom shortly about counseling, but she also gave Brandon her card with her phone number on it. "I'd be happy to talk with you again and you can call me anytime."

————

Even when their agenda was jammed with cases, the Student Threat Assessment Team often spent a few minutes during their weekly sessions talking over broader matters of school safety or relevant current events. The discussions were part of an ethic championed by Van Dreal and McCarthy for continual training and refinement of their operations. Behavioral threat assessment relied in part on what the field called structured professional judgment—essentially, the collaborative analysis built on a team's case evaluation system plus its multidisciplinary expertise. The collective effort could always benefit from considering the latest incidents or research.

On the day of the session focused at length on Brandon's case, the team briefly discussed a traumatic incident that had just occurred at a high school in nearby suburban Portland. "Have you all been following the Parkrose situation?" McCarthy had asked the group. It would've been hard to miss. The incident in mid-May at the high school of that name had been all over the news, after a student wearing a black trench coat entered a classroom just before the lunch hour and brandished a shotgun, pointing it at himself. A young football coach named Keanon Lowe, a former player at the University of Oregon, had courageously disarmed the student with his bare hands before harm was done—and then bear-hugged the despondent eighteen-year-old senior, speaking empathetically to him until Portland police arrived. The poignant scene of a staff member embracing a student on the precipice of lethal violence was captured on school surveillance footage that later became public and went viral on social media.

While news coverage highlighting Lowe's role in the frightening incident was well deserved, McCarthy pointed out some key context obscured by the hero narrative: Lowe also worked part-time in a security role at the high school and had gone to the classroom primed to respond because a worried student had spoken up. Recently, the near-culprit, Angel Granados-Diaz, had been talking of killing himself. A female classmate's warning to a staff member that morning prompted a call to school security, and it was in that capacity that Lowe had gone looking for the young man just before he arrived in the classroom with the shotgun.

The case was a reminder of how critical bystander reporting often is to prevention work, even right up to a final taut moment. In an ideal scenario, of course, the reporting would take place long before a person with deadly intent ever showed up armed at a school, workplace, or other venue. Salem-Keizer leaders had seen numerous cases over the years hinging on tips of this nature, and they had worked to foster a culture of speaking up that also marked robust threat assessment programs I'd looked into in K–12 and university systems in Colorado, Virginia, and California.

The STAT conversation around the Parkrose case also touched on the thin line between suicidal and homicidal intent. As far back as the Safe School Initiative two decades earlier, threat assessment pioneer Robert Fein and his colleagues had studied cases in which tormented adolescents had crossed over from suicidal to homicidal thoughts. The way Fein had described this progression from their perspective was, "If I'm going to die, then I'm taking others with me who caused me pain." On one of my research trips to the Colorado school district that is home to Columbine, I'd spoken with psychologist and threat assessment veteran John Nicoletti, who framed the issue both clinically and operationally. While it was instinctive and purposeful to ask suicidal adolescents why they wanted to kill themselves, an equally urgent priority for threat assessors could be to discern *where* they might be planning to end their lives. A response indicating a school or another public venue, Nicoletti said, could have immediate implications for a case.

This suicide-homicide nexus was drawing fresh attention in the field alongside rising suicide rates nationally. Despite the fact that the Parkrose incident was being celebrated for its nonviolent conclusion, it was troubling in that broader context. "One concern is that more kids seem to be committing suicide at schools," remarked Clem Spenner during the STAT discussion. "I've read reports about it also happening elsewhere." Following a long police career that included service as a school resource officer, Spenner now oversaw threat assessments as a consultant for the twenty smaller, more rural K–12 districts neighboring Salem-Keizer in the Willamette Education Service District, a long-running partnership that had extended the reach of the STAT operation to upward of eighty-four thousand students in the region (and brought the total number of Level 2 cases handled by the STAT annually to approximately 110). Oregon in particular was experiencing a rise in suicides. In the four years from 2015 to 2019, there had been a 10 percent increase in ten- to twenty-four-year-olds taking their lives, advancing a trend since the start of the decade. Salem-Keizer and its neighbors had faced an outsize share of the tragedy, including a suicide that Spenner and McCarthy were looking into from a few months before, when a student in one of Spenner's districts had shot himself on a high school ball field.

"We may never really know whether any of these kids went to the schools with some kind of intent to do a shooting and then at the last moment decided only to kill themselves," Spenner continued. He and a law enforcement officer attending the STAT session had just been discussing this deficit: a non-criminal act of solitary suicide was not conducive to further investigation of a victim's actions and background. Perhaps only with the exception of a family stepping forward to help, which was unlikely in such a difficult situation, there wasn't going to be much chance of learning about possible planning and preparation for a suicidal attack.

Yet many rampage shooters were suicidal, and threat assessment practitioners had been focusing on a related hallmark of cases: deliberate public performance. Behavioral experts at the FBI and elsewhere shared a sense that such acts, especially in the age of social media, could be heightening a perception among youth that lethal violence—whether solely self-directed or in tandem with targeting others—was a valid solution to their anger and suffering. It was alarming enough that teens were ending their own lives with greater frequency, but showing up at school to do it? As Spenner put it, "That's making a statement."

Investigators would soon build a more detailed picture of the Parkrose incident, shedding light on the shotgun-wielding student's mind-set and what had been an extremely close call. The instant before Coach Lowe had intervened in the classroom, there had been the sound of a click—Granados-Diaz had pulled the trigger. Tears rolling down his face, he'd pointed the barrel at his own torso, but the weapon didn't fire. It was then that Lowe jumped into action and wrested it away. At a court hearing five months later, Granados-Diaz's defense attorney argued that the evidence showed his client intended only to harm himself and no one else. That intent could be seen in his remorseful comments after he was taken into custody, his attorney said. Moreover, in an unusual twist for a school shooter case, Granados-Diaz had brought only a single round in the shotgun and had carried no other ammunition or weapons with him, according to a Portland PD arrest report that classified the incident as a suicide attempt.

"The situation shows you're in high need of support and intervention," the judge told the defendant, sentencing him in a plea agreement that included mental health treatment and three years of probation.

Notwithstanding that cautiously hopeful outcome, there was more to ponder about the evidence from a threat-assessment perspective. According to his defense attorney's statements in court, the despairing high schooler hadn't wanted family to find him dead at home, instead choosing the classroom so that his body would be discovered quickly in public. He had been failing in school, had gone through a recent breakup with a girlfriend, and had considered suicide for months. On the morning of the attempt, he had consumed a heavy amount of alcohol to deaden his nerves. He had also written a message on the single shotgun shell: "The last red pill, 5/17/19, just for me." That final phrase further supported the case that he'd planned to harm only himself.

Conceptually, though, his message also pointed toward the territory of cultural scripting and public performance. The term "red pill"—a metaphor originating with the 1999 blockbuster sci-fi film *The Matrix*, in which the protagonist realizes a horrifying reality after taking an eye-opening red pill instead of a comforting blue one—is associated with dark fringes of the internet, including with so-called incels, or involuntary celibates. The subculture of sexually insecure and aggrieved men first drew attention in 2014, after a bitterly misogynistic community-college dropout named Elliot Rodger targeted female students in a suicidal rampage near the University of California–Santa Barbara. Extremist themes of awakening associated with "red-pilling" and the virulent misogyny of incels have surfaced with multiple mass shooters since.

Social rejection in the form of romantic or sexual failure was a type of loss or triggering event that marked numerous case files from Salem-Keizer and other school and university threat assessment programs. Van Dreal recounted a sobering case from the 2000s involving a high schooler named David who had abruptly become withdrawn following a breakup with a girlfriend. After enduring some mockery from classmates, he'd made some veiled comments, overheard by a teacher, about "getting even." Van Dreal already knew David, who as a younger student had gone through some fairly typical bouts of depression. But the STAT had an incomplete picture, as a police officer on the team discovered when Van Dreal asked her to track down David at home and she encountered his mother, who opened the door with bloodshot eyes and a bruised face. David had been experimenting with building homemade explosives and when reprimanded by his mom had gone into a fit of rage and tried to strangle her, the officer learned. (Future threat-assessment research would confirm that strangulation attempts correlate with increased danger of further and completed lethal attacks.) The mom showed the officer David's diary, which described a plan. He was going to get a gun to take to school, first point it at his ex-girlfriend and everyone around her, and then kill himself. The STAT moved quickly to find David and get him into the custody of the Oregon Youth Authority, which worked with the family to relocate him for some long-term care.

"If he'd been able to get a gun, that one would have been a disaster," Van Dreal said. "A kid in that situation doesn't just go in and point the gun. The adrenaline kicks in and he starts pulling the trigger, shooting others along the way to his suicide."

David improved steadily with treatment and completed his high school education with a GED. He eventually returned to the Salem community and found a steady job. He had become devoutly religious and soon got married and had children, taking his family to church every Sunday. For more than a decade, he also kept in touch with a member of the Salem-Keizer team who had helped him through some of his darkest days.

Due in large part to social media, warning signs stemming from social rejection and other pain points among troubled youth became ever more out in the open in the 2010s, detectable to the trained eye in expressions of humiliation, blame, vengeance, and despair. Unfortunately, even as the STAT and teams elsewhere had emerged from the "Dark Ages" of threat assessment, as Van Dreal put it, many communities around the country had yet to pay much heed to the lessons learned in the two decades since Columbine. Often, that focus came only after tragedy hit close to home.

———

Collective memory today is distorted by a widespread belief that the era of school shootings dawned with Columbine. But the genesis of Salem-Keizer's threat assessment program traces to the year before, to a typical school morning in May 1998, when the phone lines suddenly began lighting up with calls. Anxious parents in the community pressed administrators for assurances that their kids were safe in the classrooms and cafeterias, on the playgrounds and ball fields. John Van Dreal was sitting in his district office that morning, going over a challenging case involving a fifth grader who had been menacing classmates and a teacher. The kid's behavior stemmed from a tough home situation involving parental substance abuse and domestic violence, but Van Dreal knew the territory and was prepping a plan to run by an administrator and counselor involved. He had no idea how his career in school psychology was about to transform. A sober-faced colleague leaned into his office doorway: "Hey, John, do you know what's happening down in Springfield?"

Just before eight a.m. that day, in the city about an hour's drive south of Salem, a fifteen-year-old student named Kipland Kinkel had gone into Thurston High School armed with a semiautomatic rifle, two pistols, a hunting knife, and a stockpile of ammunition. He'd headed down a mostly vacant hallway in a khaki-colored trench coat, showing no emotion as he fatally shot sixteen-year-old Ben Walker and wounded seventeen-year-old Ryan Atteberry. Then he'd entered the crowded school cafeteria and begun firing steadily, killing seventeen-year-old Mikael Nickolauson and wounding twenty-four other students in less than a minute. When Kinkel paused, the fifty-round magazine in his rifle emptied, several students rushed and tackled him, pinning him down. Injured kids were sprawled across the cafeteria floor, the metallic scent of blood in the air. As school staff and police rushed in, Kinkel screamed, "Just kill me." In custody, he soon confessed to having murdered his parents at home the previous day.

The Thurston nightmare was among a string of attacks in the two years preceding Columbine that stoked fears around the country about a school shootings "epidemic." In one case, particularly stunning for its youthful act of predation, a pair of middle school boys in Jonesboro, Arkansas, pulled a fire alarm and then positioned themselves in the nearby woods as students and teachers poured out of the building and into their view, a live shooting gallery on a school playground. Those two shooters—just eleven and thirteen years old—hit fifteen victims in the March 1998 attack, killing four girls and a teacher. Elsewhere, lethal rampages had occurred at schools in Alaska, Mississippi, Kentucky, and Pennsylvania.

During the court proceedings that would put Kinkel in prison for life without parole, there was conflicting analysis of his psychological condition. The case was an early bellwether among school shootings for questions and misconceptions about the role of mental illness.

Kinkel had been talking about hearing voices in his head, starting with a police interrogation after the shooting, and then in greater detail with two mental health practitioners who evaluated him for trial and testified for the defense that he was psychotic and possibly schizophrenic. However, the sole psychologist who worked with Kinkel prior to the rampage, Dr. Jeffrey Hicks, testified that he never saw any evidence that Kinkel was psychotic or delusional. Hicks had met with Kinkel and his mother for therapy nine times in the year before the shooting and found Kinkel to be angry and depressed. No discussion of hearing voices ever came up in those sessions, except during the initial intake when Hicks asked Kinkel as part of a routine screening for delusions whether the teen ever heard voices when no one was present. Kinkel's answer was no.

In various journal writings and notebook marginalia, Kinkel had described his alienation and violent rage, but never with any mention of auditory hallucinations. The night before he attacked the school, he penned a note at home apologizing for having just killed his parents, declaring that he loved them dearly. "I want to

be gone," he wrote. "But I have to kill people. I don't know why."
With a conspicuous use of capitalization, he added a new dimension to his narrative: "My head just doesn't work right. God damn
these VOICES inside my head."

Might it have been a ruse? A calculated effort by a bitter, profoundly troubled kid to shape his story and fashion some particular
legacy he imagined for himself? Such questions about shooters' sense
of self-perception—and public performance—would later become
of keen interest to threat assessment researchers looking into emulation and fame-seeking behavior, as would examination of a related
desire common among perpetrators to seize a feeling of control.
Many shooters anticipated what would be said about them, fueling a pattern of them leaving behind so-called manifestos and other
"legacy tokens," as the FBI came to call such case evidence.

If Kinkel's mental state was murky, what might have been dis-
cerned with greater clarity was the array of escalating behavioral
warning signs he'd shown. After watching TV coverage about the
grim schoolyard shooting in Jonesboro two months before his own
attack, Kinkel told two peers he thought the carnage was "cool"
and that "somebody should do that around here." He tried to manipulate another classmate into joining him, boasting that he had
a better plan and could outdo the boys in Arkansas—a desire for
one-upmanship and sensational attention that would continue to
mark numerous other plots and attacks. Kinkel spoke about Jonesboro and the other recent school shootings as failures, stating that
"if he was going to go out, he'd try to take as many people out with
him" as possible, according to a fourth classmate.

Beyond his emulation and suicidality, Kinkel had a recent history of violent conflict, displaying an explosive temper and fighting
with other students when he felt wronged—including one instance
when he pointed a gun at a peer who'd set him off, a form of inten-

sification that would stand out to threat assessors. He had also cultivated an interest in bomb making, giving a speech on the subject in a class the fall before the shooting. Kinkel increasingly sought to obtain firearms, first with help from his father (who thought he could mollify his son's interest) and then when he bought a stolen pistol from a peer at Thurston High and stashed it in his locker the day before he struck. Discovery of that weapon prompted his arrest and suspension from school, a final triggering event that set in motion his lethal plans.

It might seem astonishing in hindsight that all of this didn't add up enough for anyone in a position of authority. But little about such an accumulating picture of danger was yet understood in 1998, except in a few small circles of mental health and law enforcement. Most weren't seeing any picture at all: sharing of possible warning signs among relevant adult leaders was often nonexistent—a problem of "information silos."

With his focus on youth aggression, Van Dreal had been well aware of the cluster of school shootings in the late 1990s, but Thurston High was practically in Salem's backyard and the news of so many kids grievously harmed there was a gut punch. The core of Van Dreal's work was conducting broad psychoeducational evaluations of emotionally disturbed students, helping the schools to shape alternative education plans and manage reactive aggression and other disruptive behaviors. This problem felt different. As one Salem-Keizer assistant superintendent remarked during a hastily assembled leadership meeting, "I don't know what we need to do, but we can't let something like this happen here."

Van Dreal and three other school psychologists and a social worker soon gathered with their boss, Ruth Daniels, the director of student services, to discuss the implications for school safety. Statistically, the Thurston attack remained an extreme anomaly: the probability of a student homicide at a school in America was one in two million. Still, administrators were continuing to field calls from agitated parents, including state legislators with kids in the district, and like Van Dreal and others, Daniels sensed that the tragedy down the road held a new significance. "This is a big deal and it's frightening people," she said. "These were kids and teachers who look just like ours. I need you guys to work on figuring this out. If kids are threatening to kill people, can you add a specific assessment on that?"

The group of specialists were unanimous in their reluctance. "The last thing I wanted to do," Van Dreal recalled, "was go into a school to figure out whether a kid might later shoot and kill people, and tell that principal, 'Yeah, he's OK,' and then go home and try to relax. What if I made a wrong call?"

That risk was substantial. The FBI's school-shooter monograph and the other federal agencies' groundbreaking Safe School Initiative would not exist for another year and a half, and the foundational research from Robert Fein and Bryan Vossekuil was but a gleam in some distant universe of elite law enforcement. What Van Dreal and his colleagues knew was the traditional work of violence risk assessment, using clinical tools like the MacDonald Triad, a theory from the early 1960s holding that potential for violence was associated with cruelty to animals, bedwetting, or fire setting. Such evaluation methods had little relevance for moving quickly to identify and thwart predatory attacks. (There was an old insider joke among psychs who felt that the widely known MacDonald Triad was marginally useful at best: the guaranteed case would be the kid who put a dead pet in his bed, pissed on it, and then set the bed on fire.)

Throughout the meeting, Van Dreal noted that Daniels kept

glancing his way. It was obvious she wanted him to lead the effort, as he was the one who really knew rough kids.

John Van Dreal had grown up with something of a checkered youth himself, in Bakersfield, California, where his parents' encouragement to pursue his artistic impulses had helped him outgrow his restive ones. Truancy and vandalism gave way to Titian and Van Gogh, and he went off to study fine art and educational psychology at Brigham Young University, where he developed an abiding interest in youth afflicted with disturbing behavioral problems. Kids who threatened violence or harmed themselves, he felt, could be understood far beyond the fears they provoked. He first worked with "highly disruptive" adolescents in acute-care residential facilities in Utah, a role that not many others wanted, and then migrated to Oregon's public schools with a set of sought-after skills. Soon he also had an art career taking off on the side, using his weekends and summers to paint classical landscapes and portraits that began fetching him significant sums from collectors. He regarded his two professional lives as entirely separate, though he would come to highly value intuition and creativity in both.

One day, not long after he'd arrived at Salem-Keizer in the early 1990s, Van Dreal was making his rounds to an elementary school that housed a "self-contained classroom," set up for kids with acute special-education needs from around the district who were known to be volatile. Commotion had erupted just before Van Dreal got to the building, when an emotionally disordered young student began spitting and throwing punches. An instructional assistant carefully restrained him on the floor along with the teacher's help, using techniques designed to prevent harm and the use of excessive force. By the time Van Dreal walked in, the petite school principal had arrived and was also down on the ground in her slacks and blazer, helping to calm the child. "It's going to be OK," she repeated in a soothing voice.

Van Dreal got down next to the Twister-like pile. "Hi, I'm John. How can I help?" As the boy began to relax, the principal reached one hand across for a quick shake. "Hi, I'm Ruth," she said warmly. "Tap me out."

Van Dreal greatly admired Daniels for the de-escalation skills and unflappable good humor that had long since elevated her to a district supervisory role, but what she was now asking in the wake of Thurston was a tall order. The group of five specialists agreed to convene monthly to develop a strategy, enlisting social worker Bill MacMorris-Adix to come up with a flowchart that might guide them: if a kid had a history of A, then consider B, and so on. MacMorris-Adix produced a draft that the group refined as school started up again that fall.

The endeavor still gave Van Dreal much pause. His concern wasn't about dealing with rough behavior; in past work he'd had a kid bite him, and another who'd pounced one time right after he'd foolishly turned his back, allowing the kid to land a blow that split open his head. He knew well the sharply disaffected teen who'd make a show of ranting about punching everyone in the face or going after others with a baseball bat. "Obviously all that stuff was abnormal, but it was my normal," he recalled.

What his experience did not include was a student generally thought to be more typical, whose behavior went from elusive to lethal. Before Kinkel struck at Thurston, he had made people nervous, including his parents. But denial of a kid's dangerousness was a powerful emotional blind spot in parents, a dynamic that would continue to mark many cases over the years, from Columbine to Sandy Hook. And for others who were around Kinkel, any spine-tingling they felt about him may have been obscured by the common acts of delinquency he got into with peers, like shoplifting and toilet-papering houses. Deeper investigation into what preceded his horrific attack was just getting started as the Salem-Keizer crew tweaked the flowchart they intended to guide them. "I just didn't feel like we knew what we were doing," Van Dreal said.

The following spring, after Columbine, a strange paradox of hysteria and denialism percolated the country. Suddenly every kid in a trench coat seemed dangerous. At the same time, leaders in many communities settled into the belief that such an act "could never happen here," a comforting sentiment that would stubbornly persist in the face of countless mass shootings. But Columbine left the Salem-Keizer leaders even more on edge. Daniels told Van Dreal they could no longer dally on a plan.

Meanwhile, state legislation about to pass in July 1999 would expand requirements for handling "children exhibiting violent tendencies." By that fall, school districts throughout Oregon would have to implement policies for "managing students who threaten violence or harm in public schools"—including giving mandatory verbal and written notification to parents of any students targeted on apparent hit lists or otherwise threatened with violence, within twenty-four hours of discovering the problem. Students believed to have engaged in such behavior were to be removed immediately from a classroom setting and could not be allowed back in until they were evaluated by a licensed mental health professional, which the law said could be done by an outside practitioner. That option, though intended to add flexibility, could keep students out of school for days or even weeks and turn costly. Salem-Keizer leaders felt they needed to build a more efficient approach, keeping in mind a "youth services" partnership they already had going with local public health and juvenile agencies.

In late spring of 1999, a veteran security and human resources consultant with the district, Paul Keller, began outreach beyond the school system. A former state law enforcement agent who had once worked with the FBI to take down the Rajneeshee cult after a mass poisoning in northern Oregon in the 1980s, Keller remained connected in criminal justice circles. The year before Columbine, he had worked with an associate to establish a threat advisory team based at the Marion County Sheriff's Office that was focused on problematic adults in the community, in response to a recent trend of threats against school principals and local judges. The team liaised with school district leaders and other law enforcement partners. Keller now proposed that they meet at the Marion County Circuit Court in downtown Salem, in the chambers of presiding Judge Paul Lipscomb, to discuss further coordination.

The adult-focused team had been a good start, Judge Lipscomb said to the assembled group, "but what are we going to do about the schools?" Van Dreal listened as MacMorris-Adix conveyed the district's concerns about wading into matters of potentially deadly violence. Van Dreal focused his own comments on a single point: "No one person should be doing this work in the schools," he said. "We need a group of people with different professional perspectives, a team approach."

Van Dreal had long seen that as the smartest way to handle complicated decisions on behalf of troubled kids with special-ed needs, yet he had also backed into this collaborative tenet of threat assessment out of self-interest. "I already had a great gig going!" he recounted with a laugh one evening in 2019 while lounging outside his backyard art studio. Psychoeducational evaluations were low-stress and could be done on a dependable schedule, leaving ample space for his parallel career. The added urgency and liability of threat assessment work promised to disrupt that, even with responsibility distributed among partners.

A few days after the courthouse meeting, Daniels summoned Van Dreal back to her office, with Keller on hand. "Paul and the others want you to be the person to build this program," she said. "Will you give it six months?"

The law enforcement veterans felt Van Dreal was cut from the right mold, not just because he was dedicated to working with difficult kids but also because he didn't have a burning passion for it, not to the extent that he'd be swayed by emotion or take the work home with him at night. Van Dreal agreed to the role, while urging that they press local law enforcement, mental health, and social service agencies to share responsibility in what was not only a school district problem but also a community one. Van Dreal and his colleagues convened a series of focus groups, surveyed the newly emerging research in the field, and honed a set of best practices with feedback from the various partners. The animating principle was that everyone had a part to play in detecting and managing the danger and in building community trust with good case outcomes.

The 1999 Salem courthouse meeting had echoes of the gathering a decade earlier in the chambers of Supreme Court justice Harry Blackmun. Though the effort in Salem sprang from leaders within the community who knew nothing of that hidden history, the pursuit of broader collaboration by Van Dreal and others suggested that the approach was fundamentally well suited for contending with an inherently unpredictable danger.

Within a couple of years, word about the program they were building would make its way to the US Department of Education's Bill Modzeleski, who would enlist Van Dreal as a contributor on the in-depth guide to be developed from the Safe School Initiative. But first came a steep learning curve in Salem. In September 2000, as the kids flocked back into the K–12 buildings to begin the new school year, the program went operational. Within just a few weeks, Van Dreal and the Student Threat Assessment Team found themselves grappling with an intense case that would turn out to be unique in the annals of the field—and would still reverberate two decades later, influencing the approach to another complex case that was setting off alarm bells and playing out in 2019.

chapter seven

_____

A ROAD LESS TRAVELED

It was no coincidence that in the couple of years following the Parkland mass shooting, the caseload handled in Salem by the Student Threat Assessment Team was as large and active as ever. By fall 2019, the team was still periodically reviewing Brandon's case. Now a senior, he was markedly improved after a period of therapy and summer employment, and he had since found a girlfriend and seemed on track to graduate. But just as the team shelved Brandon's case again, they had another long-running one back on their hands. After years of problematic behavior and a stint away from the district, a seventeen-year-old junior named Trevor had reenrolled at Valley High School and soon begun to act in some worrisome ways.

A blond kid of average height with a toothy grin, Trevor had first come on the STAT's radar when he was in middle school. That earlier material in his case file included bullying behavior, both as an instigator and victim; vandalism of school property; and an incident where he had blurted "Heil Hitler" at a teacher who'd given him a bad grade. In another incident, he had mimed shooting a classmate from behind and passed a note to a friend that read, "Payback's a bitch." When questioned by an administrator, he said he was just joking and had no intention of hurting anyone. By Trevor's freshman year at Valley High, two antagonists had set him up for a public humiliation. The pair of boys manipulated him into asking out a popular girl who they knew would reject him, and afterward they mocked him viciously on social media. Trevor soon posted a response: "Guess what? I'll be killing you both."

The Valley High building team found no evidence that Trevor had taken any action to follow through. They defused the situation with disciplinary warnings and by modifying all three students' schedules to separate them. They gave Trevor academic help and cultivated his interest in a video production club. He was a student of average intelligence, socially immature and struggling with emotional stability, but with educational support and the building team keeping a close watch, his behavior improved over the course of his freshman year.

By the following fall of 2018, his mood turned darker. He repeatedly expressed bitterness to friends and a teacher about bullying. There appeared to be no ongoing harassment, but he maintained a distinct view of himself as a victim. When fall Spirit Day arrived, he showed up to school in a trench coat, combat boots, and a backward baseball cap. He told peers he was dressed as a Columbine shooter. As he was questioned in the principal's office, a staffer who knew him well grew alarmed by his demeanor, particularly when he angrily refused to let staff examine the contents of his backpack. Once they persuaded him to give voluntary consent, they discovered he was carrying a notebook containing multiple images of guns and a photo of himself posing in tactical

gear. He also had a map printout of the school grounds and surrounding area. The map was precisely the kind of item the STAT
leaders flagged in their trainings for the building teams—was it an
indication of planning behavior? As building staff worked to reach
Trevor's mom, the principal called McCarthy. In many cases the
STAT would have a day or more to look into a situation, but the
level of concern McCarthy heard on that call had her mobilizing
an investigation in less than two hours.

The STAT's initial findings were a relief: Trevor had no access
to weapons, and there were no signs of him planning an attack.
The map discovered in his backpack turned out to be benign; he'd
been carrying it in case he couldn't remember the route to a nearby
after-school activity. (His mom had taken away his smartphone
until he boosted his grades and proved he could stay out of conflict.) The STAT soon became aware of other red flags, however,
including notebook scribblings by him alluding to self-cutting and
suicide. The team also learned that Trevor had become focused on
weapons and started wearing camouflage attire, hiding it from his
mom by changing on the way to school. A Valley High counselor
who had been working with him and happened to be a military
reservist told a STAT investigator that he'd been struck by Trevor's
"encyclopedic" knowledge of firearms. Trevor wanted to enlist in
the Marines after graduating and had remarked that he felt "like
nothing" when he dressed in regular clothes, but that with camo
on, "people know I'm powerful." A troubled person identifying
with a warrior mentality was a behavioral pattern among plotters
and attackers that was well-known to threat assessment experts.

When the counselor had suggested to Trevor that the military
was unlikely to accept him unless he improved his school record,
Trevor pledged to do better, but underneath he stewed while cultivating another interest: Columbine. A school staff member and

two peers reported that Trevor talked repeatedly about the 1999 school shooting, rattling off specific details about the event and its aftermath. When STAT members interviewed him, he made it clear that he admired the Columbine perpetrators for standing up to bullies and taking back their power. They probed whether his focus on that myth might prompt him to act. "No, I don't want to hurt anyone," he responded. "I wouldn't do what they did, but you gotta admit you can understand it and you know how they felt."

Trevor was stirring anxiety in multiple people around him, including his mother, Linda—with a fortunate upshot in her case. The STAT often encountered varying degrees of denial or resistance in parents, which could hinder information gathering and crucial safety planning. This situation was the opposite: a single parent in her early thirties who also had a younger daughter, Linda was desperate to engage. When STAT members met with her at Valley High right after the Spirit Day incident, she described compounding problems on the home front. Trevor had taken her smartphone without permission several times; in one instance she discovered he'd been watching graphic videos about school shootings. (The team found that he had also developed an interest in the Parkland massacre.) Recently, he had brandished a kitchen knife at her after they'd gotten into a shouting match. Linda noted that she had the support of a steady boyfriend, who had developed a rapport with Trevor, but it was clear to the team that she was struggling. She had also taken Trevor to talk with the pastor at their church, but respite from that meeting was short-lived.

"I've tried everything to get him help, and no one has helped me," she said, barely able to hold back the sobs. An additional comment from her stood out as a measure of the potential danger: "If he does anything stupid, it's not on me."

Linda shared another complication, details of which a police officer serving on the STAT soon confirmed. There was an ongoing investigation into allegations from a person connected to the family that Trevor had sexually abused his younger sister, who was in fourth grade. It was not unusual for the threat assessment process to uncover serious adjacent problems, with varying impact on case management. Trevor's mom agreed to several immediate stepped-up safety measures: She would secure sharps and any other potentially dangerous items in her home (there were no firearms, she confirmed), and she would work with the team to get an immediate psychological evaluation for Trevor and access to treatment. Security staff would begin searches of his belongings when he arrived at school, and she would maintain similar vigilance at home, also closely monitoring internet use to keep Trevor from focusing on violent content. Tapping a teacher and a coach Trevor liked, the Valley High team ramped up check-and-connects with him, and had the building team's SRO inquire discreetly with his peers about how he was doing. McCarthy's team also gave Linda a contact for a county social services representative, so that she could start getting some much-needed support for herself.

The new regime worked well for just over two months. Then the building team got word from a student that Trevor might be trying to obtain a gun. As the STAT vetted that information, McCarthy got a call from Trevor's mom. He had turned volatile again at home, and it was all just too much for Linda to deal with. She had decided to send him to live with his grandfather, whom Trevor barely knew, in a small rural community in Idaho. She wasn't interested in exploring further options. Trevor would be leaving within a couple of weeks.

STAT leaders convened to discuss the situation. A move like that, to a place where Trevor essentially knew no one, was likely to be a major stressor for him. They determined that the community where he was headed had no threat assessment system and few if any resources for case management. Without adequate support and monitoring in place, they believed Trevor could easily become more dangerous. The best they might be able to do would be to give a heads-up call to unknown local law enforcement.

There were no easy answers for the team at this pivotal juncture in Trevor's case. Some STAT members had school-age kids of their own and empathized strongly with a mother who had grown to fear her son. McCarthy and her colleagues consulted further with a deputy district attorney who served on the team, who shared in their sharp discomfort with the situation. They reached a consensus: the risk associated with Trevor leaving the fold under the current circumstances was too high to accept if there was an ethical way to prevent it. The deputy DA urged the local law enforcement agency handling the sexual abuse investigation to wrap up their work quickly, then filed a court petition that would keep Trevor in the area for the near term. Soon thereafter, Trevor was taken into custody on the evidence of abuse.

In detention, Trevor's behavior continued to raise concerns, including a veiled threat he made regarding possible violence at Valley High. As his case was adjudicated, local juvenile authorities recommended a residential placement in the region where he could be under full-time supervision and receive continuing education and robust therapeutic care.

Leveraging such a legal scenario through the juvenile system was rare but not unheard of with case management and still aimed for prevention with the most constructive possible outcome. Nonetheless, it had been a difficult step to take, seen by the team as a necessary act of last resort. Linda was deeply upset but also indicated a sense of relief.

"We took the road less traveled when we decided to keep him in the community," McCarthy said, driving to a middle school for case work early one morning in October 2019, the sun beginning to climb ahead of us into a cloudless sky. "It goes against instinct, and some people would probably think we were crazy doing that, but we just couldn't in good conscience go with the increased risk." It had been a year since Trevor had been placed in a residential home not far outside the Salem-Keizer district. Later that afternoon at the weekly STAT session, his case was on the agenda for review. "Even when they go out of our hands they always seem to end up coming back," McCarthy remarked with a smile.

Trevor had since been moved to a second residential home over the summer, this one located inside the district, so that he could be closer for visits from his mom. He had improved significantly with medication and therapy, but his re-enrollment meant the team needed to examine his case closely again. Trevor had previously been diagnosed with developmental and learning disabilities, anxiety, and depression. Per his recent treatment, his file now contained an additional diagnosis of autism spectrum disorder—though a mental health practitioner serving on the STAT who had also evaluated Trevor felt that the ASD diagnosis, characterized as mild, was questionable. Among other factors, Trevor's strong "theory of mind," including his ability to manipulate and deceive others, was not consistent with ASD, in the STAT practitioner's view.

Team members also met with Trevor and his juvenile-parole officer, Connie, who had worked with the STAT on other cases, and explained to Trevor an individual education plan that laid out his restrictions and responsibilities as he prepared to return to school.

The initial reentry at Valley High went smoothly, but Connie soon circled back to the team after noticing that Trevor was wearing the same set of clothes every weekend, a kind of uniform comprised of baggy cargo pants, a Boston Red Sox cap he wore backward, and a black T-shirt with the word WRATH printed in red letters across the chest. Trevor had told Connie the outfit was an old favorite he'd dug up during the move to the new group home and that he wore it because it made him feel "more comfortable," but she sensed there was more to it than he had let on.

Though unfamiliar to her then, what Connie had described to the team was an imitation of the outfit worn two decades earlier by shooter Dylan Klebold on the day of the Columbine massacre. A STAT member followed up with supervisors at the group home and further learned that when Trevor was first getting settled in over the summer, he'd told them, "Call me Dylan." The home had confiscated some contraband tealight candles, part of a small makeshift shrine to the Columbine perpetrators that Trevor had stashed under his bed. He'd also drawn up a flowery design for a tattoo he wanted, letters spelling out a name: Dylan. In describing the longer-term trajectory of the Columbine influence in Trevor's case and its potential to exacerbate danger, McCarthy cited threat assessment expert Reid Meloy: "Fixation is what a person constantly thinks about. Identification is who the person becomes."

At the STAT session, McCarthy and another team member summarized the latest developments. Upon interviewing Trevor again, it became clear he had deceived Connie and his mother about the provenance of the clothes. He admitted coaxing his mom to go online and purchase what he needed for the outfit, its meaning also lost on her. He further suggested the getup was meant to be ironic, like the trench coat that had once landed him in trouble on Spirit Day: "Like I told you, I would never do anything like those guys. Plus, it's just free speech."

Trevor had been cooperative and affirmed that he wanted to keep going to school. Connie and the STAT members told him he would have that opportunity, but now in a more closely supervised alternative program within the district. He could no longer dress up like Dylan Klebold and would be required to wear regular clothes both in school and at the home on the weekends. With him having agreed to those restrictions, the STAT now decided to tap a modest cash reserve they kept for supplementing case management, to buy him a new set of clothes that he liked. The funds were an earlier innovation of the program, raised with an annual party Van Dreal threw at his home; they were typically put toward extracurricular programming or sometimes more creative uses. In one recent case, the team had learned that the spiraling anger of a freshman they were monitoring was rooted in the theft of his beloved bike on school grounds. As he muttered about "revenge" and fixated on blaming the school, the team saw an opening. They bought him a new bike, which quickly deescalated the case. The team felt that the gift of clothes to Trevor would boost his outlook, and they would keep a close watch via staff at the group home and school, scheduling his case for review again in two weeks.

I asked McCarthy how a kid like Trevor, so recidivist and apparently worrisome, could still be enrolled in the district. She explained that, given his present circumstances, with careful 24/7 supervision, the team assessed him to be a low-level risk for targeted violence. Clearly there were significant risk factors in terms of his mental and behavioral health, but Trevor was about as well supervised and managed as any individual could be, McCarthy said, short of confinement in a locked facility. The STAT had consistently found no evidence of pre-attack planning or preparation behaviors, and any such activity would now be very difficult for him to conceal. Meanwhile, updates from his current therapist, shared with consent by his mother Linda, indicated that he was continuing to make progress.

If and when Trevor reached a point where he was no longer on probation and was leaving the group home, the team would move rapidly to assess him again. For the eventual possibility that he could leave the school system through graduation or otherwise, they had also begun sharing the case with their partners on the community's adult-focused threat advisory team, some of whose members also served on the STAT. "This is a tough one," McCarthy acknowledged. "He's certainly someone who will stay on the radar for a while to come."

———

One day on another drive around the district with McCarthy, we stopped briefly at the Oregon State Hospital, just east of downtown. Originally built in 1883 and long known as an insane asylum that was home to hundreds of men, women, and children, the psychiatric hospital had been replaced a decade earlier with the construction of an adjacent modern facility. The original sprawling three-story brick Kirkbride building was restored and kept true in profile to the hospital's starring role in *One Flew Over the Cuckoo's Nest*, filmed inside in 1975 with a mix of Hollywood crew and longtime hospital residents. (Producer and future movie star Michael Douglas still regarded many of those residents as "criminally insane" more than forty years later, further remarking in a 2017 interview, "We had an arsonist working in the art department.") Fronted by wide lawns and rows of trees in fall oranges and golds, the building now housed the OSH Museum of Mental Health. Its contents told a history of maltreatment and progress: the tale of a ten-year-old "imbecile" locked away at the end of the nineteenth century with "uncontrollable fits of anger," and displays of straitjackets, leather restraints, and electroconvulsive therapy machines from a subsequent bygone era.

If retrograde ideas about mental illness causing violence still hindered America's reckoning with school and mass shootings, the threat assessment program in Salem illuminated the modernity of a broad-based approach to behavioral and mental health struggles. Within the school district's safety and risk management operation, the Student Threat Assessment Team's work was designed to be beneficial well beyond the small possibility of planned violence, with experts on the team who specialized in sexual aggression, substance abuse, and suicide risk. The STAT also engaged regularly in gray-area situations of lesser scope to help foster a climate of safety.

McCarthy had just helped triage such a case that morning at one of the elementary schools, where earlier in the week a student had disrupted a class by lashing out at a schoolmate sitting next to him. Upon talking with the building personnel involved, McCarthy quickly confirmed her initial sense from the student's file that he was a low or perhaps moderate risk for reactive aggression. However, because the nine-year-old had also made a provocative comment about using a gun, the teacher, new to the building, remained highly agitated and was spreading unfounded worry among staff. Lowering the temperature in this type of circumstance was also part of the STAT's mission; McCarthy could help clarify that this wasn't a school shooter in the making but rather a kid who struggled with a sensory-related behavioral issue and needed some basic environmental adjustment and special-ed assistance.

In the past year, McCarthy and her colleagues had been handling multiple threat cases involving students with diagnoses on the autism spectrum, a subject of rising research interest in the field. "A lay person isn't going to have a great understanding of either autism or threat assessment, and there's a lot of nuance involved," McCarthy said. High-profile mass shootings over the past decade had turned a misleadingly fearful spotlight on the disorder in the eyes of the public: Adam Lanza, who attacked Sandy Hook in 2012, had an ASD diagnosis among multiple other afflictions, and mass shooters who struck in California in 2014 and Oregon in 2015 reportedly did as well. But research published in 2017 by leading experts in the recently founded *Journal of Threat Assessment and Management* made clear the detriment of assigning blame to the disorder.

"Most individuals who fall on the spectrum of ASD are neither violent nor criminal," the authors wrote, a finding affirmed by multiple studies detailed in the paper. Rather, ASD in the mass killers they analyzed existed within a highly complex set of factors, and these cases required an understanding of "the crucial role" of comorbid conditions that led to the violence. In Lanza's case, according to the authors, those included severe obsessive-compulsive disorder and probable psychopathy, along with several long-building behavioral and environmental problems with his home life.

For threat assessment practitioners encountering ASD, the key is understanding how *symptoms* associated with autism might contribute to or exacerbate danger with a case subject who is not doing well broadly—the fixation behavior that could accompany the disorder, for example. (This was a counterpoint in the team's debate over the recent ASD diagnosis in Trevor's case, with his fixation on Columbine.) McCarthy further observed that kids with autism, who can struggle to develop social relationships, often face bullying and tend as they get older to become more aware of how they differ from their peers, which can compound feelings of rejection and isolation, or deepen depression.

As McCarthy navigated a range of cases, meeting with struggling youth and their parents around the district, she operated with a seamless mix of empathy and clinical coolness. Her manner seemed exactly right for the work, yet in a way paradoxical. She was not alone among threat assessment professionals who came across as gifted, emotionally intelligent people, but who also seemed to have a certain detachment or desensitization about them.

"Yeah, to do this work you have to have a cold dead heart!" she said with a belly laugh, when I mentioned the pattern. Perhaps the work necessarily attracted people, she suggested more seriously, who were biologically predisposed to slightly lower levels of emotional arousal amid trauma. Yet for her, little was more exciting than helping improve a screwed-up kid. And the highly structured and contained K–12 setting offered a great advantage: "We can provide a lot of services to kids and pretty much engineer their environment in ways that really support them." Her colleagues serving on the adult-focused threat advisory team often faced much steeper challenges in trying to steer case subjects, she noted, due to a lack of monitoring or programmatic options.

Courtenay McCarthy had earned her psych degrees in Minnesota and then Colorado, where she did field research with drug addicts suffering from HIV and hepatitis, then returned home to Oregon to build her career. Her early experience included working with troubled and traumatized youth, in the setting of child protective services. She moved into school psychology, eventually landing back in her hometown. Two of the cases she had just worked over the past several days were at the elementary and high schools she'd once attended herself. "Having a deep sense of connection to where you're doing this work is helpful," she said. (She added she was careful not to have any direct personal ties to a case, which to date had not come up.) "The hope that's intrinsic in the mission is so important," she continued. "You have to have the perspective that everybody can change for the better. Kids make bad choices. That's part of how they grow. We see some dark things for sure, cases of kids who have terrible home situations. But generally kids really like being in school, and there are many cases where we've been able to work with that and improve their situations to avoid a bad turn, and with that process you know you're really making a difference."

The mission in Salem had a revealing history of boundary pushing, recounted over lunch one afternoon by McCarthy, Van Dreal, and attorney Paul Dakopolos, who described how he and Van Dreal had navigated uncharted territory when first launching the program. Big hesitations hung over the early years with regard to federal laws restricting the disclosure of education and health records (FERPA and HIPAA, respectively), which drove them to creative thinking and the occasional use of "cowboy law," as Dakopolos put it wryly. They didn't want the outside agencies, particularly youth mental health services, to lawyer up and throw cold water on establishing active working partnerships, so they set about drafting simple memorandums of understanding.

"From a legal standpoint, the MOUs weren't worth the paper they were printed on," Dakopolos said, but they served to bring everyone to the table, where they could start building trust in the model of shared responsibility. "We needed to be able to talk to each other more about what the problems were with kids," he said. "Once we were in the room together, we could get into, 'Here's how we'll handle this, and here's what everyone agrees to do.'" They had to maintain the privacy protections for student records required by law—but that didn't mean they couldn't set up channels for talking to each other informally about a developing safety concern or collaborate on strategy for how to respond.

"Had it all blown up," Dakopolos added with a smile, "I would've been the world's most rotten lawyer."

Dakopolos had done legal work for numerous school districts in the region over the years, and like Van Dreal and others, his role was compelled by indelible events. He had been counsel for the Springfield school district for several years during the 1990s, and although no longer with the district at the time of the Thurston High School attack, he happened to be in town working with another client that morning, at a location close to a hospital. "It was horrific, with the sound of all the ambulances wailing by," he recalled. "I vowed then that for any school district I represented, I would do everything I could on my watch to guard against that happening. And if we had to step on some toes in the process, so be it."

That described their approach to threats and security issues in general, including more than one case involving a volatile parent. One year, a father who had relocated to the Midwest after a bitter divorce and custody battle had returned to Salem and was on his way to show up at his son's school. A worried building administrator got Dakopolos on the phone, unsure of what to do. "The kid is not in school today," Dakopolos told her flatly. "OK, but the student is here?" she replied, noting that the front office had him listed as checked in. "The kid is not in school today," Dakopolos repeated. She went with his recommended response. The father was not happy, but he left the school, buying administrators time to formulate a plan.

Dakopolos continued. "We've always asked the question, 'What news article would we rather not read? The one about how Dad came from Kansas and no one has ever seen the kid again since, or the one where a parent didn't get to do what he wanted to do?"

Sometimes they found themselves handling information disclosure to opposite effect—pushing the limits of sharing too much.

Oregon in 1999 had mandated notifying the parents of kids who were threatened, but how much did you tell those parents? The law was wholly unspecific in that regard. Dakopolos framed a scenario: "We might think it was important to identify for parents the individual who made the hit list with their kid on it. The legal response would be to ask, 'Wouldn't that be a FERPA violation, to disclose the name?' Well, my answer to that was always, 'Who cares?' The responsible way to view all this is, we're doing risk management at its most important level. We're talking about, potentially, children's lives."

They felt they could argue with legal confidence that telling parents what they needed to know to keep their kids safe had nothing fundamentally to do with a threatening subject's education or health records. Rather, it was a matter of behavior and circumstances, and at stake was the psychological and possibly physical safety of other students. In a few select cases, they even went beyond revealing who the threatening individual was and provided additional context, Van Dreal added, "so that if Johnny, who we're monitoring, calls up their Billy and says, 'Hey, meet me at the park,' now they know it's not a good time for their Billy to go do that."

Federal privacy laws would later loosen around the potential to demonstrate reasonable information-sharing in the context of student safety, but for them these kinds of judgment calls were also the art of threat management. "If it's a matter of protecting students," Van Dreal said, "then I'd rather be with Paul in court on a possibly wrongful release of confidential information to key parties than to be there for wrongful injury or death." Over the years there had also been plenty of times when Dakopolos told Van Dreal, "No, you can't do that," after Van Dreal had called up to float some outside-the-box strategy for a thorny case. But they felt that if they could always document pushing the boundaries in good faith, true to their goal of student safety and well-being, then they could be confident that the legal system and the majority of the community would back them. "There were a couple times when we had sabers rattled at us by aggressive parents," Van Dreal said. "We encouraged them to go to their attorneys, and then we never heard from them about it again."

Case management decisions were also about protecting the lives of the threatening students themselves. "We didn't want them going Measure 11," Van Dreal said, referring to the Oregon law passed in 1994 that imposed minimum prison sentences for various violent crimes and mandated that juveniles age fifteen and older who committed them be tried as adults. The STAT leaders had worked ever since the 1990s to prioritize "pro-social" solutions and move away from the widespread zero-tolerance policies that resulted in high numbers of school expulsions and contacts with the justice system. (Reform of the state's youth crime laws in 2019 scaled back draconian treatment of minors, including abolishing life sentences without parole. For the threat assessment program, the goal remains the same: to prevent kids from engaging in violence that could land them behind bars and ruin their own lives as well as those of victims.)

The strategy won trust among educators. In response to a 2005 survey administered by the University of Oregon's Institute on Violence and Destructive Behavior, 94 percent of school administrators and counselors from the mid-Willamette Valley region responded that the Salem-Keizer model effectively identified potentially dangerous students and situations, served a valuable role in decision making, and had positive effects on school safety. The school administrators who were surveyed overwhelmingly reported that the model boosted efficient coordination with law enforcement and outside mental health agencies, and nearly all survey respondents agreed that the procedures used in the program were respectful of the students and their families.

By the 2010s, the program could also be measured in its widespread adoption by school districts throughout Oregon and Washington, as Van Dreal increased outreach and trainings. In fall 2017, Van Dreal asked Bill Modzeleski, since retired from the US Department of Education, to conduct a handful of case reviews and an overarching analysis of the now more developed Salem-Keizer model, including its integration with the district's broader safety and risk management operations. What Modzeleski found was quality case work and a program that "far surpassed" what he had seen elsewhere. He cited the robust partnership with the adult-focused threat advisory team and with local outside agencies, and fidelity to the program's goals built on continual training and refinement of practices. Salem-Keizer also appeared to be using an equitable model. Research from a similar behavioral threat assessment program, developed by psychologist and education expert Dewey Cornell for Virginia public schools and also becoming more widely known, had shown no disparities among Black, Hispanic, and white students in cases resulting in out-of-school suspensions, school transfers, or legal actions.

A vulnerability for the Salem-Keizer program was a lack of regular auditing or scientific study of its results, which had never been made a priority amid limited resources and well-established community trust. In 2020, however, McCarthy and her colleagues began gathering data internally and planning for an analysis of the STAT caseload and outcomes by outside researchers at the University of Washington. An initial data set spanning the three school years from 2017 to 2020 was affirming. Less than 12 percent of the nearly 150 cases involved students who were expelled as a result of a threat incident and investigation, and less than 10 percent resulted in arrests, a rate that would've been still lower except for an unusual spike in the 2019–2020 school year from four arrests for possession of guns or replica firearms in school buildings.

Leaders in the field have long known that empirical validation of their work was destined to remain mostly obscure, sometimes even to them. During a training talk in Florida for threat assessment practitioners in early 2020, Van Dreal recounted how a stern police officer he knew marginally back home had approached him after a meeting a few years prior and reached out uncharacteristically to hug him. "In my past I haven't gotten the best response when I've tried to hug cops," Van Dreal quipped. Nonetheless he'd obliged. The officer's eyes welled up. "I want to thank you for saving my son's life," he said.

Van Dreal was a little astonished and unsure of how literally to take the comment. At first, he could hardly recall the case. It was not a high-octane one. There had been some vague signals from the unhappy teen that he might want to harm himself or others, and the Salem-Keizer team had intervened to make him feel more included in his school: a couple of academic adjustments, a closer connection with a teacher, a recommendation for extracurricular programming. The kid ended up doing well, went off to college, and was now an upstanding young man in the community. Van Dreal's point with the story was that the most sensational or urgent cases weren't necessarily the most illustrative. The true heart of the work was early intervention—the very earliest possible.

"Absolutely, we want to make sure we capture the eleventh-hour incident before it happens, the kid who has the weapons in his backpack and is on his way," he told the audience of counselors, administrators, and cops. "That's big, right? That's success. But I'll tell you this: It's also failure. If a kid makes it that far and is under our watch, we've failed. That kid has now committed a crime, probably a felony, and he's going to be institutionalized. Yes, we've saved the people who were in harm's way. But now we've also lost that kid. That kid goes away, and comes out a different person."

———

Early intervention in threat cases can involve numerous tactics, their purpose mostly self-evident in the support and services offered. But a full understanding of the STAT's extraordinary legal intervention in fall 2018 that kept Trevor from leaving the community and moving to Idaho requires the context of some vivid institutional memory. The fraught decision was influenced in part by the STAT's history with a singular case, one both triumphant and tragic, and which speaks like no other to core operational and philosophical challenges facing the field.

Shortly after Van Dreal and his colleagues launched the program in September 2000, a school resource officer posted at McNary High got a tip about a junior named Erik Ayala. The sixteen-year-old had told a classmate that he was angry at "preps" and was going to bring a gun to school. When the officer spoke with Ayala, the dejected youth insisted he had no intention of hurting anyone. Two months later, he tried to kill himself by swallowing a fistful of Aleve tablets. He was admitted to a private facility in Portland to undergo treatment. As Ayala recovered and was preparing to return to the high school, the STAT investigated the deeper trail of his turmoil, including comments he'd made to peers about wanting to kill. In his school notebooks, he had raged about feeling like an outsider and being rejected by a girl he liked. He'd gone online to try to buy a gun, and had drawn up a hit list. The names on it included one of his own close friends and the girl he longed for.

The team also knew Ayala's potential. "He was a very gifted, bright young man," Van Dreal recalled. The STAT was just developing their "wraparound strategy" for threat management, and this case would be a high-stakes test. Ayala returned to a team of people showing him how much they cared about him through counseling, in-home tutoring, and help pursuing his interests in music and computers. "A lot of what was done for him," Van Dreal said, "was to move him away from thinking about terrible acts."

The team kept close tabs as the school year went on. A teacher Ayala admired checked in with him frequently and passed along updates. The school resource officer struck up casual conversations with Ayala and his two close friends, Kyle and Mike, helping to gauge Ayala's stability and progress. Over the next year and a half, the high schooler did well in classes and his outlook steadily improved. When Ayala graduated in 2002, the STAT handed off his case to their partners on the community threat advisory team based at the Marion County Sheriff's Office. The model of overlapping coverage was the first of its kind in the field, expanding collaboration on cases that involved individuals beyond the school buildings, which could include those who graduated or otherwise left the school system.

Ayala now lived with his parents and got an IT job at a Fry's Electronics. He grew frustrated that his computer skills were being underutilized and occasionally still vented to his buddies, but with continued counseling and a network of support now stewarded by the adult community team, he stayed on a decent track. "We moved in front of him and nudged him onto a path of success and safety," Van Dreal said.

Eventually that path took him sixty miles away, to Portland, where in 2006 he moved into an apartment with his high school buddy Mike. Ayala's mental health struggles began to catch up with him. He couldn't hold down a job or find a girlfriend. He became increasingly withdrawn and often holed up in his bedroom playing *Resistance: Fall of Man* and other first-person shooter games. He was no longer in touch with the teams who had watched over him in his hometown for nearly five years.

On the morning of January 24, 2009, Ayala scribbled a note apologizing to his family and bequeathing his PlayStation 3, his car, and what little remained in his bank account to Mike. "I'm sorry to put all this on you buddy," he wrote. "I know it's not much consolation, but as my friend and roommate you are entitled to everything that I own. Good luck in this fucked-up world." Then he readied the 9 mm semiautomatic pistol he'd bought two weeks earlier at a pawnshop and headed downtown. Around ten thirty that night, a group of teens waited in line outside the Zone, an all-ages dance club. Ayala didn't know anyone at the club, but to him it was a hangout for the kinds of kids he'd long since perceived as causing him deep pain. In a matter of seconds he shot nine people, most of them teens, two of whom died. As a security guard moved toward him, Ayala put the barrel under his chin and pulled the trigger one more time.

Those who had worked with Ayala back in Salem could barely stomach the news. "It hit us all really hard," said Lieutenant Dave Okada, a leader on the community threat advisory team, who retired from the Salem PD in 2018 and continued to work in the field as a private consultant. "We had so much invested in him and his case."

The tragedy stood as a unique example of both the promise and limitations of behavioral threat assessment—a kind of gut-wrenching proof of concept. "Erik ended up acting out his ideas from high school on a similar, if not the same, target population almost a decade later," Van Dreal acknowledged. That suggested, perhaps as clearly as might ever be possible, that the two teams in

Salem had prevented him from going on a rampage when he was younger. Yet the outcome also laid bare daunting questions about managing a potentially dangerous person over the long term. Even if a troubled kid could be steered away from violence and set up to be a better-adjusted adult, what happened when he moved beyond the reach of those helping him? When was a case *really* over?

At a certain fundamental level, answers to those questions did not exist. One conceptual solution to the problem was to establish "trip wires," or a farther reaching network for vigilance and support. When possible, a threat assessment team would make contact with counterparts in a community where a subject was headed, share legally permissible background information, and invite further communication if and when that might become helpful (which could be mutually beneficial if the subject were to head back to their own community at some point). FBI experts had sometimes advocated this approach with the subjects of workplace threat cases going back to the 1990s, and the strategy would later figure among threat assessment operations at other federal agencies and some schools and universities. A major obstacle, however, was a lack of national scale. Many American communities had never heard of behavioral threat assessment, let alone had programs. That was especially true in smaller communities with fewer resources, part of the predicament to confront the Salem-Keizer team many years later with Trevor's imminent move away. Short of much wider adoption of the work geographically, the hope with this fundamental challenge was at least to build greater cultural awareness of behavioral warning signs.

That mission had become more evident with Columbine in 1999, as had the need to improve information sharing about individuals in crisis who might be planning violence. But after the turn of the millennium and the world-altering terrorist attacks of September 11, 2001, America's attention was riveted on a different kind of danger and a coming era of war. Mass shootings continued periodically through the mid-2000s: at schools, workplaces, a shopping mall, a church event, a nightclub concert, and yet another postal facility, this time with a rare attack by a female perpetrator, who was an ex-employee. Unrelated to international terrorism, however, these events failed to sustain much national interest. Political debate over gun laws had calcified, and the expiration of a ten-year federal ban on assault weapons promised a windfall for gun manufacturers, who cranked up production and gave away high-capacity ammunition devices to boost sales.

Meanwhile, 2007 ushered in the first iPhone, an online phenomenon called social media was taking off, and before long, the problem of mass shootings would again loom large. To the extent that the vigilance of everyday people was frequently an important first link in preventing attacks, the field of behavioral threat assessment still needed help spreading the word about a solution that remained mostly unknown.

chapter eight

VITAL CONNECTIONS

Kristina Anderson felt a ripple of panic. It was Monday morning and her pal Colin Goddard had just called. They were running late for their 9:00 French class, and he was hustling over to her apartment near campus to pick her up. "Yeah, I'm ready to go," she'd told him, still in bed. She shrugged off her minor hangover as only a nineteen-year-old could, rubbing the sleep from her bright blue eyes and quickly tidying her shoulder-length brown hair. Through the plastic blinds on the bedroom window the weather looked gray and blustery with even a light dusting of snow, rather unusual for a morning in mid-April. The Virginia Tech sophomore pulled on a pair of fitted jeans and a white polo T-shirt, then a sweatshirt. She debated for a second whether to wear her usual flip-flops in hopes of some sunshine breaking through, but that seemed wishful thinking. She put on her light-blue Puma sneakers, grabbed her book bag and headed out.

During the short ride in Goddard's car, the two friends were tempted to skip class for coffee and a bagel, but with finals approaching, they deemed that too risky. They parked and then hurried past a cluster of buildings toward the neo-Gothic stone exterior of Norris Hall.

Along the second-floor hallway at 9:15 a.m., the doors to the engineering and foreign language classes had all since been shut. "You're going in first," Anderson said with a grin as they reached room 211, figuring she might duck some awkwardness by trailing behind Goddard's six-foot-plus frame. Their professor, "Madame" Jocelyne Couture-Nowak, looked their way and continued talking as they took their usual chair desks toward the back of the nearly full classroom of eighteen students. Feeling a little overheated, Anderson took off her sweatshirt and settled in. She glanced over at her friend Ross Alameddine, a bookish, cheerful English major and ace computer gamer, who smiled at her quizzically. She was surprised a moment later when another classmate, Rachael Hill, walked in and sat down in one of the remaining open seats near the front. Hill was studious and always well-prepared for class, and it was unlike her to show up late.

Earlier that morning at the West Ambler Johnston residence hall across campus, where Hill lived, a couple of students on the fourth floor had been startled by thudding sounds around seven fifteen a.m. and wondered whether another student in a nearby room had fallen out of her loft bed. The noise was unsettling enough to prompt a call to campus police. When the first officer arrived at the building, in less than five minutes, an emergency medical team close behind, he found a grisly scene in freshman Emily Hilscher's room. Hilscher and another student, Ryan Clark, a resident adviser in the dorm, were sprawled on the floor in pools of blood. Clark was only partially dressed. Both had been fatally wounded by gunshots.

A double homicide was shocking and extraordinary on this idyllic campus nestled in the foothills between the Blue Ridge and Allegheny mountains. Initially, police suspected a domestic conflict. They questioned Hilscher's roommate, who had been off campus for the weekend and had just returned to go with Hilscher to an early class they had together. She confirmed that Hilscher had been staying with a boyfriend at a nearby college over the weekend, and said she knew of no problems between the couple. She also told police that the boyfriend owned a gun and practiced at a shooting range. Immediately he was deemed a "person of interest" and a focus of the investigation. There were bloody footprints leading away from room 4040, but no one interviewed at the residence hall reported seeing anyone leave the room or the building after the jarring noises.

As police would soon learn, the person responsible for the murders was Seung-Hui Cho, a twenty-three-year-old Virginia Tech senior. He had slipped into the lobby of West Ambler Johnston early that morning and possibly followed Hilscher, who had just returned to campus, up to her room. One early theory was that the killings were the culmination of an attempted sexual assault. Clark, who lived in an adjacent room, presumably heard the disturbance and rushed over. But Cho had no known connection to Hilscher nor any record of violence, and his attack may have been better explained as "novel aggression"—a trial run for testing his resolve and ability to kill. Cho had left the building, returned to his own dorm to change out of his bloody clothes, and headed for the post office just off campus in downtown Blacksburg. There, a clerk punched a stamp onto a package he had addressed to NBC News in New York, postmarked 9:01 a.m.

Back inside West Ambler Johnston, which housed more than eight hundred students, police continued to process the crime scene and conduct witness interviews amid widespread confusion. Many students had little idea of what had taken place, and police soon allowed them to leave the building to make morning classes, including Rachael Hill, who rushed across campus to French class.

Three-story, L-shaped Norris Hall had three large entrances framing heavy wood doors. Just after 9:30 a.m., Cho finished chaining them all shut from the inside. He posted a note on the interior door of one entrance warning that opening it would set off a bomb. Then he went up the stairs.

As the jolt of staccato cracks began in nearby room 206, and then 207, confusion gripped Anderson and her classmates. Initially they thought it could be the construction work close to the building that had been going on for several weeks, but the sounds were growing louder and anxiety was setting in. Couture-Nowak peered out the classroom door, then slammed it shut, her usual dimpled smile lost to pale dread. "Get down behind your desks!" she urged. "Call 911!" Anderson and others scattered out of their seats. Goddard reached an emergency dispatcher on his cell phone and began describing their location. Two students in the front, Matthew La Porte and Henry Lee, jumped up and pushed their lightweight chair desks toward the door to barricade it. Couture-Nowak rushed another one over, then started to back away.

Bullets pierced the door. Cho pushed it open and didn't utter a word as he walked in and immediately shot Couture-Nowak and multiple students. He fired in rapid bursts as he crossed the front of the room and moved methodically down the four narrowly spaced rows of desks. In the back of the room, curled forward over her desk seat with her knees on the floor, Anderson glimpsed a tan vest with ammunition clips in the front pockets, arms outstretched with a weapon. Her mind raced to make sense of the surreal. *Maybe it's a paintball gun. Maybe this is some sort of horrible social experiment or crazy reality TV episode about to be revealed to them.* She closed her eyes and braced against the chair. *Your turn is coming.* The deafening bangs felt like a wave closing in. A bullet struck her in the lower back. The sharp slap of it was surprising, though it hurt less than she expected, more of a burning sensation. It was all happening so fast and still impossible to believe.

Suddenly it was quieter, the room still, the pounding of gunshots more distant. Anderson could hear the muffled ringing of a cell phone from somewhere a few feet away. The air was bitterly floral with gunpowder. She kept her body curled as tightly as possible on the seat of the desk chair. "Don't move," Goddard said, lying nearby on the carpeted floor, a wound in his leg. "He could come back." She noticed that a classmate nearby kept coughing. *Why on earth isn't she staying quiet and playing dead?* Anderson turned her head to look, and then realized why, as the sound from her classmate faded.

Cho reentered the room, peering from the front to see who was still alive. The overturned desks and the book bags and bodies in the narrow aisles made the rear of the room less accessible. He reloaded and resumed shooting. Anderson could feel herself panting and willed herself to stop. A round hit the wall just above her head, throwing off a puff of debris. She raised up slightly to wipe at the sprinkle of dust on her arm—an instinctive reaction, and a grave mistake. He pointed the pistol and fired again, hitting her from behind a second time, just below the waist. He squeezed off more shots farther across the room, then left again.

Virginia Tech police and officers from the Blacksburg PD tactical team swarmed the exterior of the building. With no precedent here for a situation like this, no one, not even members of the tactical unit, had axes or other tools for breaching the chains. Officers attempted to blast through an entrance with two shotgun rounds,

but those failed. They scrambled for a locked entrance to a mainte-
nance area, shot the lock off that door and began moving in.

Now crumpled all the way down on the floor of room 211,
Anderson lay in shock as she held hands with Goddard, who was
now also bleeding from additional wounds. "Stay quiet," he whis-
pered. The crack of gunfire continued elsewhere on the second floor.
Sirens were wailing outside, and voices were shouting from the floor
below and getting closer. Then there was motion along the front of
the classroom again. Then, a single bang followed by a dropping
thud—the last shot Cho would ever fire.

They lay there for several more minutes. Anderson felt thirsty.
She noticed a stinging pain in her midsection growing sharper, the
sights around her receding into a blur.

"Shooter down," she heard the first officer into the room call out.
Then: "We have a lot of blacks in here." Anderson would only later
learn that the odd-sounding description was code for fatalities. The
SWAT officer moved quickly, calling out she was alive. "Yellow,"
he said as he came close, but then corrected himself. "Red." Whatever that meant, she knew the diagnosis wasn't good. Next she was
in an officer's arms and floating past bodies.

At the building exit, a second officer helped take hold of her
legs as they emerged into daylight. That moment, captured at
10:22 a.m. by a photojournalist standing about two hundred yards
away on Virginia Tech's iconic central Drillfield, would soon appear
on TV broadcasts and front pages around the world: Anderson in
her white polo shirt, jeans, and sneakers, about to be laid down on
the grass.

Paramedics began opening her clothes, telling her she was going to be OK, but she felt cold from head to toe and her thoughts
were spiraling to strange places. For a moment she wondered self-
consciously what they would think when they discovered she was

wearing red underwear. She just wanted to go to sleep. Straight above her stretched the vast gray sky.

———

Anderson woke from four hours of emergency surgery to the tearful faces of her parents, who'd raced by car to the hospital from 250 miles away. Later, once the narcotic haze diminished and the parade of doctors and nurses around the clock gave way to the removal of some bandages, she gazed at the various tubes still in her and the staples down her midsection.

She'd been struck by three bullets. The surgeons had removed her gall bladder, much of one kidney and parts of her large and small intestines. A third shot that morning had ricocheted into the tip of her right foot, though she hadn't registered it. The fact that her big toe wasn't shattered beyond repair was likely thanks to her choice of the thick-soled Pumas instead of the flip-flops.

Anderson would have to relearn over time how to sit up, how to eat, and how to walk. Then, how to live free from fear and sadness, and guilt. She had survived the deadliest school shooting in American history. Thankfully, so had her friend Goddard and others. But many of their talented and fun-loving classmates, including Rachael, Ross, Matthew, and Henry, had not. Twenty-seven students and five faculty members were murdered at Virginia Tech on April 16, 2007, and twenty-seven other people were wounded or otherwise physically injured during the mass shooting, including a handful who jumped from second-story windows to escape. The attacker had fired a total of 174 bullets inside Norris Hall, 61 of them in Anderson's classroom alone. One student was shot 19 times. The toll was steepest in the French class, where eleven of the eighteen students present and their teacher died.

After four grueling months of physical recovery and rehab living at her parents' home in northern Virginia, Anderson returned to campus that fall, determined along with her fellow survivors to jump back into college life. She felt twinges of pain whenever she coughed or laughed too hard, and she struggled with frustrating digestive problems. She found herself getting anxious in classrooms and at parties, and soon the once enjoyable moments of social life felt cumbersome, even painful. One night that December, she collapsed on the floor of her apartment, sobbing uncontrollably. (She would soon better recognize the PTSD symptoms.) She found her way to a trusted therapist and began to talk about the equally fearsome emotional wounds. Later, she took a lead role in a student group working to help heal the Virginia Tech community and began connecting on social media with survivors of other school shootings, including those from the next big one, in February 2008 at Northern Illinois University.

Following her graduation in 2009, Anderson did a stint teaching English in the south of France and dabbled in marketing work back home on the East Coast. She felt restless, but she had also begun doing something else: with her parents' encouragement, she shared her ordeal in a couple of talks at private events for CEOs and community leaders. She felt compelled to urge better awareness and to honor the first responders and the victims lost.

At first, telling her story to an audience was nerve-wracking and at moments even tormenting, but Anderson grew steadier and more confident as she saw how strongly it resonated. In Washington, DC, she met Bill Modzeleski, who became a mentor and pointed her to the Safe School Initiative. The research insights about preventing attacks were a revelation. She saw how threat assessment embodied hope. With interest in her story growing among educators, mental health professionals, and law enforcement leaders, she realized she could be a unique kind of connector, a voice for community preparedness and individual responsibility to speak up when a person or situation seemed worrisome or off. She soon forged a training partnership with Gene Deisinger, a psychologist turned cop who had developed an early threat assessment program after a mass shooting at the University of Iowa in the 1990s and later became Virginia Tech's deputy police chief in the wake of the April 2007 massacre.

At speaking events and trainings around the country, Anderson relived her ordeal over and over again with extraordinary poise, weaving in what she was learning about better prevention and response. There were moments of palpable emotion, like when she teared up at the thought of her mom learning of her shooting. Other moments lent catharsis. She joked that with those paramedics outside Norris Hall scrambling to assess and stop her bleeding, red probably hadn't been the best color underwear to get shot in. Her story riveted students and educators and drew standing ovations from roomfuls of cops, some of them uncharacteristically reduced to tears.

Anderson knew that audiences expected to witness her emotions, yet nothing about how she summoned the memory of her horrific experience felt gratuitous. She took sparing aim with the painful details. Her targets were misconception and complacency.

"We know these events have been averted and that they're preventable," she told me on a spring afternoon in 2016, standing on the bluff-top campus of Pepperdine University in Malibu, California, where she and Deisinger were giving a two-day seminar. "We just don't really talk about it very much. But we should."

Gun policies were not a subject of her work, yet people would sometimes approach her afterward on a stage or in a lobby and ask the "good guy with a gun" question. Her memory required a certain reconciliation between how the massacre had happened lightning fast and yet how time had also seemed to seize up and then move in slow motion. But she'd never felt a shred of doubt about how little opportunity there was to react. The fight-or-flight response in people varies widely and is unpredictable, but some of her deceased classmates hadn't even had a chance to dive from their chairs. Each time she was asked the question, she would kindly suggest in response that the idea of a student or a teacher with a gun saving the day was a fantasy.

Looking for a secluded place to talk after several hours inside a low-lit auditorium, we'd gravitated along with Deisinger toward the Heroes Garden, a memorial high on the campus honoring an alumnus and others who'd been aboard the hijacked airliner that crashed into a field in Pennsylvania on 9/11. Anderson, usually cheerful and a caffeinated talker, was in a more pensive mood standing in the afternoon sunshine. Nearly a decade had passed since that morning in Blacksburg, and she did not plan to be known as "the girl who got shot" for the rest of her life. "I know my work will have to evolve," she said, gazing out at the sapphire Pacific Ocean. "For now I still sort of look like I'm in college, and I can travel around like a maniac doing this, but one day when I'm hopefully pregnant and starting a family, no one is going to believe me crying onstage. One of my goals right now is to maximize sharing my story and the emotional impact while I can."

Shooting survivors had always spoken out to some degree, but she and others had become a rising presence since the early 2010s, leveraging social media to influence school safety policies, gun regulations, media coverage, and beyond. Deisinger, who was sitting on a bench nearby listening quietly, joined in to comment about another goal of their presentations: demystifying the mass shootings problem. I noted that both he and Anderson used the term evil in their talks about what had happened at Virginia Tech, which could perhaps seem contradictory to that purpose.

"It's meeting people where they are in their conceptualization of the issue, and then bringing them along to some understanding," said Deisinger, since retired from his law enforcement role. "Even as a scientist and a psychologist, I do have a belief that evil exists. Those are the extreme cases, the outliers, and threat assessment work is not going to stop those. Force is going to stop those. As a crime-scene investigator, I've seen the effects from those on bodies, on families— and the effects are evil." And yet Deisinger also spoke of how gratifying it was to show people that a majority of disruptive and violent behaviors could be perceived in a less frightening and debilitating way, making them an approachable challenge: "In all the thousands of threat cases I've worked over the past twenty-three years, while some were pretty freaky up front, these were people who were going through crises, and most were amenable to some level of intervention. That's not how a lot of people view this problem, unfortunately, because they're just thinking it's 'the worst of the worst.'"

With Anderson's story serving as a clarion call, Deisinger's training presentation drove home the imperative of having a centralized system for information sharing. The lack of that at Virginia Tech had been disastrous. Teachers, counselors, administrators, and the Virginia Tech PD had become aware of different aspects of Cho's bizarre and troubling behaviors during the course of his college career. Some sounded the alarm and tried to help Cho, particularly within the English Department, where he produced graphically violent writings, harassed female students, and scared multiple classmates. But those efforts were isolated—the enduring "silos" problem—and were further hindered by misguided fears about the federal laws that keep students' education and health records confidential. As the Virginia Tech Review Panel, a state-mandated group of independent experts investigating in the aftermath, concluded in its official report: "No one knew all the information." Deisinger cited a line from Virginia-based psychologist and threat assessment leader Jeff Pollard on this crucial point: "You can't connect the dots if you don't collect the dots."

As seasoned with the work as Anderson had become, she still had lingering questions about her assailant's path to mass murder and the university's handling of the before and after. They were not about culpability or catharsis, matters she'd left behind long ago. Rather, she wondered how she might continue to gain insight for her work reaching out to survivors and championing better preparedness and prevention. When a new opportunity materialized in 2019, she set out to uncover yet more about the cataclysmic event she'd survived.

———

The bizarre package stamped at 9:01 a.m. at the Blacksburg post office that day in April 2007 had made it easy to write off its author as insane and incomprehensible. Inside it, Cho had included an eighteen-hundred-word rambling diatribe, pictures of himself posing with weapons, and video recordings of him reciting grievances and justifying the massacre. It was an incoherent screed made of rage and despair, but it was also calculated. He had spent weeks putting the material together. It was a performance. He figured the media would help him publicize his ideas about the "Apostles of Sin," and about why, just like those two "martyrs" at Columbine High eight years earlier, he intended to start a "revolution." This was the culmination of Cho's years' worth of homicidal and suicidal ideation, threatening communications, and emulation behavior, from the violent marginalia he'd scribbled beginning in middle school to his trying to look menacing in the handful of mailed photos. In one scowling image, he wielded a raised hammer: an homage to the rampaging protagonist of a Korean vengeance-themed film, *Old Boy*. Cho wanted this mimicry to look chilling and tough, but he was just following another version of the cultural script, identifying with a fictional antihero and seeking infamy. According to the report from the Virginia Tech Review Panel, whose eight members included retired FBI violent-crime expert Roger Depue (the originator of the term *leakage*), the materials from Cho conveyed "a grandiose fantasy of becoming a significant figure through the mass killing, not unlike American assassins of presidents and public figures."

Cho had a history of serious behavioral and mental health problems long predating college, which were unknown to authorities at Virginia Tech. But by the time he was a junior in fall 2005, following a series of disruptive behaviors and a message Cho sent to a roommate indicating he was suicidal, Cho was picked up by Virginia Tech police and detained overnight for evaluation in a local psychiatric hospital. Remarkably, no one notified his parents. Hospital psychologists determined Cho was not an imminent danger to himself or others, documenting that there was "no indication of psychosis, delusions, suicidal or homicidal ideation" and that "his insight and judgment are normal. . . . Follow-up and aftercare to be arranged with the counseling center at Virginia Tech; medications, none." At a hearing immediately thereafter, Cho was ordered by a magistrate to undergo outpatient counseling. The details of his evaluation and treatment remained confidential within the counseling center he went to—and crucially, a weakness in state law for reporting adjudication of mental health issues to a federal background check system meant that Cho was later able to legally purchase the two handguns he used in the attack.

Yet even apart from any explicit knowledge of Cho's mental health record, he had displayed multiple serious behavioral warning signs, particularly from fall 2005 through his final weeks of planning and preparation in spring 2007. He produced multiple graphically violent writings in English classes, upsetting peers and drawing notice from teachers. He was caught surreptitiously photographing female classmates and responded angrily to reprimand. He stalked and harassed several female students, who told residential advisers they were frightened by him and filed complaints with university police. He stirred anxiety and fear in other peers, including some who stopped attending classes where he was present. Socializing one night with a group in a female student's room, he pulled out a knife and began stabbing it into the carpet.

In the final weeks before the mass shooting, Cho acquired weapons and tactical gear, was seen lingering around Norris Hall, and made trips to a gun range, where he was observed practicing reloading while shooting.

A good deal of these accumulated warning signs went public after the massacre, revealed initially by journalists and then in the state panel's 150-page report, released in August 2007, which detailed Cho's personal history, authorities' actions and decisions on the day of the attack, and recommendations for policy changes. However, the work of the Virginia Tech Review Panel was completed in just four months, and the group gained access to some key investigative evidence only in the final days before publication. Two years later, the panel produced an addendum to the report, which included various additions and corrections, while stating that its key findings remained unchanged. The addendum also made evident the limitations of the information it had given the public; the panel acknowledged that it had left out investigative material for purposes of clarity. Incorporating more than two hundred interviews, four public hearings, and upward of a thousand pages of documents, the addendum stated, "The Review Panel wanted to avoid obfuscating the major findings in a cloud of lesser important or repetitive details, focusing on the findings and recommendations that were key to improving campus safety."

Though that approach seemed well intentioned, the upshot was that some details of Cho's path to mass murder remained buried—material that could perhaps shed further light on warning behaviors and on how, with greater community awareness, he might have been stopped.

In May 2019, Kristina Anderson and I spoke by phone about taking a trip to the Library of Virginia in Richmond to dig into a little-known trove of documents from the Review Panel's work, which had been unsealed a decade after the massacre as part of a state settlement with victims' families. A few weeks later, just around the corner from the state capitol, we walked up the wide stone front steps and through the glass doors, where we met with Roger Christman, a friendly archivist who escorted us to a restricted section of the building. Christman said he was glad that the material, which he'd organized to some degree after its arrival in a state of considerable disarray, was about to get some use. Over two days, Anderson and I pored through the lion's share of more than sixty boxes of documents containing materials examined by the panel, as well as members' extensive internal commentary and communications about the investigation.

Inside one box was a document from several months after Cho's detour into mental health treatment in the fall of his junior year: a program for the Graduate Student Assembly's annual Research Symposium and Exposition, an event that showcased "outstanding scholarly pursuits and achievements" throughout the university. A Review Panel member had notated the document for filing, though no mention of it had been included in the panel's public report. Listed among the twenty-one works in the program's Advanced Undergraduate section was a poem called "Spear Me Down, Heaven," by Seung-Hui Cho. The entry was like nothing else in the section, which otherwise held research-focused presentations from biochemistry, engineering, psychology, animal sciences, and so on, titles like "Understanding the Effects of Myo-Inositol Oxygenase on Signaling Pathways" and "Teeth Clipping in Baby Pigs: Impacts on Growth and Injury Scores." Cho's entry stood out even more for its decidedly inartistic ramblings, which were grim and macabre from start to finish. Among the paragraph-length jumble he'd submitted were such lines as: "This thing, my life, all an agony, of Hell of torture" and "feelings-thwarted by sun's beams ready to attack, averted by smiling faces ready to rape—come, a wish to annihilate my self." It also contained references to Jesus Christ and to a personal state of "decaying," "patheticness," and "humiliation."

The writing may not have seemed so unusual on its face, but the context in which it had been elevated certainly was, and it appeared that a segment of the university community much broader than Cho's immediate classmates and teachers had been in a position to notice that something was amiss. Exactly how Cho's poem got into the program, and whether he presented it in front of an audience as scheduled on a Wednesday morning in late March 2006, have remained a mystery. The chair of the English Department, who had previously intervened with Cho and tried to help by tutoring him one-on-one, later said she'd known nothing about the symposium entry. Event organizers and a handful of participating students said they couldn't recall the poem or whether Cho had shown up to read it. Apparently no one had noticed or openly reacted to the material, yet there it was, a year before the massacre, a conspicuously bizarre cri de coeur and expression of suicidality.

Moreover, in a lapse even more important from a threat assessment perspective, authority figures who had been seriously concerned about Cho were by then apparently no longer paying attention to what he was doing around campus. He had already generated major anxiety at the university. In the prior fall, of 2005, various email communications among faculty, administrators, and a Virginia Tech police detective detailed safety concerns around Cho. They included discussion of adding extra security for classes he was attending and for one-on-one meetings between Cho and faculty members. Faculty conveyed to the detective that students were "very upset" by Cho's behavior and that he had reacted angrily to being confronted about it. Separately, various communications among the university's Residential Life staff warned that female students being harassed by Cho in the dorms were frightened by him, and at least one residential adviser said she was "creeped out" by Cho and would not interact with him alone.

These details expanded the picture of concern and fear among the community seen in the Virginia Tech Review Panel's report, which had included the fact that one English faculty member, when looking into a noticeable drop of attendance in her class, had learned from a student that it was because of Cho's presence: "Everyone's afraid of him." That instructor subsequently told the department chair that she wanted Cho transferred out of her class, declining an offer to have an added security presence and threatening to resign for the first time in her twenty-year career if Cho wasn't removed.

At the time, the university had in place what was essentially a lesser, ineffective version of behavioral threat assessment—what it called a Care Team, whose purpose was to identify and work with students who were having problems. As the Review Panel concluded in its report, the Care Team's failure to contend with the many red flags that were "so apparent with Cho" was in part due to inadequate participation by the Virginia Tech PD—which knew Cho repeatedly had been warned about his stalking and harassment behavior, had threatened suicide, and had been temporarily detained by a magistrate and submitted to emergency psychiatric care. "The Care Team did not know the details of all these occurrences," the Review Panel found. Nor did that team have the full picture from alarmed residential advisers and their supervisor about Cho's menacing behavior in the dorms.

The panel determined that academic faculty "spoke up loudly" about Cho, but that conflicting conclusions were drawn about Cho's mental health state, which underwrote a global failure to follow up on the case after the array of ominous behaviors in fall 2005. "No one sought to revisit Cho's progress the following semester"—in spring 2006, when his macabre poem turned up in the annual grad symposium—"or inquire into whether he had come to the attention of other stakeholders on campus," the Review Panel found. The Care Team lacked threat-assessment expertise, it concluded, and was further hampered by overly strict interpretations of federal and state privacy laws.

The warning signs kept coming through Cho's final year, including a piece of short fiction he wrote whose protagonist set out to commit a school massacre. Filled with alienation and rage, his character, named Bud, left home early in the morning; he was armed and wearing a "strappy vest with many pockets," and was careful about evading police as he headed for the school, where he soon approached an "arbitrary classroom." In one standalone line, Bud thinks, "This is it. This is when you damn people die with me." After Bud fails to follow through, he despairs at his inability "to kill every god damn person in this damn school."

A story Cho wrote for a different English class the following semester featured Ax Manson, a character publicly humiliated in school and savagely beaten and murdered by his own father, who was sexually involved with a teacher hated by the protagonist. Cho's writings were glaringly dark, crude, and clumsy, reflecting little writing skill. Nonetheless, the instructor who fielded the "Ax" story—a name Cho would later use to sign the rantings he mailed to NBC News—sought to encourage him, even though Cho had also conspicuously refused to speak a single word in her class, an advanced fiction workshop that required oral participation and extensive group interaction. "Your stories are original & memorable, & you handle violence in interesting ways," she wrote on an evaluation of his portfolio, giving him a B grade.

The collective failure to detect or address the danger nearly a decade after Columbine must have been tough for any survivor to realize. During two days of plumbing the archive, there were several moments when I observed Anderson looking through documents that connected to her personally, from a list naming the shooting casualties to internal communications about how victims' families were interacting with university officials and attorneys. She acknowledged that the experience felt a bit strange, though she didn't find it surprising or upsetting. In her years of work, she had interviewed law enforcement agents, first responders, faculty, and survivors all directly involved in the calamity, and she had spent countless hours revisiting her own experience, both publicly and in private conversations. Once, a few years back, a police officer who had helped rescue her that fateful day had told her, "I thought you were dead."

"That wasn't so nice to hear," Anderson recalled with a faint smile.

But she kept choosing to go there. In the decade-plus since the attack, there were only two specific types of evidence she would not expose herself to: images or audio from the scenes of the massacre.

Anything else was fair game and might have value in the mission to improve understanding, for herself and others.

Inside one archive box was a file of newspaper clips that had been collected by the Review Panel from the immediate aftermath, stories Anderson had never seen. One of the pages, mildly yellowed with time, displayed a photo of parents weeping over their daughter's coffin, which had been signed by classmates before it was to be lowered into the ground.

"I can't say that I'm not affected by the material," Anderson acknowledged, gazing at the image for a moment. She had long relied on therapy and a discipline of allowing herself to experience whatever emotions came with new information, even if not right away, and then setting aside those feelings as she pursued her research with purpose. If she failed to uphold that process, she knew she was vulnerable, that she could slip into seeing the world in darker terms and feeling more on edge.

Reflecting on the two days in the archive, Anderson pointed out some material she'd found vexing, from among a handful of internal university emails unknown to the public. The correspondence among faculty and administrators revealed them expressing to each other how fine a job they were doing handling Cho and supporting each other in the process. Clearly they had become alarmed over time and cared about the situation, Anderson remarked, "but how did they not all get into a room and figure out what actual steps to take?"

In 2007, there had still been a pronounced false sense of security and unwitting denial in play. There had to be better ways to recognize such danger before it was too late.

chapter nine

THE NEW MINDHUNTERS

With a toll unprecedented at the time, the Virginia Tech massacre marked the beginning of a deeper focus on rampage shooters for a small team of FBI special agents. Six years earlier, the tectonic events of September 11, 2001, had thrust much of the premier federal law enforcement agency toward the mission of counterterrorism, including within the FBI's elite Behavioral Analysis Unit. In June 2007, however, BAU agents specializing in threat assessment gained an additional priority after President George W. Bush tasked three of his cabinet members to respond to the catastrophe in Blacksburg; they subsequently called for a joint effort by the FBI, Secret Service, and Department of Education to examine the danger of targeted violence on college campuses. That initiative resulted in "Campus Attacks," a collaborative overview study of 272 cases that in part reiterated behavioral warning signs increasingly known to the field since Columbine, from entrenched grievances and threatening communications to stalking behavior and attack planning and preparation.

Completed in 2010, the research also called out an important distinction, noting that behavioral threat assessment on college campuses is a more formidable challenge than in K–12 schools, where in general students are far more contained. (It would be hard to imagine Salem-Keizer's STAT failing to act in a case like Cho's.) College students have greater autonomy and grapple with a broader range of new life challenges and stressors, the study observed. Substance abuse is an easier pitfall, sexual assault is more prevalent, and so on. And workplace violence is another expansive layer: the largest universities function essentially like small cities, including sizable workforces.

Nationally, few institutions of higher education had formal threat assessment operations in place prior to the Virginia Tech tragedy. In the aftermath, many began to put together teams, including throughout Virginia, which in 2008 became the first state to mandate their presence at all public colleges and universities, and soon thereafter, at K–12 schools. (A handful of other states would follow suit over the next decade-plus.) The FBI's Behavioral Analysis Unit, with its expertise in serial killings, child exploitation, and other grievous crimes, had a history of collaborating with local authorities, including on threat assessment, though mass shootings usually were investigated and prosecuted as state offenses. Leaders at the BAU, based near the FBI training academy in Quantico, Virginia, contemplated what more could be done to help stop rampages in schools, workplaces, and other public venues. With the multidisciplinary work of the FBI's National Center for the Analysis of Violent Crime as a model, they designed a team for standout agents and analysts from the FBI and other federal agencies to pool their expertise. The plan was to offer nimble operational support to state and local leaders anywhere in the country who were alarmed about a potentially violent threat and sought help.

Launched in 2010, the FBI's Behavioral Threat Assessment Center included specialists from the Naval Criminal Investigative Service, the Bureau of Alcohol, Tobacco, and Firearms, and the US Capitol Police, as well as expert consultants in forensic psychology and psychiatry. The mission was twofold: violence prevention and deep research. The BAU team helped to evaluate and manage threat cases at the request of local authorities, particularly in smaller communities that lacked resources. The team also investigated in the aftermath of attacks, continuing to build the field's underlying knowledge. Confusion still lingered in the world of law enforcement about when to involve federal authorities in mass shooting investigations, but following Sandy Hook in 2012, with the passage of the Investigative Assistance for Violent Crimes Act, Congress ensured that the FBI would have jurisdiction to pursue its growing mission.

The agents with the BAU were a new generation of "mindhunters," as the prior era's FBI serial-killer team had become known, but they pursued a different goal than their predecessors at gruesome crime scenes. In cases of mass shootings, there was no point to assembling characteristic profiles to help identify an unknown predator and track him down. These offenders were already in jail or the morgue. The mission instead was to expand the knowledge of warning behaviors by scrutinizing the thinking and actions of shooters leading up to and during their attacks. The profile, so to speak, was not of a person but of that behavioral process itself.

As FBI evidence technicians at the scenes of massacres dealt with bullet casings and other forensic material, the BAU agents were looking for nuances in how the attackers had moved and acted, the clothing or other attire they wore, and perhaps certain objects they'd carried or discarded. As intricately as possible, the agents were mapping the final stages of behavioral escalation. Beyond the crime scene, they examined the perpetrators' home, work, and other familiar environments and interviewed people who knew or had encountered them. Then the team stepped back to study the panoramic view, "to try to really understand these individuals from cradle to grave," as FBI supervisory special agent Karie Gibson, a member of the BAU team and a clinical psychologist, told me in November 2017. "We want to see how they lived, what the risk factors were, and where the turns in the road were for them. The picture becomes three-dimensional and very informative when you take all that data and overlay it with the specifics of their pathway to intentional violence. From a threat management standpoint, we can see where and how that began to build, and learn from that for developing effective interventions."

The ways in which a person's history and deteriorating life circumstances combine to produce an act of mass murder can easily seem inscrutable, but the unit's deep analyses, Gibson suggested, showed otherwise. "I've seen in so many cases the points where, if just one person in these individuals' lives had taken notice and helped them, it could've made a difference." A major triggering event like job loss or divorce could set off a plan to kill, but before that, the troubled person often faced an accumulation of stressors: financial woes, health problems, personal conflicts, and difficulty in school, work, or a relationship. In someone lacking resilience, even the subtle trigger points could carry a lot of weight, and working to remedy those could matter greatly to dissolving the potential for a violent outcome.

The idea that the nation's top law enforcement agency was more invested than ever in this type of prevention work seemed extraordinary, though also a measure of a numbing familiarity that had just scaled up again a few weeks before, in early October 2017, with the unprecedented carnage on the Las Vegas Strip. About an hour's drive south of Washington, DC, the headquarters of the Behavioral Analysis Unit was located within a row of brick buildings in a generic office park near Quantico, where I was met by supervisory special agent Andre Simons, a longtime BAU leader. Moving through security inside the building's unmarked entrance, the better-known historical roots of the BAU briefly happened to be highlighted. "Did you see the latest about the guy in Florida?" a security officer asked Simons in a moment of small talk, as credentials and communication devices were checked. The officer was alluding to the uplifting news that an alleged serial killer had just been taken into custody after a recent string of unsolved murders had sown fear in Tampa.

Seated at a large table inside a windowless conference room, Simons and current unit chief John Wyman discussed a history of the team's work and some evolving challenges with the ascendant problem of rampage attacks. Simons, whom I'd first met at the J. Edgar Hoover Building in Washington three years earlier to learn more about the work of the unit, was not a stereotypical picture of a G-man. Five-eight and fit with a close-shaved head and a charismatic gaze, he was a conspicuously skilled listener. His interest in the synergy of mental health and law enforcement traced to a degree in counseling psychology and a background in crisis-intervention policing before joining the FBI more than two decades before. Simons had played a central role in developing the Behavioral Threat Assessment Center, which he helped lead for half a decade.

Like other leaders in the field when asked about results, he was reluctant about the unit being credited with thwarting hundreds of mass shootings. "Success for us is the absence of an event," he said. "It's hard to share success stories, because you're talking about people who have moved or been navigated away from committing violence. So how do we prove that the intervention made the actual difference?"

Wyman added that they found many local leaders enthusiastic about building their own threat assessment teams after high-profile attacks were in the news, but that the interest often faded with budget constraints and a general understanding that gun rampages remained a low probability. "'Show me how many specifically you've prevented,' they'll say to us. Well, we can't."

Since 2010, the team had handled between 150 and 200 new cases per year in partnership with agencies and institutions around the country, from local police departments to large public universities. Not one subject of those cases had gone on to commit an act of targeted violence, a track record that would continue through the end of the decade. "It's certainly possible that there were subsequent minor issues or acts of violence that weren't reported back to us," Simons said, "but there have been no lethal or mass casualty events, the fear of which is generally why the cases would come to us." He emphasized that his summary was not a scientific analysis, but that those results stood on a decade's worth of empirical knowledge. "I've seen people who, but for the intervention of many dedicated practitioners, would've attacked without a doubt."

Most cases that landed with the BAU were in a murky middle zone. They didn't typically involve people armed to the teeth and acting highly volatile, who were more likely than not to have been arrested by local authorities. Nor did the cases tend to feature those who were behaving oddly or blowing off steam but upon a closer look appeared clearly to pose no danger. The unit got involved most commonly when local law enforcement or institutional authorities reached out to the FBI with a distinct unease, when they were dealing with people who were provoking significant anxiety or fear but hadn't violated any laws or policies. Those cases were the real work.

Reached typically through liaison agents in any of the FBI's fifty-six national field offices, the BAU team served in an advisory role and was never the "case owner," even when consulting directly behind the scenes on an assessment or threat management strategy. The modus operandi was to provide expertise without muddying case custody or local decision making. For those reasons, the BAU leaders would not disclose details even from successfully managed threat cases that were retired. However, some local authorities who had turned to the BAU for help later agreed to share case information with me, revealing insight into how the collaborative work with the FBI specialists played out.

One case from a small town in Minnesota in the mid-2010s involved a high school junior named Jason. After breaking up with a girlfriend, quitting the school football team, and failing a couple of his classes, Jason had pondered suicide, superficially cutting his wrists with a razor blade one night and then dialing 911. Around the same time, he had begun making conspicuous comments about school shootings. He was proficient with and had access to hunting rifles. A few months before the case began, the local sheriff had attended a threat assessment training conducted by a regional FBI field office; he drew on that knowledge to work successfully with the parents and the high school principal to get Jason into some temporary mental health treatment. The sheriff remained concerned, however, that Jason might be a danger after returning to school, so he reached back out to the FBI for advice. An agent and a psychologist with the BAU consulted with the local leaders and Jason's parents on a management plan and stayed in periodic contact over the following year.

Jason improved over time, though his case was touch-and-go.

A science teacher noticed him researching bombmaking, but that turned out to reflect his interest in the popular TV show *Breaking Bad*, not in causing harm. Months later, according to the local Minnesota team's case files, the BAU experts warned of a "potentially dangerous period" as Jason finished high school and began the transition into young adult life. There were indications of possible psychosis in his mental health records, and the BAU noted that he was in an age range when psychotic breaks were most common. But Jason had responded well to longer-term treatment and had solid support from his parents and an uncle, who had made it his mission to teach Jason about photography. The struggling high schooler also benefited from a friendly rapport with the sheriff, who checked in with him regularly.

"He knew the family and others were trying to help him, and I do not believe that was lost on him," the sheriff recalled.

About a year after Jason graduated, he enrolled in a residential program that sent him to another state where he would have continuing access to counseling support while training to be a chef. He quickly took to the culinary work. Afterward, he moved to a nearby city, landing a job at a prestigious local restaurant. Soon he was engaged to be married. Perhaps now only his cooking skills might ever land him on the local news.

———

At BAU headquarters, Simons described how the several years after Virginia Tech were pivotal for ramping up broader historical research as well as investigations on the ground. Whatever the team could learn in the aftermath of attacks could potentially help stop future killers. The next stage of that mission would also be on a university campus, in a case that would prove illuminating on multiple levels for Simons and his colleagues. In February 2008, less than a year after Virginia Tech, a former graduate student entered a lecture hall at Northern Illinois University in DeKalb and fatally shot five students, wounded twenty-one other people and then killed himself. Twenty-seven-year-old Steven Kazmierczak had left behind no clear explanation of motive, but the BAU investigators who deployed to the scene soon gleaned a great deal about his mind-set and actions around the crime, including elements they would see in future cases.

Kazmierczak was no loner. He had been in contact with a girl-friend, family members, and colleagues at another university to which he'd moved, but he had kept his interactions compartmentalized. Mapped out, his relationships formed a starburst pattern: single isolated lines emanating from one central point. A stable person's life usually looks more like a spiderweb, Simons explained, with strands also linking across those lines to form concentric circles of connection among the people around the individual. The agents could not determine clearly whether the lack of interaction among those who knew Kazmierczak was inadvertent or by design, but it had made his deterioration and his attack planning and preparation less detectable. He was also skilled at "impression management," an ability to mask his inner turmoil and intentions and to project a deceptive image of himself. The people connected to him appeared not to have noticed signs of suicidality, nor his smoldering rage against NIU over what he had perceived to be detrimental changes to a graduate program that had forced him out.

In the final three days, Kazmierczak had isolated himself in a Travelodge motel room, where he drank cans of Red Bull, readied a sawed-off shotgun and semiautomatic pistols he'd recently purchased, and called and emailed people to say good-bye. The BAU team called this behavior "cocooning."

"It's not only to get logistically ready but psychologically geared up for the attack," Simons said. "Oftentimes the offender views the attack as a transformative event, where he has now fully blossomed into the omnipotent, controlling, dominating person he sees himself as."

Cocooning and a related behavior known to practitioners as an "energy burst" would mark numerous other attacks, including the one in Tucson in 2011, where in the final twenty-four hours Jared Loughner shopped for ammunition at two local stores, checked into a motel, left a voicemail for a friend, and posted a "good-bye" message on social media. (Seemingly aware of consequences that might await him, he searched online for "assassins" and "lethal injection.") Gearing up for an attack also sometimes involves drug use or other methods of desensitization. In Aurora in 2012, James Holmes took Valium and played loud techno music in his earphones as he opened fire inside the movie theater.

Kazmierczak's actions at the NIU crime scene revealed specific clues to the behavioral process of his attack. He had entered the large lecture hall through a rear vestibule and then kicked open the inner door and walked onto the stage. His theatrics included wearing a black T-shirt with the word TERRORIST overlapping an image of an assault rifle. Showing no emotion, he said nothing as he fired his shotgun onstage and then used handguns as he moved into the auditorium rows, which that day held about 120 students. NIU police in the area alerted by a 911 call had immediately raced to the building, and the BAU agents determined that Kazmierczak had understood that officers were quickly bearing down on him. His reaction was to stop firing—even though he still had a lot of ammunition, many more potential victims trapped in the rows of auditorium seating, and a tactical advantage for a gun battle with the approaching police. Instead, he pivoted and marched back up to the center of the stage, where he fatally shot himself.

Who knows how things would have ended if he'd kept going? "It's more important to some offenders to follow their mental scripting of the event and commit suicide in a place and manner of their choosing, to preserve their sense of omnipotent control," Simons explained. The BAU team would see more of this behavior, including from the mass shooter in upstate New York the following year, who was heavily armed and outfitted in body armor yet avoided imminent confrontation with police by killing himself.

This virulent mix of grievance, deterioration, and aberrant narcissism would also be revealed by perpetrators who lived. The legacy of behavioral science research at the FBI had been built to a great extent on interviews with lethal offenders, and Simons and his fellow agents pursued those as well. There was no substitute for the primary sources themselves when it came to scrutinizing their behavior. "We saw the narcissism characteristic popping up again and again at a level that was, shall we say, disruptive to what would be considered normal functioning," Simons said. He recalled one rampage shooter they interviewed in prison after publishing the "Campus Attacks" report in 2010: "He greeted me and immediately launched into criticizing what he thought were errors in our conclusions and in the way we had approached the work." Simons smiled wryly. "That was rather instructive." On the second day of interviewing the offender, Simons decided to point up the behavior and suggest it was perhaps worthy of the offender's own consideration, which proved effective. "He was very willing to have that discussion, and others."

The deep research into killers' pre-attack thinking and behaviors would continue for years. The gun massacres kept coming. While working attack sites was grimmest for first responders and evidence technicians, that aspect could also test the BAU investiga-tors. "One of the tough parts is to be at the scene of such devasta-tion and not be able to engage that side of it," Simons said. "We have to look at it very clinically. We're trying to squeeze out as much information as we can from the behavior, independent of the tragic parts." Sandy Hook in 2012 was especially trying. "I hate even to use a positive word like 'motivating' to describe such a hor-rendous act," he continued, recalling how it galvanized the team. The elementary school massacre had unmistakably magnified the need to do everything in their power to advance the prevention work, to find the constructive amid the darkness.

Their approach almost sounded trite in light of the BAU's well-known serial killer history, Simons acknowledged, yet its utility was clear. "It's important for us to walk in the same path as the offender, to see what he was seeing, so that we can start to identify what was important to him. Often that can include things brought to the scene that have no tactical purpose. If there was something so important to him that he had to have it there, yet it had no operational value, then we know it has psychological significance. Sometimes that can be very nuanced."

In the vestibule of the NIU lecture hall in 2008, Kazmierczak had left behind a black backpack containing two magazines and a book. One magazine had a major pop star on the cover, the other a gallery of infamous killers. The book was a collection of political satire. The materials seemed intended to be enigmatic, to mock the idea that investigators would be able to figure out the perpetrator—another bid to control the narrative and define his own infamy.

In similar psychological territory, the crime scene at Virginia Tech had also turned up a notable item. Cho had brought along the hammer he'd used to pose in a photo like the killer from the Korean vengeance film. The hammer had played no part in his attack but held deep meaning for him, threat assessment experts later concluded. Kazmierczak, too, had identified with a violent antihero, which he expressed through his physical appearance. The fall before the attack, he had dressed up for Halloween as the sadistically moralizing killer from the *Saw* horror film series and also had the character tattooed on his forearm. These kinds of details held significance not in a causal sense, but rather in what they could reveal about the way killers to be construct narratives for themselves and whom they identify with as they escalate toward violence.

Investigators began seeing more connections among the killers' narratives. An official report from NIU published two years after the attack included a comparison of Kazmierczak and Cho that listed nearly two dozen behavioral and background factors they shared, including emulation behavior. Both had hailed the Columbine killers. And Kazmierczak subsequently admired Cho and studied his tactics. Shortly after the Virginia Tech massacre, Kazmierczak noted to a friend what he thought about the devastation in Blacksburg. Cho, he remarked, "obviously planned it out well."

With their case data and analysis expanding in the 2010s, the BAU team was poised to advance the field's knowledge of pre-attack behaviors, and Sandy Hook underscored the need to share that knowledge more widely. The FBI had long offered training and expertise to the nation's various law enforcement communities, and after the elementary school massacre the bureau conducted a "road show" via its field offices to spread the word about the BAU team's capabilities for assisting with prevention work. But as Simons later recounted, the team had also begun realizing an urgency to share more of what they were learning with educators, mental health professionals, and other frontline personnel, who often were best positioned to notice and evaluate aberrant behaviors and potential warning signs. "Seeing that the shootings problem was growing was also important and heavy on our minds," Simons, who retired from the FBI in 2019, later recalled.

As the painstaking state and federal investigations into Sandy Hook had continued, Simons and his colleagues dialogued with Newtown parents, among them Nicole Hockley, whose blue-eyed, mop-topped first grader, Dylan, had perished after being shot five times in the attack. Alongside other devastated parents, Hockley had spoken with fortitude at public hearings and campaigned in the nation's capital for stricter gun regulations. She had soon also taken an interest in prevention strategies. Simons recalled a meeting with Newtown parents at which his team shared some of what they were learning from the case; Hockley had pressed them about FBI outreach. Why weren't they spreading the information on warning signs more widely, including to parents and students?

In the broadest sense, the field had its own version of the silo problem. It was rooted in a certain pragmatism, Simons suggested: threat assessment data are complex and nuanced, and case work requires rigorous training to ensure its fairness and efficacy. However, Hockley had raised a strong and ultimately superseding point, he told me. "If we're going to catch these early, then we also need the people who are often even better positioned to see the warning behaviors."

Simons noted an added challenge, however, that came with prospects for vigilance among close friends and family. They might well be disinclined to recognize or respond to warning behaviors precisely because the concerning individual was a loved one. It could be extremely difficult to see a buddy or a son as potentially dangerous, or to invite any sense of jeopardy in taking action. This hurdle was evident among parents historically, from Thurston and Columbine to Sandy Hook and beyond; the Salem-Keizer caseload too, over time, had included numerous examples of reluctant peers or parents in denial. But in Simons's estimation, this too ultimately supported the argument for greater sharing of what the field was learning. "These are the people who may actually be the most in need of the information about what to look for and where to seek help."

The thinking of BAU leaders had already begun evolving away from a long-held concern that future perpetrators might pick up on publicized threat-assessment concepts or data and try to exploit that knowledge. Cultivating public engagement in the strategy was now becoming the greater priority. The goal of developing and demystifying the prevention research with a broader audience in mind resonated strongly with Simons, who valued the perspective of a longtime mentor of his, threat assessment pioneer Robert Fein. When the two had worked together over the years, Fein had often reiterated a guiding principle: "What good is research if it's not usable?"

In 2018, Simons, along with consulting criminal-justice expert James Silver and BAU researcher Sarah Craun, completed work on a major new analysis of sixty-three gun rampages spanning more than a decade, in schools, workplaces, and other public venues. The multiyear investigation published by the FBI advanced several key concepts showing that such attacks were preventable. At its core was a clear refutation of the belief that shooters burst out of extreme social isolation. In fact, most lived with or had social connections to other people—who usually witnessed disturbing pre-attack behaviors rooted in depression, anger, and paranoia, from conspicuous levels of interpersonal conflict to communications signaling violent intent.

The team reiterated that the warning behaviors were not predictive and could be easier to recognize in hindsight. Even so, the promise for early intervention was unmistakable. Each of the sixty-three shooters had, on average, displayed four or five troubling behaviors that were observable to people around them: their friends, classmates, teachers, spouses, or domestic partners. In a majority of the cases, the first known instance of such behavior came more than two years prior to the attack. By no means did these observable warning behaviors foretell violence with clarity, but the research showed in the greatest detail yet that these rampages were not really surprises.

Moreover, windows of opportunity to intervene continued to exist even if the *early* warning signs went unnoticed. More than three-quarters of the perpetrators had spent a week or longer planning their attacks, while two-thirds spent at least a month planning, and some took far longer. Once they reached the stage of tactical preparations, about half of the shooters took a week or longer, from conducting surveillance to obtaining firearms, ammunition, and body armor or other gear.

The BAU's work cast additional light on the process leading up to attacks and further debunked familiar myths. Few of the assailants had significant violent criminal histories. Nearly all of them used legally obtained firearms—including the 40 percent of shooters who purchased at least one gun specifically for use in their attacks. Almost three-quarters had personal connections to the venues where they struck, most often a current or former workplace or a current or former school. This was especially instructive. Familiarity, accessibility, and grievances were the factors driving the selections of attack sites—not, as so often suggested in the media and political debate, randomness, insanity, or prohibitions of firearms in these places.

The FBI had documented a record high of thirty rampage shootings in the United States in 2017, but an uphill battle remained against the common perception that these assailants were alien and undetectable. Many of the perpetrators from the decade-plus worth of cases analyzed by the BAU had been facing multiple stressors, a well-established correlate of criminal behavior, and had coped poorly with these various social, financial, legal, or health setbacks.

"It's important for people to understand that active shooters are people in the community," remarked Silver, who served as an assistant US attorney before going into academia. "They have jobs. They're in school. They do talk to people. They come from all walks of life."

The more that everyday people registered this context, the BAU team believed, the better the chances that they would feel validated in their sense of unease or fear about someone and decide to seek help. That could be key to improving on the enduring bystander problem. People around the shooters, the team found, had notified law enforcement in fewer than half the cases—despite the fact that, in every single case, at least one person in proximity to the shooter had noticed a concerning behavior, and that in many cases, multiple people had noticed. Those behaviors observed by the bystanders had stemmed from recognizable situations: sharp interpersonal conflicts, unsettling verbal or online communications, aberrant use of firearms, focus on violent media, deterioration in personal routines or hygiene, and physical aggression.

Another finding in this territory really struck the BAU team. More than 80 percent of the bystanders did in fact respond to a troubling behavior—by communicating directly with the shooter. That made a certain sense, effectively asking a person whom they knew, "Hey, what's going on?" Beyond the BAU study, empirical evidence of this scenario went at least as far back as Robert Bardo in 1989, when his sister in Tennessee had called him four days before his final bus ride to Los Angeles, sensing his malevolent intentions for Rebecca Schaeffer, but Bardo had brushed her off with sarcasm: "Yeah, you think you got it."

Now the BAU had confirmed a pronounced pattern: despite perpetrators' self-isolating or erratic behaviors, no fewer than four out of five had shown the social wherewithal to navigate past empathetic or suspicious questioning. The research firmly established, in other words, that many shooters engaged in leakage behavior *and* subterfuge.

In Simons's view, family members or others close to the subject of a threat case would benefit from knowing about this dynamic: "We need to say to them, 'Listen, the person is likely going to deny it.'" Therein also lay the importance of educating the public and gaining their confidence in the work. "They have to be able to hear that and then trust that a threat assessment team will be able to determine thoughtfully and fairly whether or not that denial is being used to conceal authentic plans."

The team's work also took on the most formidable bogeyman of mass shootings: mental illness as the prime cause. Most of the sixty-three shooters they studied had exhibited mental health issues, and nearly half were suicidal, which strongly echoed previous research elsewhere. But emotional struggles underpinning violent transgressions are not the same thing as having a clinically diagnosable mental illness. This crucial distinction was made clear by another key finding: the team could only verify that 25 percent of the shooters were known to have been professionally diagnosed with a mental illness of any kind prior to their attacks. Just three cases involved a psychotic disorder.

Simons, typically reserved in conversation, waxed zealous about what this meant. Given the enduring myth that all rampage shooters are insane, much of the public might conclude that the FBI research simply had missed the mental illness in the other

75 percent. But while it was plausible that such conditions had gone undetected in some of the remaining shooters, he said, the BAU team had further determined that many of them clearly would *not* have qualified for a clinical diagnosis of mental illness. That had been borne out by the team's unparalleled deep dive into investigative files and other resources uniquely at their disposal for analyzing the perpetrators. "Nobody would say that they were mentally healthy, or that they were resilient and coping well, but these were people who were angry," Simons emphasized. "They decided to use violence as the solution to whatever their problems or grievances were, or for their own satisfaction or entertainment."

The possible intersection with clinical mental illness was important to consider in threat cases, but the research further indicated that mental health problems were most likely to be an exacerbating rather than root factor, causing disruptions in perpetrators' lives that could compound other stressors. An affliction like depression might make it harder to hold down a job, for example, leading to financial distress or the loss of a relationship and accelerating a downward spiral.

Simons and his colleagues had felt strongly about digging into this complex side of the shootings problem, with stigma as a major reason. From anxiety to mood disorders, psychiatric research shows that nearly half of all Americans are diagnosable with some form of mental illness over their lifetimes. The number of rampage shooters isn't even remotely in the same universe, but a serious cost comes from political leaders and gun industry lobbyists continually reiterating to the public that "mental illness pulls the trigger," as was the message once again after a pair of mass shootings in Ohio and Texas in August 2019. The consensus among leading threat assessment experts is that this false belief can hinder people who are in serious need of counseling or therapy from seeking it, for fear of being labeled dangerous or a killer. A similar chilling effect has also stopped people close to mentally ill individuals from encouraging them to get help, according to practitioners knowledgeable of cases where that has occurred.

The inaccurate blanket statements about mental illness tend to segregate an entire population in the public's mind, Simons observed. "Speaking personally, I think it also denies in some ways the responsibility we have as a society to acknowledge that the active shooter problem transcends the question of whether a person has a mental illness. Ascribing blame for all these attacks exclusively to mental illness fails to recognize the complexity of the motivations that lead a person to choose catastrophic violence."

There is another potentially grave consequence. Bystanders who might help save the day could also fall for the widespread assumption that all shooters are deranged lunatics. "That dramatically narrows the aperture for what people would be looking out for," Simons said. "You could have someone thinking: 'Boy, my friend over here is saying some really concerning things, and lately he's gotten really interested in guns and has been talking a lot about Columbine. But I know he's not mentally ill, so there's no way he could be a shooter.'"

It was no coincidence that Simons's hypothetical subject of a threat case alluded to the 1999 high school massacre. By the mid-2010s, the BAU team had picked up on a troubling trend. Amid the explosive growth of social media, emulation behavior among perpetrators was accelerating. Through the remainder of the decade and into the start of the next, the emergence of that trend and others underscored a principle of the field: preventing these attacks always requires a degree of adaptability. Cases are dynamic and evolving by definition of the model, and so too is the world in which they occur.

chapter ten

EVOLUTIONS

The digital media age has exerted profound influence on how we see the mass shootings phenomenon. Through Twitter and other social media platforms, the public begins to learn of these attacks as they unfold in real time. Misinformation and political outrage also spread swiftly. A popular satirical news story from *The Onion* often recirculates in the aftermath, mocking widespread resignation with its well-known headline: 'NO WAY TO PREVENT THIS,' SAYS ONLY NATION WHERE THIS REGULARLY HAPPENS.

Digital media have also become directly consequential to the mass shootings problem, at once fueling emulation and threats and becoming indispensable to threat assessment work. The effects on perpetrator behavior have a unique dimension. They show that journalists and public officials can be instrumental to changing a misguided cultural narrative about mass shooters and stopping the harmful elevation of them.

No prior scenario illustrated this opportunity more sharply than the aftermath of the attack at a movie theater in Aurora, Colorado, on July 20, 2012, where twelve people were murdered and seventy others were injured during a midnight premiere of *The Dark Knight Rises*. The twenty-four-year-old perpetrator had thought about how he might get public attention, searching online beforehand for tips on posting photos from his mobile phone—yet he had no idea what wild heights of notoriety awaited him. Just hours after the country woke to the news on that Friday morning, the smiling face of James Holmes, a socially dysfunctional PhD dropout, filled computer and TV screens nationwide, with news networks breaking into daytime programming to broadcast special reports on the "Batman Massacre." Soon the public learned that Holmes had fashioned himself into the comic superhero's evil arch nemesis.

"He had his hair painted red," announced New York City police commissioner Raymond Kelly at a press conference, relaying details of a law enforcement briefing. "He said he was the Joker."

ABC News' *Nightline* aired Kelly's remarks followed by a law enforcement commentator weighing in on Holmes: "He's a guy that has so left reality that he's part of the Batman world," said Brad Garrett, a former FBI special agent. "And he's gonna go in and play this character, and through that character, he's gonna kill people." As other major media reported the Joker details, citing unnamed federal officials, ABC News anchor Diane Sawyer opened a separate broadcast with a related scoop: "Police in Colorado are studying the Batman movies and comic books to learn more about the mind of the killer in Aurora."

According to global headlines, life was imitating art to sinister perfection. There was just one problem: The story wasn't true. "We found nothing showing it had to do with Batman," said George

Brauchler, the Colorado district attorney who prosecuted Holmes in 2015 on 164 counts of murder and attempted murder.

The Joker story had fulfilled public hunger for a narrative explaining the horrific event, enduring despite even basic flaws like the fact that the comic villain's hair was well known by fans to be green. Case evidence showed that Holmes's decision to dye his hair bright red stemmed from feelings of desperation about a young woman he liked who had rejected him five months before the mass shooting. He thought it made him look more attractive and "brave." In Holmes's apartment, which he had rigged with explosives intended to divert police from the movie theater attack, investigators had found a Batman mask—but they concluded the item was an afterthought, acquired once Holmes had surveilled and selected the cineplex based on tactical calculations and body count potential. Investigators concluded that the highly anticipated premiere could just as easily have been for another blockbuster, say, *The Avengers* or *Skyfall*. The prosecution team didn't concern themselves with correcting the record about the Joker falsehood during the 2015 trial, according to Brauchler, because it wasn't germane to convicting Holmes on the extensive evidence of his planning for the attack.

Holmes himself was surprised by the tale about his motive. His thoughts after learning about it in prison from fellow inmates were revealing of his interest in notoriety. "They kind of turned me into a super villain," he told Dr. William Reid, a psychiatrist who evaluated him for trial. "At least I'm remembered for doing something."

Early misinformation had become a general problem with mass shootings in the digital era, including false claims about more than one attacker that often arose from the initial chaos and circulated on social media and in news reporting. Some victims in the Aurora theater had at first been in a state of disbelief, a common reaction that was particularly understandable in a darkened cinema where

Holmes deployed tear gas and was dressed from head to toe in body armor and other tactical gear. One moviegoer reported thinking the shooting was a promotional stunt. The unreliable account of Holmes claiming to be the Joker appeared to have originated with an eyewitness who spoke to police on the scene. (Raymond Kelly did not respond to media inquiries about the account he gave after it was first debunked three years later by a *Denver Post* columnist.)

Kelly's press conference the day of the attack clearly had been intended to reassure the public in a densely populated top movie market: "As a precaution against copycats and to raise the comfort levels among movie patrons, the New York City Police Department is providing coverage at theaters where the *The Dark Knight Rises* is playing in the five boroughs," he stated. Law enforcement leaders in other cities announced similar steps, while AMC Theaters said it would no longer allow people wearing costumes or masks into screenings.

The ubiquitous Joker story, though, draped the message of vigilance and safety in a dark irony—by potentially fueling inspiration for a follow-up attack. Growing case research showed that such sensational news content—*behold the super-villain!*—epitomized the kind of attention numerous mass shooters craved and knew they could provoke through shocking acts. *Nightline*'s in-depth report featured Holmes's face a half dozen times and narrated the Joker details with a slow zoom in on a still image of the murderous character's diabolically smeared visage as famously depicted by actor Heath Ledger in the Batman movie franchise. The broadcast concluded with a point of caution sourced to law enforcement officials, described without irony by chief investigative correspondent Brian Ross: "Across the country there are concerns that there could be something else from the copycats," he said, "someone trying to capitalize on the same publicity that Mr. Holmes has received."

As the FBI's Behavioral Analysis Unit and others in the field were deepening their research on pre-attack behaviors around this time, they were finding emulation among far more plotters and shooters than even experts had previously understood. Further scrutiny of major cases from years past affirmed the metastasizing trend: The mass shooter at Northern Illinois University in 2008, for example, had taken note of the chaining of the doors by the Virginia Tech shooter as he'd planned to trap his own victims in the NIU auditorium. A mass shooter the following year in upstate New York had also looked at the Virginia Tech shooter's tactics; he blocked off a rear exit to the building where he struck, mailed a grievance-laden manifesto to a TV news station, and used weapons and tactical attire similar to those of the Virginia Tech shooter.

By 2015, sensational news coverage, unfiltered social media content, and shooters' quests for notoriety were streams merging into a raging current. As forensic psychologist Reid Meloy and several colleagues observed that year in research on identification behavior, "Cultural scripts are now spread globally within seconds." Their analysis further detailed how some perpetrators saw themselves as "warriors" fulfilling a mission or fighting for a cause for which they wanted to surpass the impact of previous attackers.

In August 2015, the problem reached a logical next stage when a disgruntled ex–TV reporter stalked two former colleagues as they conducted a live broadcast on location in Roanoke, Virginia. The perpetrator had fumed about being fired from WDBJ-TV back in 2013 after a series of angry clashes with colleagues, and he had vowed a response that would "be in the headlines." Using a semiautomatic handgun and filming his attack with a body camera, he fatally shot reporter Allison Parker and cameraman Adam Ward and wounded their interview subject, Vicki Gardner, as the station's anchor and others in the studio reacted with confusion to the live feed. After fleeing the scene, the perpetrator posted the body-cam footage on Facebook and Twitter, then killed himself a few hours later as police caught up to him in a car chase.

The ghastly snuff video had gone viral in less than thirty minutes after its posting and was soon dubbed in news commentary as the first-ever "social media murder." Tech companies blocked the footage as the day went on, but it continued to circulate online, and cable news networks looped snippets of it in their ongoing coverage. HollywoodLife.com, a celebrity-news site, produced a three-minute video report that replayed the initial few seconds of the killing no less than seven times and was viewed by at least a hundred thousand people. Video stills from the attacker's perspective made the covers of tabloid newspapers, inviting the public to gaze along the barrel and muzzle flash of the Glock 19 used to kill Parker, her face frozen in a final moment of terror: EXECUTED ON LIVE TV, blared the *New York Daily News* headline.

Five weeks later, a deeply disaffected twenty-six-year-old man carried out a suicidal gun massacre at Umpqua Community College in Roseburg, Oregon, after posting comments online about the Roanoke killer: "I have noticed that so many people like him are all alone and unknown, yet when they spill a little blood, the whole world knows who they are. A man who was known by no one, is now known by everyone. His face splashed across every screen, his name across the lips of every person on the planet, all in the course of one day."

Attempts by mass shooters to gain attention in freshly shocking ways were on the rise as digital media offered vast new opportunity for them to feed their pathological narcissism. In the next several years, at least two assailants went online in real time while they were carrying out attacks. In Florida in 2016, a gunman searched on his smartphone for news of a "shooting" and "Pulse Orlando" while he was inside the nightclub of that name committing a massacre. In California in 2018, an attacker at a bar in Thousand Oaks posted messages on social media accounts both immediately before and during his suicidal rampage. A user on the fringe site 4Chan had recently posted a message evoking the grim trend: "Has anyone ever livestreamed a mass shooting with a GoPro helmet?" An answer came in March 2019, when a far-right extremist carried out a terrorist attack at two mosques in New Zealand and wore a camera streaming footage of the massacre on Facebook Live.

The Columbine mass shooting, meanwhile, remained the biggest source of emulation behavior and exerted influence that now spanned generations. In a cluster of three separate attacks in early 2018, two of the offenders were mere infants when Columbine took place, and a third hadn't even been born yet. "I'm thinking about doing my school the same way," a nineteen-year-old commented about a Columbine video on YouTube prior to opening fire at his former high school in Ocala, Florida, nineteen years later to the day. "Everybody will know my name," he added. The perpetrator who attacked Marjory Stoneman Douglas High School in Parkland that February had researched Columbine and recorded himself on video, saying, "When you see me on the news, you'll all know who I am." A high school junior who went on a deadly rampage that May at Santa Fe High School just south of Houston wore a trench coat and insignia mimicking the Columbine shooters' attire.

Perhaps most unsettling was that there were many others like them, mostly young men (and a few young women) who plotted or carried out attacks marked by the "Columbine effect," as I called the phenomenon in my investigative reporting based on case data I'd begun collecting in 2013. After two decades had passed since the Colorado tragedy, the data grew to contain more than a hundred Columbine-inspired plots and attacks in thirty-four states, which revealed several disturbing patterns: Like the shooter in Ocala, eigh-teen other case subjects planned to strike on the date of the Col-umbine mass shooting. (Most were thwarted, and two ended up attacking on different dates.) Many case subjects identified with the pair of perpetrators from 1999 specifically as "heroes," "martyrs," or "gods." And several made pilgrimages to Colorado, from as far away as North Carolina and Washington state, to visit Columbine High School before returning home to carry out shootings.

Those were just the cases discoverable in the public record. "There are many more who have come to our community and have been thwarted," John McDonald, the director of security for Colorado's Jefferson County school district, told me when I met with him at Columbine High School to learn about Jeffco's threat assessment operations. "They want to see where it happened, want to feel it, want to walk the halls. They try to take souvenirs."

In 2016, after *VICE* published an article about an online sub-culture of "girls who love the Columbine shooters," several different young women from out of state showed up within a month, eager to get inside the building. McDonald's team had grown adept at intercepting even the most casually suspicious visitors approaching the campus. For some it was just about prurient fascination, but for others, something worse. More than a decade after the tragedy, a high schooler from Utah who had requested an interview for his student newspaper had spent much of an in-person meeting with Columbine principal Frank DeAngelis asking for details about the 1999 carnage and security measures since put in place. The sixteen-year-old was arrested back home the following month, along with a co-conspirator, after another student alerted school authorities to ominous text messages she'd received alluding to the pair's bud-ding plot to bomb the high school.

Suspected copycats came from as far away as overseas, added

McDonald, who began managing security in 2009 for the district's 157 schools and roughly 86,000 students. "It's a cult following unlike anything I've ever seen before," he remarked. "The problem is always on our radar."

The problem's reach is measurable in additional ways: By 2019, more than a dozen attacks had occurred abroad, in Canada and several other countries from Europe to Latin America, in which the assailants had researched Columbine or cited it as an inspiration. Threat assessment leaders in the United States have encountered numerous Columbine-influenced cases unknown to the public, including Los Angeles–based forensic psychologist Kris Mohandie, who has evaluated multiple youth offenders fixated on the 1999 attack. The Columbine perpetrators "had this grandiose fantasy that they would be remembered," he noted. "What's perverted about the whole thing is that, in a way, they got what they wanted."

The Columbine effect also became a problem of language. Whereas gun rampages had once become known generically as "going postal," now they were "doing a Columbine." News media and public officials alike had grown accustomed to referring to school shootings as "Columbine-style attacks," and the emulation problem reached a stark new level of impact just ahead of the event's twentieth "anniversary"—another term whose default usage in reference to mass shootings may well lend them unwanted significance. In April 2019, an eighteen-year-old woman who authorities said was "infatuated" with the Columbine massacre flew from Miami to Denver and headed to a retail shop in Littleton, where she bought a pump-action shotgun. Authorities closed and locked down hundreds of schools in the Denver region as a precaution while police searched for her, soon finding her dead from a self-inflicted gunshot wound in the nearby mountains.

———

The deleterious effects of digital media also have a promising side. Through the 2010s, FBI researchers found that rampage shooters were announcing their grievances and violent ideation on social media with greater frequency before attacking—a significant development among a pool of offenders who were otherwise often socially withdrawn. In some instances, open-source content could reveal a lot to investigators about whom a threatening subject might be targeting and why.

A broad-based investigation remained key, however, as partial information could be misleading. In a case at a government agency in the nation's capital shortly after the 2013 mass shooting at the Washington Navy Yard, for example, the subject, who was socially awkward and kept to himself around the office, had freaked out coworkers by riffing about guns on social media and leaving pictures of unusual-looking weapons on his desk. Threat assessment professionals who went to speak with him at his home found that he was an avid collector of antique and exotic firearms and had no interest in violence.

Yet it was becoming a lot less feasible to evaluate case subjects effectively without understanding how those individuals behaved in the digital realm. Andre Simons and his BAU colleagues had come to see that a growing number of plotters and attackers were, as Simons put it, "living more vividly online than in the physical world."

It is crucial to understand that shooter-focused news coverage and social media content do not *cause* a person to commit violence, nor is there scientific evidence that graphically violent video games, movies, or music do. In the world of behavioral threat assessment, the more useful way to think about influences from media and entertainment is to recognize their possible association with warning behaviors—as potential additional clues to an individual heading down a dangerous path. An example of this came in a form of leakage that marked a murder-suicide in 2013 at Arapahoe High School in suburban Denver. The day before the shooting, capping off months of troubling aggression and other warning signs, the eighteen-year-old perpetrator announced in front of peers and a teacher that he had recently bought a shotgun and named it after a legendary rock star. "Don't make me show you Kurt Cobain," he sneered at a classmate who angered him. Other comments and photos of the weapon that he shared were reported by one student to a school psychologist. The relevance was not that the music of Nirvana was somehow responsible for motivating what was to come; it was the fact that Cobain had taken his own life with a shotgun. The perpetrator's use of the namesake was a signal of suicidal rage and despair as he neared the end of his pathway to violence.

Various other cases indicate how a focus on violence-themed entertainment can connect with warning behaviors. It can be a type of fixation, or what earlier threat assessment research referred to as "aggression immersion," a way for perpetrators to nurture their grievance-based ideas about committing an attack. The 2011 hit song "Pumped Up Kicks" from indie band Foster the People, whose lyrics are told from a school shooter's perspective, turned up in menacing communications in cases handled by Jeffco's team as well as in a case in New Jersey involving a threat from a high school student. The catchy pop tune had been a focus for a twelve-year-old who opened fire at his middle school in Nevada, as well as for the Parkland perpetrator, whose brother had witnessed him strutting around the house to the song while mimicking attacking with a shotgun he'd acquired. Salem-Keizer threat assessment leaders saw cases over the years where they theorized that first-person shooter video games had served as a tool of psychological "rehearsal" for individuals planning attacks—not as a motive for what they planned to do, but as a way they felt they could prepare themselves for the act.

In contrast to age-old debates over "dangerous" pop culture, however, the influence of sensational news attention on mass shooters suggests a unique opportunity for the media to contribute to prevention. Because many perpetrators behave with an expectation of gaining notoriety, altering the scale and tone of coverage might help diminish some plotters' motivation and the overall copycat effect. News organizations can rethink (as some have) where and how to name and describe attackers, and how to handle material like shooter images and "manifestos." It is a matter of proportion, about better balancing reporting in the public interest with denying offenders any sense of glorification or a megaphone for their screeds. News outlets are the driving force in this regard, although because social media users sometimes spread photos, videos, or manifestos found online through other avenues, tech companies also have a role to play in diminishing shooter content, as exemplified in vivid terms by the ex–TV reporter's snuff footage from Roanoke.

After Aurora and then Sandy Hook in 2012, some major news media began changing their approach, in part thanks to efforts by Caren and Tom Teves of Colorado, whose twenty-four-year-old son, Alex, was murdered in the movie theater attack. The grieving parents' push to change media behavior through a "No Notoriety" campaign was embraced by CNN's Anderson Cooper, who started declining to name shooters or show their faces on the air and instead prioritized reporting on victims and survivors. Three years later, amid the Aurora perpetrator's trial and the first "social media murder" in Roanoke and the subsequent community college massacre in Oregon, the advocacy movement gained momentum. In late October 2015, *People* magazine announced a new policy to "use strong caution when deciding whether to show these murderers' photos or use their names, and not allow ourselves to be a platform for their messages." It was a long way from the 1980s when the magazine ran an article spotlighting Theresa Saldana's near-lethal stalker, including his tactics later picked up on by Rebecca Schaeffer's killer.

Threat assessment experts recommended in particular avoiding the posed images that offenders post online to look tough or cool, as I had reported earlier that fall in an investigation of media influence on mass shooters. Those experts further suggested hewing to dispassionate language in news coverage and avoiding descriptions of perpetrators that might bestow a sense of prestige, such as "lone wolf," or even "school shooter." The time was also long past due to bury the pair from Columbine, whose smiling portraits were once framed on the cover of *Time* magazine as "The Monsters Next Door."

"Those two offenders should be made as anonymous as possible," Kris Mohandie told me two decades after their attack, when the "infatuated" suicidal young woman who'd traveled from Florida caused the widespread school closures in the Denver region. "I think the reporting needs to downplay the people who did it, while underscoring what we've learned about how to manage these kinds of people, the things wrong with them."

In fall 2019, a big movie premiere showed why better practices could really matter, putting an unwanted legacy on display. When the Hollywood blockbuster *Joker* was set to open seven years after the Aurora massacre, director Todd Phillips and star Joaquin Phoenix found themselves fending off sharp criticism that their graphically violent film could inspire attacks. Movie theater chains once again were compelled to prohibit fans from wearing costumes, and the Los Angeles Police Department stepped up patrols around screenings, citing the film's "historical significance." An article in the *Hollywood Reporter* noted that James Holmes, who was serving life in prison with no possibility for parole, would be "forever linked to the Batman film." Moreover, the copycat effect was now specifically present in this context. Further research under way from the US Secret Service would include the case of a nineteen-year-old who had threatened to shoot up his high school gradua-tion ceremony—who had dyed his hair red in homage to Holmes and expressed a desire to meet him in person.

Despite a push by some survivors and academic researchers in recent years for news media to implement a total blackout of mass shooters' identities, it remains strongly in the public interest to identify and report on the perpetrators, not least to ensure ac-curacy about these high-impact events. Going back more than a decade, innocent people have been falsely identified online as the culprits of mass attacks. In the aftermath of the Virginia Tech mas-sacre carried out by the Korean-born Seung-Hui Cho, a *Chicago Sun-Times* columnist picked up on bloggers' erroneous blame of a young man of Chinese background, who was also fingered as a suspect on the air by Fox News's Geraldo Rivera and faced a wave of death threats. That was even before the explosion of social me-dia, whose exacerbation of the problem included a college student wrongly accused for the Boston Marathon bombing in April 2013, and the spread of a false claim in October 2015 that the commu-nity college shooter in Oregon was Muslim.

Advocates for change further suggested that media should ad-here to "strategic silence" on mass shooters, a misnomer whose gist was to downplay rather than wholly ignore the perpetrators. A bet-ter term instead might be "strategic diminishment." Clear-eyed re-porting can cast essential light on how and why people commit these attacks while intentionally shrinking the frame around the offenders. Notably, journalism uncovering the behaviors and back-grounds of mass shooters has long been valuable to building threat assessment knowledge. From the Secret Service's Exceptional Case

Study Project in the 1990s to the FBI BAU's various in-depth research initiatives in more recent decades, experts in the field have long cited news reporting as a significant source of context and data.

After the staggering attack on the Las Vegas Strip in 2017, American news media made some heartening progress. National television broadcasts generally refrained from highlighting images of the perpetrator, and in the initial days after the attack, print editions of the hometown *Las Vegas Review-Journal*, *USA Today*, the *Los Angeles Times*, the *Wall Street Journal*, the *Washington Post*, and the *New York Times* all focused their front pages around vivid scenes of first responders and survivors. Three of the papers included unglamorous thumbnail-size photos of the attacker, while on the front pages of the three others, his image was nowhere to be found.

In March 2019, the world saw strategic diminishment modeled brilliantly by New Zealand prime minister Jacinda Ardern with her response to the attack on the two Christchurch mosques. Her government moved quickly to suppress the massacre footage, and she personally embraced and brought global attention to the victims and survivors. Although the assailant had been publicly identified and his court proceedings would later be broadcast, Ardern drew a bright line when she addressed Parliament in the aftermath: "He is a terrorist. He is a criminal. He is an extremist. But he will, when I speak, be nameless."

———

Deeper study of mass shooters through the 2010s revealed more about key areas of warning behavior, including domestic violence, misogyny, and identification with extremists. In some cases, those elements were converging in new ways, with digital media playing a significant role.

Experts began to learn more about the incel phenomenon in 2014, after evidence showed that Elliot Rodger had planned his suicidal shooting spree in Southern California as a "War on Women," in which he intended to slaughter "the very girls who represent everything I hate in the female gender: The hottest sorority of UCSB." His attack brought attention to the fringe subculture of involuntarily celibates, or sexually aggrieved individuals like Rodger, who commune online in their loathing for women. Threat assessment researchers had long since found that a failure to establish or succeed in intimate relationships is seen in some mass attackers. One earlier example was the Virginia Tech perpetrator in 2007, who had hired a prostitute in a motel room three weeks before he struck, for what was apparently his first and last sexual experience.

The emergence of dangerous incels starting from 2014 pointed to an evolving picture, in part for how they intersected ideologically with various other misogynistic online groups: the "pickup artists," the "men's rights activists," the "red pill" believers, the "men going their own way," and other antifeminist elements of the "manosphere." Some among these disaffected men were now translating their online grievances into real-world violence. Rage exacerbated by sexual failure turned up again in the perpetrator at the Oregon community college in 2015 and in another suicidal shooter who opened fire at a Florida yoga studio in 2018. The killer in Florida, like Rodger, had posted videos of himself on YouTube seething at women and espousing bigotry. The Oregon and Florida attackers both considered Rodger a hero. A man who used a van to fatally mow down ten pedestrians in Toronto in 2018 had also praised Rodger online, hailing him as the leader of an "incel rebellion," and in 2020, a failed plotter in Virginia emulated misogynistic details from Rodger's widely published book-length "manifesto" and self-recorded YouTube videos. Rodger's written screed, which he titled "My Twisted World," had been commonly described in news coverage as a 137-page document per its uploaded format, but the text was in fact more than 105,000 words long, about 400 pages in book form. The fact that it was so extensively quoted and made available in full by media outlets right after his 2014 attack undoubtedly suggested to aspiring killers how much attention they might also command.

Collectively, this was a grievance script about entitlement and sexual insecurity that in its final stages only thinly disguised nihilistic desperation. The phenomenon was a new twist on misogyny and domestic violence that was helping to drive media commentary about "toxic masculinity," which marked mass shooting cases more than generally recognized. Over the course of the decade, the perpetrators of at least twenty-two public mass shootings had a history of domestic abuse, had targeted women in general, or had stalked and harassed specific women. Dozens of multiple-victim murders entailing these behaviors also occurred through the decade in private homes, where men gunned down intimate partners, children, and other family members.

Contrary to the misconception that mass shooters are overwhelmingly young white males, the twenty-two misogynistic public attackers ranged in age from nineteen to fifty-nine, and fewer than half were white. The set of cases included the massacres at the Pulse Nightclub in Orlando in 2016 and at a church in Sutherland Springs, Texas, in 2017. In all, they accounted for 175 victims killed and 158 others injured. At least two of the attackers voiced revenge fantasies against women online in the vein of incels—a subculture whose majority appears to be young adult men but overall is more racially diverse than is widely perceived. (Rodger himself was half

Asian.) A young man who threatened a mass shooting at a women's march in Utah and another who opened fire outside a courthouse in Dallas also appeared to be influenced by incel themes. By 2020, according to research from the Naval Postgraduate School, at least ten "attempted or completed mass murders" were connected to incel ideas.

These developments arose during a period when the FBI's BAU researchers were examining sexual stressors as part of their deep study of pre-attack behaviors, and finding a notable pattern. Among a subset of eight shooters whose cases involved sexual grievances, seven had attacked completely random groups of victims, meaning they had no personal connection to the people or places they targeted. By comparison, among shooters without sexual grievances, the number of such randomly targeted attacks dropped to under 30 percent. Threat assessment experts saw that difference in targeting behavior as potentially informative amid continued study of "target dispersion," referring to how some offenders progressed from a desire to go after specific individuals to focusing their animus on broader groups, communities, institutions, or fully random crowds. The initial research showed that target dispersion accelerates the risk of an attack, and where detectable, it would likely demand more urgent intervention.

Another strain of extremism was evolving in this period. Ever since 9/11, the threat of homegrown jihadist terrorism had been a prime focus for the field, but as mass shootings and other threats and attacks by far-right extremists increased sharply during the years of Donald Trump's presidency, leading threat assessment experts tailored trainings in response to that ascendant danger. Violent far-right extremism had long posed at least a marginal danger, particularly after the Oklahoma City bombing stirred a next generation of anti-government believers, but its proponents emerged greatly emboldened under a president who embraced bigotry and demagoguery and refused to clearly oppose white supremacist hate.

Threat assessment leaders typically are stoic in the face of tumultuous current affairs, but after an intense 2020 election year battered by a politicized pandemic, several top experts I spoke with described feeling deeply unsettled by the way dehumanization and themes of existential social war had become normalized in American politics. As one of them put it, "History shows how bad it can get when you really start convincing people that differences of opinion or political affiliation are coming from 'enemies' to be feared and despised because they're threatening to destroy your way of life." That virulent demagoguery is a difficult problem to confront, observed another expert, in a society that fundamentally cherishes the freedom of speech.

Political demonization and unhinged conspiracy theories were percolating fringe subcultures, with social media forming an ever more interconnected pathway to radicalization, according to forensic psychiatrist Philip Saragoza, a threat assessment practitioner with expertise on incels and other extremist groups. "One thing we emphasize in trainings is how cross-linked these categories have all become," he told me, describing the growing pattern. "You have these disaffected young males who live online, and they'll wade into a community on 4Chan or 8Chan, and in one thread they'll find all kinds of misogynistic content from incels or other manosphere groups that's also wrapped up with MAGA movement politics, QAnon, or 'great replacement' and other racist conspiracy theories. It's a real hive of choices, almost like à la carte extremism."

Few individuals may partake to an extent that fuels real-world dangerousness, Saragoza noted, but the proliferation of such content has upped those prospects, he said, particularly as it intersects with ascendant political demagoguery. He pointed to widely viewed speeches from a manosphere figure posted on YouTube since 2020 exemplifying this crossover. As the speaker rails against feminism and promotes retrograde and misogynistic views of women, he sports a bright red hat with white lettering: MAKE WOMEN GREAT AGAIN.

Since 2018, Reid Meloy and several colleagues, including Dr. Tahir Rahman, a psychiatrist at Washington University in St. Louis, have published research that speaks to the dangers from extremist ideology of all kinds, including the resurgence of the far right. Their work focuses on a theory of targeted attacks arising from "extreme overvalued beliefs." The concept, which traces to ideas from the nineteenth-century German neuropsychiatrist Carl Wernicke, describes a person who is dug in and becoming dangerously motivated by entrenched political or ideological views—as distinct from being driven by delusions or obsessions that are attributable to clinical disease. "The belief grows more dominant over time, more refined and more resistant to challenge," Rahman explained in one paper. "The individual has an intense emotional commitment to the belief and may carry out violent behavior in its service."

On the cold gray afternoon of January 6, 2021, violent political extremism materialized in brazen new form when thousands of Trump supporters stormed the United States Capitol. FBI investigations of hundreds of participants who were arrested revealed copious evidence of fervent belief among them in the lie spread by Trump and his political allies that the 2020 election had been "stolen" through fraud. The grim assault on the seat of American democracy included a convergence of extremist belief and misogyny. Among the core group of the most violent offenders charged with federal crimes, including attacking police officers, were several who had records of harassing, abusing, or beating up women.

Some of those and others had viciously targeted House Speaker Nancy Pelosi; they called her profane names and made graphic death threats against her in menacing online communications, as well as in videos they or others around them recorded during the Capitol siege.

In further research that had been completed just two weeks before and was published online the day after the January 6 insurrection, Rahman, Meloy, and their colleagues continued to make the case that "extreme overvalued beliefs" were important to distinguish as a driver of targeted violence and should be considered for an entry in the latest edition of the *Diagnostic and Statistical Manual of Mental Disorders*. They had also recently addressed the danger in relation to digital communications—which proved to contain an astonishing depth of criminal evidence in the January 6 cases: everything from self-incriminating celebration on social media to longer-term planning to disrupt Congress and unleash violence in the nation's capital.

The ongoing research, though focused on targeted violence by lone offenders, resonated strongly with the unprecedented attack on the peaceful transfer of power in Washington, which had been mobilized primarily online. "Social media has become the host and the vector for the virus of extreme overvalued beliefs," the threat assessment experts wrote. "The vulnerable user refines his belief over time and begins to relish, amplify, and defend it. The process can occur quickly with the addition of online group effects (e.g., thousands or millions of retweets, 'likes,' or emoticons). Emotional contagion is present and measurable in social media."

Threat assessment research on the effects of digital media, sexual grievances, ideological extremism—and their various convergence—continued apace at the start of the 2020s. With that and the deepening knowledge of pre-attack behaviors, leaders expressed optimism about how far the field had come in four decades. Still, from stubborn cultural misconceptions about mass shooters to chronic inaction by Congress, it remained unclear whether the work could become a bigger part of a national strategy.

chapter eleven

BUTTERFLY EFFECTS

At the outset of the 2020s, life in America felt exceptionally fraught
with instability and danger as the country endured a historic pandemic, mass protests over police brutality and racial injustice, and
national elections laced with demagoguery and rage. Gun sales
soared, marked by record-breaking demand for FBI background
checks in the millions and a surge in first-time buyers. Logically,
this seemed a time of rising prospects for mass shootings.

And yet, while gun homicides increased in large cities from
coast to coast and stoked fears about escalating violent crime, the
first year–plus of the new decade turned out to be conspicuously
quiet in terms of high-profile public massacres. One widely remarked theory about the shift, plausible if unknowable, was that
far fewer people simply were present in schools, offices, and other
public venues during the pandemic's first year, reducing prospects
for such attacks. When the danger from Covid-19 receded and

more normal conditions of life began to return, so too did this painfully normal American problem. In March 2021, two young men committed mass shootings within the span of less than a week, one at massage parlors in Atlanta, and another at a grocery store in Boulder, Colorado. A familiar muddle of simplistic claims about motive filled national news coverage on both perpetrators, though neither attack was easily explained. The Atlanta shooter's case included elements of misogyny, racism, and sexual grievance, and the Boulder shooter had a history of violence and signs of angry paranoia.

A month later, a suicidal nineteen-year-old fatally shot eight people and wounded five others at a FedEx facility in Indianapolis where he had recently worked. Half of the murder victims were Sikhs, and the perpetrator's online activity raised questions about whether he was motivated by far-right extremist views. But FBI and local investigators concluded that there was no evidence of racial bias, and that he chose the FedEx location in lieu of other possible targets because of his familiarity with the site.

The spate of cases reiterated how easy it is for dangerous people to get guns. The attackers in Atlanta and Boulder purchased weapons legally just before those massacres. The attacker in Indianapolis—who'd had a shotgun taken away the prior year by police after his mother warned he might commit suicide by cop—later bought two rifles legally. The problem further resumed its numbing regularity in spring 2021 with two other workplace mass shootings in California. In fall 2021, a fifteen-year-old student who had stirred concerns at his Michigan high school used a pistol newly purchased by his father to go on a rampage.

Amid this resurgence, I found myself pondering again why behavioral threat assessment wasn't more widely in use and what might be required for it to scale. After first looking deeper into the method years before, it had struck me as a solution of last resort. If heavily armed America couldn't muster the courage and political consensus to transform our underlying policies on guns, then at least we might assemble teams of skilled people to reduce the menace of mass shootings case by case. After all, other affluent societies had successfully confronted these attacks by reckoning directly with their means. Australia, historically another frontier culture with a deep attachment to guns, had endured rampages starting in the 1970s, but after an assailant killed thirty-five people and wounded eighteen in 1996, the country had invested heavily in gun buybacks and enacted stricter laws. Suicides and murders with guns plummeted, and Australia has rarely experienced public rampages in the two and a half decades since, and nothing remotely on the scale seen in 1996. Britain instituted strict gun control following a mass shooting back in 1987, and though a decade later the nation endured a devastating massacre of its own at an elementary school, in Dunblane, gun violence in that country also has remained rare.

Hardly ever during my years of reporting did I observe threat assessment professionals openly discussing gun regulations, an apparent third rail in a field populated by a wide range of political views, often conservative ones. But the presence today of nearly four hundred million firearms in the United States—concentrated in the hands of about a third of the population, yet more than enough to arm every single man, woman, and child—is a stark reality with which practitioners must contend. They know that possession of a firearm is not a meaningful predictor of targeted violence, but they also know that readily available semiautomatic weapons and large-capacity ammunition devices make attacks easy and highly lethal, allowing a perpetrator to squeeze off thirty-one shots in thirty seconds at a Safeway store in Tucson or to strafe an entire concert audience from a Vegas hotel window, and so on.

From Columbine and Virginia Tech to Sandy Hook and Parkland, each of the highest-profile school massacres since 1999 has brought a surge of interest in behavioral threat assessment. The biggest yet followed Parkland in February 2018, prompting a flurry of trainings and legislative efforts. Just a year and a half later, at least six additional states, including Florida, had enacted laws requiring the formation of threat assessment programs for their public school systems, with several more states considering similar legislation.

As an additive solution, use of this method could have powerful synergy with gun regulations already shown through scientific research to help reduce shooting injury and death, from broader and more stringent background checks to gun prohibitions for domestic-violence offenders. But if behavioral threat assessment programs really were to scale as part of a national policy, the field yet faces steep challenges. Far too few communities even know about the work, forensic psychologist Russell Palarea told me in fall 2021, shortly after completing a four-year tenure as president of the Association of Threat Assessment Professionals. "A big challenge we face is buy-in," he said. "We need to get more people to understand what this work is, that it's a problem-solving model using components mostly already in place, and that it needs to be community-based."

Over the past few years, ATAP leaders had worked with a bipartisan group in Congress to establish $300 million in funding for ramping up threat assessment programs and training nationwide, but the effort stalled and was dropped in 2020, in part due to pushback from civil liberties groups, including the ACLU, who voiced sharp concerns about privacy and the school-to-prison pipeline. Palarea and his colleagues remain adamant that such opposition misunderstands the work. "We're trying to help people who are struggling, before they get arrested or hurt themselves or others," he said. "There's no downside to that."

Ron Schouten, a leading forensic psychiatrist and legal expert who spearheaded ATAP's efforts on federal funding, suggests that school systems, corporations, and government agencies can no longer afford *not* to be proactive in this way, given the growing understanding of how attacks can be prevented. "I would argue that it's now the standard of care to have such a policy in place," Schouten said, adding that legal liability could increase for institutions in the event of an attack preceded by recognizable warning signs.

The election of President Joe Biden in 2020 heralded policy changes that could open new frontiers of expansion for the field, in part through potential synergy with broader violence-prevention efforts. Amid the spate of mass shootings that marked the waning pandemic, Biden proposed an unprecedented $5 billion to fund community-based initiatives over eight years that are aimed at combating gun violence of all kinds as a public health crisis. Long-running violence "interrupter" programs focused on reducing gun homicides disproportionately harmful to people of color in American cities, such as the Boston-based Operation Ceasefire and Los Angeles–based BUILD, have much in common with the work of behavioral threat assessment. They bring together various community stakeholders to help identify and intervene with individuals who are fueling cycles of violence, working to alleviate their stressors and grievances and offering them opportunities.

The strategy, as described by Aquil Basheer, the founder and executive director of BUILD, hinges on the concept of "shared safety"—a collective responsibility to address the personal trauma and socioeconomic struggles underpinning violent antisocial behavior. As seen with many subjects of threat assessment cases, individuals involved in gang battles or other forms of violent retribution view killing as a justifiable solution to their problems, and often the only one at their disposal. The intervention work, according to Basheer—from offering health care and employment opportunities to personal mentorship—is fundamentally about helping these perpetrators realize they have options other than using a gun.

The Biden administration's plan also sought to elevate a legal tool known as an Extreme Risk Protection Order, or "red flag" law, which allows family members, and in some cases law enforcement officers, to seek a civil court order removing guns from individuals who pose a violent threat to themselves or others. Modeled on domestic-violence restraining-order laws, the red-flag policy generally can be used to bar a person from possessing firearms for up to a year based on a judge's ruling. Connecticut in 1999 was first to establish such a law, followed by Indiana in 2005, but the policy rarely saw use and didn't begin to spread nationally until 2014, when California passed legislation in the wake of Elliot Rodger's deadly rampage near the University of California–Santa Barbara. About a month before Rodger's attack, local authorities received a tip about him possibly being suicidal, but the sheriff's deputies who subsequently visited Rodger at his apartment for a welfare check were unaware of the guns he'd legally purchased, and they found him to be "shy, timid, and polite," with no cause to put him on an involuntary mental health hold.

Buoyed by strong public support, red flag laws spread by 2021 to more than a third of the states in the nation, with a handful more considering versions. Preliminary research on twenty-one cases in California from the mid-2010s showed no violent outcomes among individuals who, after threatening mass shootings, suicide, or in some cases both, had their guns removed under the policy. The potential boon for threat management work was evident when the ·

Biden White House urged Congress to pass a national version of the law, announced incentives for more states to do so, and rolled out model legislation in June 2021 from the Department of Justice.

Leaders in behavioral threat assessment readily acknowledge that the bar for quality work is high, given the necessary training and experience and the fact that the field's underlying science is still maturing. They point to strides made with the latter, including the 2014 launch of their dedicated research periodical from the American Psychological Association, the *Journal of Threat Assessment and Management*, as well as the development of specific sets of protocols for evaluating threats that have been validated in preliminary peer-reviewed study. Over the past decade, ATAP has built an ethical code of conduct and a curriculum for training practitioners, with leadership certification requiring at least five years of operational experience and extensive knowledge of the field's literature. The nonprofit organization's membership has more than doubled in size since 2015 to more than twenty-six-hundred people from the various relevant professional disciplines.

As in any field expanding amid rising demand, however, its leaders also face a familiar problem. "Snake oil" has grown more abundant, as Palarea puts it, as prevention work comes to be viewed as a moneymaking opportunity. Just as the post–Sandy Hook era led to the hawking of "bulletproof backpacks" and the like, so too have commercial interests cropped up selling dragnet-style surveillance for social media, or prevention "training seminars" run by people who have no operational experience with threat assessment. Pandemic-era stresses have further heightened demand and strained caseloads, Palarea notes, only underscoring the need to ensure the professional integrity and credibility of the work.

What the field may need above all to scale engagement and trust is a model for built-in oversight. Salem-Keizer leaders only

recently began pursuing a more robust data analysis of their program, after long relying on a level of community buy-in that likely
doesn't begin from scratch. In Virginia, home to another vanguard
threat-assessment model for public schools, state law allows for but
does not require oversight going beyond the sharing of quantitative
program data with a state hub for threat assessment policies.

The sensitive nature of the work makes for a delicate balancing
act with accountability. On the one hand, threat assessment teams
need to have a degree of transparency to build trust, articulating
for the public how they monitor operations to ensure the fair treatment and well-being of case subjects even as they work to protect
the communities those subjects may be endangering. On the other
hand, public disclosure can be tricky as practitioners seek cooperation from case subjects and those around them by promising a veil
of discretion and confidentiality. Nor is it realistic or advisable to
publicize every investigation, which could unfairly stigmatize case
subjects and complicate constructive interventions.

In the view of Nebraska-based threat assessment leader Mario
Scalora, the key is for programs to show what guardrails they have
in place. "You have to make clear that this is not being used to
harass people or to go after political speech," he says. "Accountability is important, and so is consistency. As this becomes imple-
mented more widely, it's not just the messaging to the public, but
then operating in ways consistent with that messaging." This approach has become all the more crucial in an era when trust in law
enforcement has been called into question by a broad swathe of
the American public. "You don't build community trust with just
words," Scalora says. "You build trust with actions. You can't say
you're treating different groups of people the same, and then they
see examples of that not happening."

Scalora, John Van Dreal, and other threat assessment leaders concur that greater investment in public accountability could be an important next phase for the field. It's a perspective rooted in ethical pragmatism that could help solve the long-running by-stander problem. The field has learned a great deal through research about why people who know a potentially dangerous family member or friend still fail in many cases to report their concerns. How to change that reluctance is the more difficult question. In Scalora's view, combating general misunderstanding about threat assessment work remains crucial. "It's really important to be sensitive to feelings of vulnerability in people who come forward, their concerns about their own personal safety and privacy," he says, emphasizing that the public also needs to trust that the response won't be heavy-handed. "We have to show by our actions that we aren't overreacting to these reports but actually trying to get struggling people help, rather than punishing them."

Scalora and his longtime University of Nebraska–Lincoln research partner Denise Bulling have continued to pursue concepts of community collaboration that deemphasize the criminal justice component, focusing on alternative institutional leaders who could act as natural gatekeepers. "People may not go to cops right away," Scalora notes, "so who do people trust, and how do we work with those people? They may be mental health practitioners or education or faith-group leaders, and our goal is to work with them and reinforce for the public that the trust is worthwhile."

Effective ambassadors of this message tend to hail from the mental health side of the field, though law enforcement professionals who have backgrounds in psychology or who have led behavioral threat assessment teams can also be persuasive, in part because they tend to defy stereotypes about cops. In recent years, torchbearers for the field's growth have also included a few people who never imagined getting involved.

The ever expanding population of Americans harmed by mass shootings is known among some of those survivors as "the club no one ever wants to join." Once the initial shock and the world's attention dissipates, those who have lost loved ones face a desolate quietude and questions about how to carry on. Some have responded by focusing their energy on violence prevention, including the mission of behavioral threat assessment.

Following the death of her six-year-old son, Dylan, at Sandy Hook Elementary School, Nicole Hockley at first took a more familiar path, traveling to the nation's capital in April 2013 to join a group of survivors lobbying Congress intensively for universal background checks for gun buyers. Like others with her and many people elsewhere around the country, she felt anguish and disgust when the regulation supported by a strong national majority was voted down narrowly in the Senate. If the slaughter of tender youth didn't finally provoke serious federal progress, then what would?

At that point, Hockley made a decision: she wanted to work for change in a different way, one that wasn't so throttled by partisanship the moment anyone uttered a word about guns. She began to focus on the concept of early intervention along with two other survivors from Newtown: Mark Barden, a professional musician whose seven-year-old son, Daniel, was among the first graders killed, and Bill Sherlach, whose wife, Mary, was fatally shot while trying to protect the children. Mary was the school psychologist, whose professional website had advertised that she was "always ready to assist in problem solving, intervention, and prevention." The three began reading voraciously about school violence and prevention strategies, brushed up on past movements for social change, and established a nonprofit group called Sandy Hook Promise.

A turning point for Hockley came in July 2014, when she and other Sandy Hook survivors met in a hotel conference room in a nearby Connecticut town with several members of the FBI's Behavioral Analysis Unit, part of a broader ongoing dialogue between some Newtown families and state and local authorities involved in the investigation. Prepared to share insights from their analysis of the perpetrator, the BAU agents indicated that they hadn't before undertaken such a meeting with victims' families. In Hockley's recollection, some of them seemed even a little nervous about the gathering, as she certainly was feeling herself.

Although the perpetrator had lived right across the road from Hockley's family in Newtown, she'd never really seen the reclusive young man or known anything about him. Like so many others, she thought Adam Lanza had woken up that unimaginable morning and just snapped. She learned about the contours of his long pathway to mass murder, which had included various disturbing online communications, an extensive spreadsheet he'd assembled about previous mass shootings, and other accumulated warning signs going far back in time. As the BAU experts welcomed questions, one family member asked whether the killer's behaviors were unusual. Lanza had acted like other perpetrators in several ways, and in that regard, one of the experts replied, the case was "a typical school shooting."

Hockley appreciated the FBI's engagement with the families and felt that the BAU agents treated them with kindness and empathy. But the content of that answer floored her. "As a mom whose six-year-old boy had been killed, I was incredibly angry," she said. "As far as I was concerned, there was nothing typical about a school shooting."

As the BAU experts drew a fuller picture of the offender and what led up to his attack, including some of his acute clinical and circumstantial problems, Hockley felt compelled to speak up with a question of her own: "If you know all this, why aren't you teaching it to everyone?"

The complex and sensitive nature of the work wasn't the only reason for its obscurity. The agents said the FBI didn't have the resources to go beyond trainings for law enforcement partners. It struck Hockley that the void they were describing was a mission-in-waiting. *If they can't do it*, she thought, *we will.*

Sandy Hook Promise sought help from education and threat assessment experts and soon built a curriculum on behavioral warning signs and other aspects of prevention to take to communities nationwide. They pursued fund-raising, eventually drawing support from millions of donors that would help them conduct outreach and trainings for more than twelve million students and educators.

Hockley had also felt they needed to do more to reach kids directly. She deployed her professional skills in marketing and communications to develop a series of short videos with a creative agency that would raise awareness under a banner of "Know the Signs." One result of that work was "Evan," a two-minute spot launched in December 2016, four years after the Sandy Hook massacre. Set in an idyllic-looking school to a winsome pop song, a short montage showed the story's handsome teen namesake pursuing a budding romance. Just as he encountered the girl of his dreams in the crowded school gym, another kid entered through a side door in the background, pulled out a rifle, and prepared to open fire. As the crowd of students screamed and scattered, the screen went black and then displayed a couple of lines: "While you were watching Evan, another student was showing signs of planning a shooting. But no one noticed."

The video then rolled back through the montage, this time spotlighting the shooter-to-be in the backgrounds of various scenes: there he was, sullen and alone in the cafeteria; then staring at firearms on a library computer; then getting roughed up by bullies at his locker; then posing with a semiautomatic pistol on social media; then flexing a thumb and fingers as he mimicked shooting a teacher behind her back.

After working obsessively on the script and high-gloss production, Hockley was apprehensive about how it would be received. She showed the final cut to her partners, who, even despite their own intense focus on prevention, missed most of the warning behaviors flashing by during the first minute. That's when Hockley knew they had something compelling in their hands.

The video went viral overnight and was viewed more than 155 million times in the first three weeks. Sandy Hook Promise soon heard from schools where students had huddled around desks watching, or where parents were calling school leaders to ask about discussing "Evan" at home with their kids. Corporate leaders began requesting permission to use the video for their own internal trainings on safety and situational awareness. It was the impact of any marketing professional's dreams, and a bittersweet achievement.

Hockley and her partners could take pride in having done more than just remind the world of a terrible tragedy. Raising awareness memorably was one way to affect change, and they'd done so for a prevention strategy that quite literally needed people to notice what most never consciously had. Was that enough to stop bullets?

———

The ambition to prevent unpredictable violence is rooted, ultimately, in optimism. For a survivor whose role includes sharing her most devastating life experience, involvement in such a mission, particularly over a long time, might seem improbable. But it can also be about something that mass shooters themselves so desperately lack: resilience.

"It's not easy, because I'm constantly retraumatizing myself, but I know why I'm doing it," Nicole Hockley told me when we spoke again in fall 2021. "People engage at an emotional level. Once they've opened up their hearts, then I find it's easier for them to open up their minds to what's possible. That arc to hope is what I'm constantly working for in every interaction. My message is, 'This is what happened to me, and by doing these things, we can ensure it never happens to you.'"

Soon, a decade will have passed since that day when Sandy Hook parents faced the unthinkable and many others across America absorbed the news and then hugged their little ones at schools, parks, or recreational children's museums with stomachs aflutter. Hockley looks ahead to how she can continue to improve and expand upon her work. "I think people relate in a different way to survivors who've experienced this if you give them a tangible path forward," she says. "Otherwise, you're just a victim, which is something I never want to be seen as."

Hockley regards her mission as an evolutionary journey in which Sandy Hook Promise can respond to a changing landscape. On her mind in fall 2021 were kids all over the country returning to school in a pandemic era that has created "a powder keg" of mental health crises among students. In a time of important renewed attention on social justice, equity is also a priority for the work, she says, including a focus on how to approach and partner with communities where law enforcement is not well trusted.

The work remains her pathway to honoring Dylan's memory. In outreach and trainings, Hockley speaks about her son with love and resolve. D, as she calls him, was "a flapper." He was autistic, and that was his unique expression of associated repetitive movement. "He flapped a lot," she says. "He did it especially whenever he was excited and happy." She, Dylan's dad, and his older brother all loved that about him. "We used to joke that one of these days he was just going to take off into the air."

One day, after Dylan had been making good progress catching up on speech development, Hockley had asked him, "Why do you flap?"

He'd looked up at her with bright eyes. "Because I'm a beautiful butterfly," he said.

As often happens for those who suffer acute trauma, certain parts of Hockley's memory from the early aftermath are forever lost to her. But others remain crystal clear. She knew almost immediately after the catastrophe that she would work to bring about positive transformation. She had no idea back then how she would try to do so, only that she would.

When she'd spoken at Dylan's funeral a week after his death, she had decided to include a few words about a theoretical idea known as the butterfly effect. The way it evoked the vast connectivity and chance of life resonated for her at a moment when the world felt so bereft of meaning. In the years ahead, she would continue to be carried by its essential concept. A flap of tiny wings somewhere in the world could potentially give rise to a hurricane somewhere else. Or, as time and courage might have it, prevent one.

ACKNOWLEDGMENTS

Writing a book is an arduous task in normal times, but the further complication of doing it during a global pandemic, while mostly sequestered at home with two young children, is why I'm breaking with the common practice of authors thanking their life partners last. My wife and the love of my life, Lisa, stepped up with invaluable help of so many kinds, all while navigating her own professional career in a time of frequent uncertainty and stress. Without her unwavering support and sacrifice, this book simply would not have been possible. She is my hero.

A great many people in mental health, law enforcement, education, and other relevant fields shared their knowledge and insights with me. My deep gratitude in particular goes to Robert Fein, Courtenay McCarthy, Reid Meloy, Russell Palarea, Mario Scalora, Andre Simons, and John Van Dreal, all of whom were exceptionally generous with their time and expertise, and with their trust in the work

I was pursuing. Thanks as well to Denise Bulling, Gene Deisinger, Chuck Klink, Peter Langman, John McDonald, Bill Modzeleski, Kris Mohandie, John Nicoletti, Dave Okada, Kendall Plageman, Marisa Randazzo, Jack Rozel, Gene Rugala, Shelley Rutledge, Phil Saragoza, Ron Schouten, Jim Silver, Chuck Tobin, Bryan Vossekuil, Stephen White, and Bill Zimmerman. A few others who I am not at liberty to name also have my great appreciation.

I had the privilege of learning directly from shooting survivors who shared their personal experiences with me, a number of whom do not appear in the book. All of them have my gratitude and respect. It is difficult to imagine what it would really be like to lose a child to a shooting. My heartfelt thanks to Nicole Hockley, whose openness, fortitude, and commitment to her work are an inspiration. I am profoundly grateful to Kristina Anderson, a person of extraordinary courage, intelligence, and optimism, who not only helped me to dive deeper into important material for the book, but who was also an inspiring fellow traveler and font of friendship.

Anyone who makes a career of writing knows the importance of having a great editor, and I was lucky to have one in the talented Matthew Daddona. His thoughtfulness, sharp eye, and easygoing approach to grappling with issues big and small were instrumental to helping shape this book to its fullest potential. My thanks also to Rosy Tahan for her great editorial support, to Ploy Siripant for the excellent cover design, and to everyone else at Dey Street and HarperCollins who had a hand in bringing *Trigger Points* to fruition.

My stellar literary agent, Howard Yoon, played an essential role in helping me hone my vision for this book, from early development to eventual execution. I'm grateful for his enduring support and faith in my work, and for his top-notch guidance in the world of publishing.

For the past decade, my journalistic home has been at *Mother Jones*, whose extraordinary leaders, Monika Bauerlein and Clara Jeffery, have been supportive the whole way. It has been my additional great fortune to have them as mentors and friends. Thanks to all my talented MoJo colleagues who have worked with me over the years on the gun-violence beat, in particular to Dave Gilson, a terrific editor and trusted sounding board. A big shout-out and thanks to inimitable producer and editor James West, who taught me much about video journalism and has been an ace collaborator when traversing the country for reporting projects. Many thanks also to David Corn, Mike Mechanic, and Dan Schulman for their camaraderie and support on all things book related, and specifically to Dan for pointing me toward Howard when I began talking with various agents.

Longtime friends helped me throughout this undertaking, whether giving me smart feedback on drafts, advice on book design, a place to land during reporting trips, or just a bit of creative spark when needed. Big love and appreciation especially go out to Amanda Field, Ann Bowlus, Scott Rosenberg, and Rob Waller.

Thanks to my always supportive siblings, Julie and Andy, and their wonderful spouses, Rich and Mary. I can hardly begin to express sufficient gratitude to my amazing parents, Joyce and Gary, for a lifetime of love and encouragement, including the early gift of instilling in me a desire to never stop learning. And finally, to Charlie and Eleanor, whose radiance clarified for me daily why this work was worthwhile. May they and all of their generation grow up in a more peaceful world.

ENDNOTES

INTRODUCTION: LIGHT IN THE DARK

x   **public opinion polls over the past three decades:** From independent national surveys conducted annually by Gallup.

x   **three quarters of those killers acquire their guns legally:** "A Guide to Mass Shootings in America," *Mother Jones,* July 20, 2012.

xi   **Study of disparate state laws:** Research detailed in "States with Weak Gun Laws Suffer from More Gun Violence," US Senate Judiciary Committee, Sept. 24, 2019.

xi   **nearly 40,000 shooting deaths and 115,000 injuries annually:** Data from the Centers for Disease Control and Prevention, University of California–Davis Health, and the Pew Research Center, Aug. 16, 2019.

xi   **de facto prohibition of federal funding for gun-violence research:** "The True Cost of Gun Violence," *Mother Jones,* Apr. 15, 2015; and "Ex-Rep. Dickey Regrets Restrictive Law On Gun Violence Research," National Public Radio, Oct. 9, 2015.

xii   **the FBI had helped thwart more than one hundred "active shooters":** Transcript of Attorney General Holder's prepared remarks to the International Association of Chiefs of Police Annual Conference, US Justice Department, Oct. 21, 2013.

xiii   **"Mass murder just may be a price we must pay":** Northeastern University criminologist James Alan Fox, a widely published expert on mass killing, from "Mass Shootings in America: Moving Beyond Newtown," *Homicide Studies,* Jan. 2013.

xiii **outsize psychological, financial, and cultural impact:** "True Cost of Gun Violence"; and "The Mass-Casualty Incident at Virginia Tech: Ten Years Later," *Journal of Threat Assessment and Management*, Nov. 2016.

xiii **drills could be harmful to children's well-being:** "Participation of Children and Adolescents in Live Crisis Drills and Exercises," *Pediatrics* 146, no. 3 (Sept. 2020); and "When Active-Shooter Drills Scare the Children They Hope to Protect," *New York Times,* Sept. 4, 2019.

xiv **"these responses are not likely to be effective":** "Evaluating Risk for Targeted Violence in Schools: Comparing Risk Assessment, Threat Assessment, and Other Approaches," *Psychology in the Schools* 38, no. 2 (2001).

xiv **a multibillion-dollar industry:** "After Newtown, Sales Boom for Kids' Body Armor," *Mother Jones*, Dec. 18, 2012; "A Pennsylvania School District Is Arming Its Teachers with 600 Miniature Baseball Bats," CNN, Apr. 12, 2018; "This School District Is Arming Students with Rocks in Case of a Shooter," CNN, Mar. 24, 2018; and video footage of a Boyle County, Kentucky, active-shooter drill, from CBS affiliate WKYT, Aug. 3, 2018.

CHAPTER 1: IT'S A SMALL WORLD

4 **increased both in frequency and lethality:** "Rate of Mass Shootings Has Tripled Since 2011, Harvard Research Shows," *Mother Jones*, Oct. 15, 2014; "More and Deadlier: Mass Shooting Trends in America," *Washington Post*, Aug. 5, 2019; and "Guide to Mass Shootings in America."

6 **two distinctive modes of aggression:** As described by Meloy and detailed in *The International Handbook of Threat Assessment*, Oxford University Press, ch. 1, pp. 5–9 (2014).

6 **obscure professional niche:** Prior to 2014, behavioral threat assessment was virtually nonexistent as a subject in news media; even among mental health and law enforcement, I encountered numerous professionals during the course of my reporting who had never heard of the field, whose own leaders often noted its obscurity.

7 **defied a steady decline in America's overall murder rate:** From 1991 to 2016, the murder rate nationally fell roughly by half. "Crime Trends: 1990–2016," Brennan Center for Justice.

9 **disinhibiting effects of social media:** "The Online Disinhibition Effect," *CyberPsychology & Behavior* 7, no. 3 (2004): 321–26.

10 **a sensation connected to evolved survival instincts:** "The Ecology of Human Fear: Survival Optimization and the Nervous System," *Frontiers in Neuroscience* 9, no. 55 (2015).

12 **guns have been the weapon of choice:** "Guide to Mass Shootings in America"; database of mass attacks from *USA Today*; and "Campus Attacks: Targeted Violence Affecting Institutions of Higher Education," US Secret Service, Department of Education, and FBI, Apr. 2010.

13 **declared the school a "genocide college" and "illegal":** Loughner's video

(which he'd posted on YouTube), obtained by author from a threat assessment source.

13 **"could just as easily have come back and shot up the school":** Quote from an email contained in documents released by Pima Community College, as reported by the *Tucson Sentinel*, Aug. 16, 2011. Approximately five weeks before the attack, Loughner legally purchased the Glock pistol he used: *United States of America v. Jared Lee Loughner*, US District Court, District of Arizona, Case No. 11–0035M.

13 **served just hours earlier with a restraining order from a girlfriend:** "One Small Town's Plan to Prevent Another Mass Shooting," *Mother Jones*, Mar. 7, 2017. For more on domestic-violence murders associated with restraining orders, see: "In Some States, Gun Rights Trump Orders of Protection," *New York Times*, Mar. 17, 2013.

13 **rejected assailant Richard Farley's romantic advances:** Author interview with threat assessment practitioner Russell Palarea; *People v. Farley*, Supreme Court of California, Case No. S024833; "One Small Town's Plan"; "Unwanted Suitor's Fixation on Woman Led to Carnage," *Los Angeles Times*, Feb. 18, 1988; and "Sudden Death in Sunnyvale," *Washington Post*, Feb. 18, 1988.

14 **"pushed him over the edge":** Black, as quoted by Gavin de Becker in *The Gift of Fear*, Random House p. 149 (1997); and similar comments by her in an archival interview from ABC News's *Prime Time Live*.

16 **"a translator of mindset and behavior":** From author interview with Palarea; also as described in "Operational Psychology: An Emerging Discipline," *AP-LS News*, Fall 2007.

17 **a national investigative commission stated they could forecast:** "Preventing Assassination: Secret Service Exceptional Case Study Project" (ECSP), US Department of Justice, National Institute of Justice, May 1997, ch. 3, p. 44.

17 **one a mother and employed full-time as an accountant:** Refers to Sara Jane Moore, who tried to assassinate Gerald Ford in 1975. From ECSP, and cited in "Evaluating Risk for Targeted Violence in Schools."

17 **the FBI produced an "offender profile":** *FBI Law Enforcement Bulletin*, Vol. 68, no. 9, Sept. 1999; Band S.R., and Harpold J.A.

17 **overlooking the nearly two dozen young men:** Data from psychologist and school shootings expert Peter Langman, available at SchoolShooters.info.

18 **investigation by FBI threat assessment researchers into sixty-three active shooters:** "New FBI Study Shows Mass Shooters Aren't Loners Who Suddenly Just Snap," *Mother Jones*, June 20, 2018. Discussion of mental illness as a rare primary factor also from author interviews with FBI supervisory special agent Andre Simons (one of the FBI study's authors). A US Secret Service study of thirty-seven cases published in Aug. 2020, "Mass Attacks in Public Spaces," found seven cases in which motive was "related to symptoms of mental illness or psychosis," and a Secret Service study of sixty-seven plots to attack schools, published in March 2021, "Averting Targeted School

Violence," found much more broadly defined "mental health symptoms" in a majority of cases but emphasized that those "should not be viewed as causal explanations for attack planning."

19 **far more likely to be victims of violence than perpetrators:** "Mental Health Myths and Facts," from MentalHealth.gov, with information provided by the CDC, the National Institute of Mental Health, and other agencies; and overviews of schizophrenia and bipolar disorder from the Mayo Clinic.

19 **shot his ex-fiancée in broad daylight:** "College Romance Costs Two Lives," *Chicago Tribune*, Apr. 30, 1909; and "Senior at Smith College Shot for Breaking Her Engagement," *Santa Rosa Press Democrat*, Apr. 30, 1909. Additional case details in contemporaneous archival stories from the *Boot and Shoe Recorder*, the *Washington Evening Star*, and other publications.

19 **a 1983 attack at a middle school in suburban St. Louis:** "'It Just Happened, and Now It Is Over,'" United Press International, Jan. 24, 1983; and "Police Say Eighth Grader Planned Shooting," UPI, Jan. 22, 1983.

20 **"crazed lunatic full of hate":** Las Vegas mayor Carolyn Goodman, as quoted in *USA Today*, Oct. 2, 2017; and *Jimmy Kimmel Live*, video from broadcast on Oct. 2, 2017. The number of those wounded by gunfire in the attack was a little under five hundred, but many others were also physically injured in the chaos. Further details on victims injured and killed are available in an official investigative report from the Las Vegas Metropolitan Police Department, Aug. 3, 2018.

20 **"What made him snap? I don't know":** "Las Vegas Shooting: Stephen Paddock Was 'Upbeat, Happy' as He Bought Guns," *USA Today*, Oct. 4, 2017. One of many other examples of the "snap" theme perpetuated in the news media, from "What We Know, and Don't Know about the Las Vegas Shooter," National Public Radio, Oct. 3, 2017: "And so that's the mystery. What caused Stephen Paddock to snap, to act in a way no one who has spoken out so far would have predicted?"

20 **Las Vegas Metropolitan Police Department concluded about Paddock:** As described in a public briefing by Clark County Sheriff Joe Lombardo: "What we have not been able to definitively answer is the 'Why Stephen Paddock committed this act,'" from "Police End Las Vegas Shooting Investigation; No Motive Found," National Public Radio, Aug. 3, 2018. Further details on the question of motive are in the Las Vegas Metropolitan PD report.

21 **"The alternative to the myth of pure evil":** Steven Pinker, *The Better Angels of Our Nature*, Penguin Books, 2011, p. 569.

CHAPTER 2: BEYOND THE MAGIC MEDICINE

23 **Bridgewater State Hospital for the Criminally Insane:** The official name of the hospital at the time; the latter half of the name was later dropped.

24 **Bridgewater's dark history:** "Horrors at Bridgewater State Hospital," ABC News *Nightline*, 1989; "Homicide at Bridgewater State Hospital," *Boston Globe*,

Feb. 15, 2014; "Inside Look at BSH's Reforms," WCVB 5 Boston, Sept. 21, 2017.

24   **run by stern correctional officers:** Author interviews with Robert Fein, based on his nine years of working at Bridgewater.

25   **unshackled for public audiences:** "Mass. Court Lifts Ban on 24-Year-Old Film," *Washington Post*, Aug. 2, 1991.

25   **The era of nationwide deinstitutionalization:** Author interview with Fein; and E. Fuller Torrey, *Out of the Shadows: Confronting America's Mental Illness Crisis*, excerpt in "Deinstitutionalization: A Psychiatric 'Titanic,'" *Frontline*, May 10, 2005.

25   **"the most psychotic and violent men" in state custody:** Shervert Frazier, et. al., "Problems in Assessing and Managing Dangerous Behavior," in, "Behavioral Science and the Secret Service: Toward the Prevention of Assassination," National Academies Press, Mar. 1981.

25   **Inside at the mantrap entrance:** My narrative account of Fein's experiences at Bridgewater is drawn from my series of in-depth interviews with him between 2017 and 2020, corroborated by supporting documents he provided to me, as well as my own independent research.

30   **Sherv, as Frazier was known among colleagues:** Author interviews with Fein; and "Shervert Frazier, 93: Catalyst in Mental Illness Field," obituary, *Boston Globe*, Mar. 12, 2015.

30   **Case details from Charles Whitman's 1966 attack:** From various sources, including: "Behind the Tower: New Histories of the UT Tower Shooting," research project, University of Texas–Austin Department of History, 2016, http://behindthetower.org; "96 Minutes," *Texas Monthly*, Aug. 2, 2016; "The Reckoning," *Texas Monthly*, Mar. 2016; "The Brain on Trial," *The Atlantic*, July–Aug. 2011; and Gary M. Lavergne, *A Sniper in the Tower*, University of North Texas Press, 1997.

31   **He immediately formed an investigative team:** Shervert Frazier, et. al., Texas Governor's Fact-Finding Committee, *Report on the Charles J. Whitman Catastrophe*, Sept. 8, 1966; and "Shervert Frazier, 93." Additional context here is from an interview with psychiatrist Stuart L. Brown, who worked on the report to the governor under Frazier: "Discovering the Importance of Play through Personal History and Brain Images," *American Journal of Play*, Spring 2009.

31   **lengthy suicide letter justifying the deaths:** Documents from the "Behind the Tower" project; and *Report on the Charles J. Whitman Catastrophe*.

32   **malignant brain tumor revealed by Whitman's autopsy:** *Report on the Charles J. Whitman Catastrophe*.

32   **hereditary psychopathy was another possible factor:** According to a 1966 FBI document, after separate interviews with Whitman's father shortly after the massacre, Frazier and two colleagues each assessed him to be "dangerous," diagnosing him with "homicidal tendencies, psychopathic personality," and, if pushed the wrong way, "capable of [the] same type of incident his son perpetrated." Communication to FBI director from special agent in charge at

FBI's Houston field office, Aug. 17, 1966; via Internet Archive; and, psychopathy as a heritable trait, from author interview with Reid Meloy.

32   **"Violence and Social Impact":** The essay, widely cited in other mental health research, is found in *Research and the Psychiatric Patient*, ed. Joseph C. Schoolar and Charles M. Gaitz (Bruner/Mazel, 1975).

CHAPTER 3: ON THE TRAIL OF ASSASSINS

35   **Many clutched flowers . . . hand-drawn signs . . . carried on the wind:** Archival photos; CBS Radio *World News Roundup*, Dec. 15, 1980; and archival footage, WNBC TV, New York, Dec. 14, 1980.

36   **reportedly called out, "Mr. Lennon":** My account of the killing and the immediate aftermath draws from various sources, including: NBC/TODAY archival footage from Dec. 8–9, 1980, including a press conference given late on Dec. 8 by James Sullivan, NYPD chief of detectives; contemporaneous footage from *ABC News with Ted Koppel*, and from WNBC TV, New York, Dec. 14, 1980; additional details from Jack Jones, *Let Me Take You Down: Inside the Mind of Mark David Chapman, the Man Who Killed John Lennon* (Villard Books, 1992). It's worth noting that some historical accounts describe Chapman as having fired five shots; only four bullets struck Lennon.

36   **The timing was now a little uncanny:** Author interviews with Fein. The origins of this law enforcement–mental health collaboration are also detailed in "Research and Training for the Secret Service: Behavioral Science and Mental Health Perspectives," Institute of Medicine, Feb. 1984. The Secret Service took some initial steps in this direction in the late 1970s; by 1980, the director had approached the IOM seeking a more robust initiative.

36   **One in every four presidents . . . had been the target:** Institute of Medicine, *Behavioral Science and the Secret Service: Toward the Prevention of Assassination* (National Academies Press, March 1981).

37   **even more fraught with danger for top political figures:** Author interviews with Fein; also as described in "Research and Training for the Secret Service," the 1984 IOM report: "an ever-increasing number of intelligence investigations" at the Secret Service by the late 1970s.

37   **"I'd go away if I were you":** "John Lennon of the Beatles Is Killed," *New York Times*, Dec. 9, 1980.

37   **He had dropped his weapon:** From video of NYPD chief of detectives' press conference, Dec. 8, 1980.

37   **"more popular than Jesus":** The famous Lennon interview was published in the *London Evening Standard*, Mar. 4, 1966. Chapman's religious background and disillusionment with Lennon, detailed in, "Mark Chapman: the Man Who Shot Lennon," *People* magazine, Feb. 23, 1987.

38   **"cultural script":** Author interviews with Reid Meloy and other threat assessment experts; "The Concept of Identification in Threat Assessment," *Be-*

havioral Sciences and the Law 33, no. 2–3 (Feb. 2015); and "The Autogenic (Self-Generated) Massacre," *Behavioral Sciences and the Law* 22, Dec. 2003.

38   **the "Werther effect":** Author interviews with threat assessment experts; "The Influence of Suggestion on Suicide: Substantive and Theoretical Implications of the Werther Effect," *American Sociological Review* 39, no. 3 (June 1974); and "*13 Reasons Why* and Suicide Contagion," *Scientific American*, May 8, 2017.

38   **met with Secret Service agents from Boston and Washington:** Author interviews with Fein; and the March 1981 IOM paper, *Behavioral Science and the Secret Service*.

39   **"threat statute":** Author interview with Fein, and as detailed in the IOM committee report, Feb. 1984.

41   **still operated in old-school ways:** Author interview with Fein. Former Secret Service director John Simpson (deceased) talked about the "close-knit" culture of the agency as well: "Secret Service Changes Amid Danger Signals," United Press International, Dec. 7, 1981.

41   **The top federal protective agency was created:** From "The U.S. Secret Service in History," Clinton White House archives (1998); and the Secret Service's history documentation online, including timeline from 1865 to 1902.

41   **hundreds of concerning people designated with QI status:** Institute of Medicine, "Research and Training for the Secret Service," Feb. 1984.

42   **fraught politics and budgets of the federal bureaucracy:** Author interviews with Fein, retired Secret Service special agent Bryan Vossekuil; and Institute of Medicine, *Behavioral Science and the Secret Service*, Mar. 1981.

42   **One ricocheting bullet . . . pierced Reagan's torso:** Archival news footage; and "Command and Control: Tested Under Fire," *Dallas Morning News*, May 13, 2015.

42   **a copy of Bremer's diary:** "Arthur Bremer Shot Gov. George Wallace to Be Famous. A Search for Who He Is Today," *Washington Post*, Dec. 3, 2015.

43   **Hinckley strumming a rendition of Lennon's love song "Oh Yoko!":** "TAPE BY HINCKLEY IS SAID TO REVEAL OBSESSION WITH SLAYING OF LENNON," *Associated Press*, May 15, 1981.

43   **Among evidence considered by the jury:** "EXPERTS IN HINCKLEY TRIAL CITE POEMS AND PUZZLINGS OF TROUBLED MIND," *New York Times*, May 31, 1982.

43   **Hinckley's meteoric infamy had produced a copycat case:** "Man, 22, Is Arrested in Manhattan for Threatening the President's Life," *New York Times*, Apr. 8, 1981; and "Tests Set for Man Charged in Threat," *New York Times*, Apr. 9, 1981. The account of the perpetrator stalking Jodie Foster at her Yale theater performance is from contemporaneous news reports as well as Foster's personal essay, "Why Me?" *Esquire*, Dec. 11, 1982.

44   **"I wanted to kill about forty people":** "High School Senior Kills to Gain Attention," United Press International, Nov. 14, 1966; "Boy Kills Five to Make

Himself Well Known," UPI, Nov. 14, 1966; and "Robert Benjamin Smith: An Analysis," research by school shootings expert Peter Langman. For more on mass shooters seeking to surpass predecessors' body counts: "How Media Emphasis on Body Counts Could Motivate the Next Mass Shooter," *Mother Jones*, Nov. 17, 2017.

44   **"His acts and their consequences have become his masters":** From *The Sane Society* (Holt, Rinehart & Winston, 1955), via Fromm-Online.org.

44   **set to nearly double in size to three thousand agents:** "Secret Service Changes Amid Danger Signals," United Press International, Dec. 7, 1981; and John Simpson obituary, *Washington Post*, Feb. 15, 2017.

44   **connect with the new Secret Service director:** Author interviews with Fein; John Simpson obituary; archival C-Span footage of Simpson giving a talk at the White House, Oct. 21, 1982; and Carol Leonnig, *Zero Fail: The Rise and Fall of the Secret Service*, Random House, 2021.

45   **the split-second valor of the agents:** Timeline of the Reagan shooting, "Command and Control," *Dallas Morning News*. The head trauma surgeon who treated Reagan recalled that the president "was close to dying": "Saving the President," *GW Today*, June 30, 2010.

47   **Hopper had testified:** "Psychiatrist States He Never Saw Signs of Mental Illness in Hinckley," *New York Times*, May 11, 1982; and "Hinckley's Psychiatrist Sued in Reagan Attack," *New York Times*, Mar. 19, 1983.

47   **"mental dysfunction" in a possible killer:** From the Feb. 1984 IOM committee report, "Research and Training for the Secret Service."

48   **Fein was aghast at the situation:** Author interviews with Fein. These kinds of flaws that he and Frazier discovered in the Secret Service case files in the early 1980s are also referenced in the Feb. 1984 IOM committee report, albeit with considerable understatement: "Agents should develop the ability to evaluate critically the reports of mental health professionals, some of which may be based on inadequate evaluations and therefore should be discounted accordingly."

48   **The McLean team's research had emphasized:** Author interviews with Fein. The concepts here are also detailed by Shervert Frazier in "On Interviewing Potentially Dangerous Persons," another component of the research presented at the IOM conference, published in December 1981. Involvement of agents in stewarding subjects' care is further detailed in the February 1984 IOM report, "Research and Training for the Secret Service."

49   **His beloved Dottie:** As referenced in Blackmun's personal letters, Harry Blackmun Papers, Box 1454, folders 8–10, US Library of Congress.

50   **"There was a room upstairs at the Court":** Former Blackmun law clerk Bill McDaniel, interviewed on NPR's *All Things Considered*, Mar. 5, 2004.

50   **The FBI urged local authorities . . . most likely "accidental":** "Shot Fired Through Blackmun's Window," *Washington Post*, Mar. 5, 1985; "Bullet That Hit Blackmun Home Seen by Police as a Random Shot," *New York Times*, Mar. 7, 1985; "Two Supreme Court Justices, Senator Get Death Threats," United Press International, Mar. 5, 1985; and Linda Greenhouse, *Becoming*

Justice Blackmun: Harry Blackmun's Supreme Court Journey (Times Books, 2005).

50 **"We are fine and shall carry on as usual":** Blackmun's personal letters to friends and colleagues regarding the shooting, from Harry Blackmun Papers, Box 1454, folders 8–10, US Library of Congress.

51 **Vossekuil had begun his Secret Service career:** Author interviews with Vossekuil.

51 **the Secret Service faced four serious threat cases:** Author interviews with Fein and Vossekuil.

53 **He aimed to review everything written on assassination:** Author interviews with Fein; and Robert Fein and Bryan Vossekuil, "Assassination in the United States," *Journal of Forensic Sciences* 4, no. 2 (Mar. 1999).

54 **eighty-three offenders going back to 1949:** The earliest case, from 1949, involved a female perpetrator, a delusional woman named Ruth Ann Steinhagen, who stalked and shot Major League Baseball player Eddie Waitkus. That event was part of the inspiration for Bernard Malamud's debut 1952 novel *The Natural*, adapted for a hit Hollywood film in 1984.

55 **an otherwise extremely rare occurrence:** Only three federal judges were assassinated in the twentieth century. For details, see: Frederick S. Calhoun, *Hunters and Howlers: Threats and Violence against Federal Judicial Officials in the United States, 1789–1993* (US Marshals Service/US Department of Justice, Feb. 1998).

55 **for a meeting at the Supreme Court:** Author interviews with Fein and Vossekuil; additional details here are from Blackmun's video interviews in the Justice Harry A. Blackmun Oral History Project, and Harry A. Blackmun Papers, both at the Library of Congress; and from Greenhouse, *Becoming Justice Blackmun*.

56 **No Supreme Court Justice in the twentieth century:** Supreme Court press officer cited in "Shot Fired Through Window of Blackmun Home," *New York Times*, Mar. 5, 1985.

56 **When they arrived, they told Mark Chapman:** Author interviews with Fein and Vossekuil.

57 **turned up in a third of the eighty-three perpetrators:** "Preventing Assassination—a Monograph: Secret Service Exceptional Case Study Project," US Department of Justice/National Institute of Justice, May 1997. This groundbreaking research is known in the field simply as the Exceptional Case Study Project, ECSP for short.

58 **"I got a letter from Robert Bardo":** Author interviews with Fein and Vossekuil; and ECSP.

CHAPTER 4: THE PATHWAY TO VIOLENCE

59 **The Federal Bureau of Investigation had done threat assessment work:** "The School Shooter: A Threat Assessment Perspective," US Department of Justice/FBI, Jan. 2000; "Criminal Profiling Research on Homicide," DOJ/OJP, 1985; and *Mindhunter*, a 1995 memoir by former FBI special agent

John Douglas about the FBI's Behavioral Science Unit and its pursuit of serial killers.

59   **worked out of an old converted basement boiler room:** Author interviews with William Zimmerman, a founding detective of the US Capitol Police threat assessment unit.

60   **a rash of activity included women in four separate cases:** Author interview with John Lane, retired LAPD detective and a founder of the LAPD Threat Management Unit. The spate of four stalking-murder cases was further detailed in a co-presentation by Lane and retired U.S. Congressman Ed Royce, in August 2015. Additional data and narratives on stalking in Los Angeles from "The RECON Typology of Stalking," *Journal of Forensic Sciences*, Jan. 2006; and "Fear Factor," *Los Angeles Magazine*, Nov. 20, 2008.

62   **Bardo fired a single shot from a .357 Magnum:** Voluminous material is available on Robert Bardo's murder of Rebecca Schaeffer, with no shortage of conflicting details. My account of Bardo's and Schaeffer's backgrounds, and my reconstruction of the murder, are drawn from court documents, forensic reports, and interviews I conducted with experts familiar with the case, as well as from more than two dozen other sources, including news articles, books, and video documentaries. I included what I determined to be the most credible and well-corroborated details, bolstered in particular by my interviews with Robert Fein (who interviewed and studied Bardo for the ECSP) and with a senior FBI special agent from the Behavioral Analysis Unit, to build a thorough description of the case through the lens of behavioral threat assessment. Select source material includes: the Exceptional Case Study Project; *The People of the State of California vs. Robert John Bardo*, California Supreme Court—Petition for Review #S041806 (filed Aug. 30, 1994); "The Legal Perspective on Stalking," by Los Angeles prosecutor Rhonda Saunders, from *The Psychology of Stalking: Clinical and Forensic Perspectives*, (Elsevier/Academic Press, 1998); and more than a dozen contemporaneous news and investigative reports from the *Los Angeles Times*, the *Oregonian*, *U.S. News & World Report*, and other media publications.

62   **Bardo later claimed that he felt Schaeffer had turned "callous":** "Psychiatrist: Bardo Interested in Other Stalkers," United Press International, Oct. 9, 1991; and "Suspect on Tape Tells of Actress's Last Words," *Los Angeles Times*, Oct. 22, 1991.

62   **he recounted contradictory details:** Beyond Bardo's unreliability as the sole surviving witness, Los Angeles prosecutor Marcia Clark challenged Dr. Dietz's acceptance of Bardo's account as credulous: "Fan Convicted of Murder in Actress' Slaying," *Los Angeles Times*, Oct. 30, 1991. The 1994 Petition for Review from the state of California also contains substantial discussion of contradictory details in Bardo's descriptions of the events.

63   **"The entertainment community was up in arms":** Author interview with, and presentation by, John Lane.

63   **"There really is no way you can make it a crime":** "Stalking in L.A.," *New Yorker*; Feb. 24, 1997.

64 **"thirty calls to get through the next time":** Additional details about the early history and further operations of the LAPD TMU are from my interviews with Lane and a subsequent leader of the unit, Jeff Dunn, as well as a report from Dunn: "Operations of the LAPD's Threat Management Unit."

64 **several women in neighboring Orange County:** "Ex-Boyfriend Jailed Under 'Stalking Law,'" *Los Angeles Times*, June 10, 1991; and "Stalking History," research document provided by the Los Angeles district attorney to the California Senate Committee on Judiciary for bill analysis hearing, June 22, 1993.

64 **"Once a victim is attacked physically, then we can act":** Former Rep. Ed Royce, in co-presentation with Lane, Aug. 2015.

65 **sensational coverage of the phenomenon:** Myriad tabloid-style examples exist from that era; the trend was also noted in "Domestic Violence, Stalking, and Anti-Stalking Legislation," a research report from the National Institute of Justice published in April 1996.

66 **the victims' own current or former intimate partners:** "The Dangerous Nature of Intimate Relationship Stalking: Threats, Violence, and Associated Risk Factors," *Behavioral Science and the Law* 17 (1999): 269–83; and "The RECON Typology of Stalking."

66-67 **Ten people were convicted . . . but prosecutions under stalking statutes remained rare:** California Assembly Committee on Public Safety, bill analysis for AB 1178 (Apr. 1993 hearing); "The Criminal Justice System Response to Intimate Partner Stalking," *Journal of Family Violence*, Feb. 2020; "A Statewide Study of Stalking and Its Criminal Justice Response," National Institute of Justice, Sept. 2009; and "The Defenders," *People*, Oct. 19, 1998. The difficulty of investigating and prosecuting stalking crimes is further detailed in "Stalking Laws and Implementation Practices," Institute of Law and Justice/National Institute of Justice, Sept. 16, 2002.

67 **By 1996, all fifty states:** "Clinton Signs O.C.-Born Bill Outlawing Stalking," *Los Angeles Times*, Sept. 21, 1996

67 **face-to-face with Robert Bardo:** This account is from my interviews with Fein and includes some details also contained in the ECSP.

69 **took a plea deal:** "Actress' Bright Success Collided with Obsession," *Los Angeles Times*, July 23, 1989.

69 **Bardo gave a letter to an older sister:** Los Angeles Superior Court testimony from Arleen Wiedrich, as reported in the *Oregonian*, "Bardo's Sister Sensed Trouble Before Actress Was Shot," Sept. 28, 1991; also detailed in the 1994 California Petition for Review.

70 **a Hollywood "screen whore":** Contents of Bardo's letter to his sister and details of his diary writings and unsent letters were described by LA prosecutor Marcia Clark during Bardo's trial, as reported by various news outlets, and are detailed in Saunders's "The Legal Perspective on Stalking."

70 **Numerous dangerous stalkers:** From my interviews with multiple threat assessment experts; examples of this type of grievance have marked other cases

with communicated threats, such as "If I can't have you, no one can" and "I'm going to kill both of us and take us both to hell." From "Stalking Their Prey," *Los Angeles Times*, Nov. 12, 1996.

70   **Bardo had communicated homicidal and suicidal thoughts:** "In the Mind of a Stalker," *U.S. News & World Report*, Feb. 17, 1992.

70   **The police who captured Bardo in Tucson:** "Police Directed to Evidence in Actress' Death," *Los Angeles Times*, July 21, 1989.

70   **"I was fumbling around":** "Suspect on Tape Tells of Actress's Last Words," *Los Angeles Times*, Oct. 22, 1991.

72   **"That's where I got the idea to hire a private investigator":** Audio segment from Bardo interview with Dr. Park Dietz.

72   **"I'd have done to her what Arthur Jackson did to Theresa Saldana":** "Psychiatrist: Bardo Interested in Other Stalkers," United Press International, Oct. 9, 1991; and ECSP, ch. 6, p. 36.

73   **"historical deed, to gain your respect and love":** "Hinckley's Communications with Jodie Foster," trial archive of Professor Douglas Linder, University of Missouri–Kansas City School of Law.

74   **"going postal":** Origin and use of the term is contextualized in a monograph from the FBI's National Center for the Analysis of Violent Crime, "Workplace Violence," published in 2003; also as described in "Violence at Work Tied to Loss of Esteem," *St. Petersburg Times*, Dec. 17, 1993.

74   **Before developing the truck-bombing plan:** "McVeigh Considered Assassination of Reno, Other Officials," *Fox News*, Apr. 27, 2001.

75   **"targeted violence":** "Threat Assessment: An Approach to Prevent Targeted Violence," National Institute of Justice, July 1995.

76   **"I decided I was going to dress up like a law enforcement person":** Author interviews with Fein and Vossekuil; the ECSP; and "Mind of the Assassin," *60 Minutes II*, Mar. 14, 2000.

77-78 **instigated by the mail bombing assassination:** *Hunters and Howlers*. "This book was born of death," Calhoun wrote, "and I began to ask why only one federal judge had been killed between 1789 and 1979."

79   **a phenomenon known as suicide by cop:** Robert Fein and Bryan Vossekuil, *Protective Intelligence & Threat Assessment Investigations: A Guide for State and Local Law Enforcement Officials*, US Department of Justice, Jan. 2000.

79   **how often a desire for notoriety kept turning up:** Author interviews with Fein and Vossekuil; and "Assassination in the United States," *Journal of Forensic Sciences* 4, no. 2 (Mar. 1999). In another case they examined from that era that remains unknown to the public, a young man from Florida who pursued a plan to shoot Reagan had sent a letter to Lee Harvey Oswald's widow, Marina, hoping to learn more from her about the experience of the JFK assassination.

79   **getting his name "permanently in history":** Author interviews with Fein and Vossekuil. Some details of this threat case have not previously been reported; others were included in "Fame Through Assassination: A Secret Service Study," *Morning Edition*, National Public Radio, Jan. 14, 2011.

81   **viewed on live television by upward of ninety-five million people:** "25

Years Ago Today, America Stopped to Watch the Cops Chase O.J. in a White Ford Bronco," CNN, June 17, 2019.

81 **He had thus made it known through prison associates:** The account of the interview with Sirhan Sirhan, and the stir caused by Manson at Corcoran prison, are from my interviews with Fein.

81 **a swirl of epic Kennedy-worthy conspiracy theories:** Much ink, unsurprisingly, has been spilled about these; see *Confessions of a Guerrilla Writer*, a memoir by journalist Dan Moldea, who wrote an in-depth investigation of the Sirhan case, *The Killing of Robert F. Kennedy* (W. W. Norton, 1995). A sampling of news stories referring to the theories includes: "Prosecutors Say Too Late to Reopen Robert Kennedy Case," Reuters, May 7, 2011; and "The Assassination of Bobby Kennedy: Was Sirhan Sirhan Hypnotized to Be the Fall Guy?" *Washington Post*, June 4, 2018.

82 **"with twenty years of malice aforethought":** "Sirhan Sirhan: Lawyers for RFK Assassin Allege New Forensic Evidence," Associated Press, Nov. 29, 2011. Moldea, in his memoir, reported that by the time of his first jailhouse interview with Sirhan at Corcoran state prison in 1992, Sirhan had already claimed no memory of the shooting.

82 **Sirhan was another perpetrator who had considered multiple targets:** Author interviews with Fein; and "Assassination in the United States."

82 **"a part of him that wasn't going to lie":** Intriguingly, an earlier 1994 jailhouse interview with Sirhan by Moldea—who had set out with his book to prove a conspiracy theory behind RFK's assassination but ended up concluding that Sirhan acted alone—strongly supports Fein's analysis of Sirhan. From Moldea's memoir:

"Were you a participant in a conspiracy?" I asked.

Sirhan replied, "Do you think I would conceal anything about someone else's involvement and face the gas chamber in the most literal sense? I have no knowledge of a conspiracy."

"But, yes or no, were you part of a conspiracy, Sirhan?"

"I wish there had been a conspiracy. It would have unraveled before now."

"Then, why do you even talk about the possibility of being mind-controlled?"

"My defense attorneys developed the idea of *The Manchurian Candidate* theory."

"Then, once again, why don't you just accept responsibility for this crime?"

"If I was to accept responsibility for this crime, it would be a hell of a burden to live with—having taken a human life without knowing it."

"Then you are saying that you are willing to take responsibility, but you have no memory of committing the crime?"

"It's not in my mind, but I'm not denying it. I must have been there, but I can't reconstruct it mentally."

83 **wanted to seek a retrial:** "Sirhan Sirhan: Lawyers for RFK Assassin Allege New Forensic Evidence," Associated Press, Nov. 29, 2011.

83   **to gain a level of attention and status he so desperately craved:** Author interviews with Fein; and "Assassination in the United States."

83   **"He was my hero . . . a betrayal":** Video of Sirhan interview with Frost, *Inside Edition*, 1989.

84   **a city electrician in Los Angeles who was angry:** "City Worker Held After 4 Supervisors Are Slain," *Los Angeles Times*, July 20, 1995.

84   **upward of two hundred threat cases annually:** Author interview with LAPD TMU's Jeff Dunn.

85   **Rugala and his colleagues:** Author interviews with Rugala.

86   **"I just bought an AK-47":** Author interviews with Rugala. Additional context on the FBI approach discussed can be found in *Workplace Violence: Issues in Response*, eds. Eugene Rugala and Arnold R. Isaacs (DOJ/FBI, 2002). Notably, the type of weapon from the case, an AK-47, had been used in a 1989 mass shooting in Stockton, California, in which the assailant had killed five schoolchildren and wounded thirty other people: "Weapon Used by Deranged Man Is Easy to Buy," *New York Times*, Jan. 19, 1989.

87   **lethal violence of any kind constituted just 1 percent:** *Workplace Violence: Issues in Response*; further perspective here from my interviews with Rugala.

CHAPTER 5: THE KIDS AREN'T ALRIGHT

89   **Beginning just before noon Colorado time:** My account of the Columbine mass shooting in this chapter draws from my interviews with threat assessment leaders in Colorado, at the FBI and elsewhere, as well as from an array of research documents, news articles, archival TV news footage, and books, including the definitive volume, *Columbine*, by Dave Cullen (Twelve Books, 2009).

90   **"We don't know yet all the hows or whys of this tragedy":** Archival video of Clinton's remarks from the White House.

91   **Payback for bullying . . . they had killed indiscriminately:** Author interviews with threat assessment leaders; "The Search for Truth at Columbine," report from Peter Langman (SchoolShooters.info, 2008/2014); and Cullen, *Columbine*. An illustrative example of the general media atmosphere and framing in the initial aftermath of the attack can be found in "Shooter Pair Mixed Fantasy, Reality," *Washington Post*, Apr. 22, 1999.

91   **Clinton White House had begun in the immediate hours after the rampage . . . more SROs:** "Policy Response to School Shootings"; White House memo from Bruce Reed and Jose Cerda III to Bill Clinton, April 20, 1999, from the Clinton Presidential Library Archives.

92   **atop the list of the gravest possible crimes:** From a survey of police chiefs nationally, cited in Robert Fein and Bryan Vossekuil, "Assassination in the United States."

93   **Riley accepted the offer to collaborate:** Author interviews with Modzeleski.

93   **the FBI published its dubious offender profile:** Stephen R. Band and Joseph A. Harpold, "School Violence: Lessons Learned," *FBI Law Enforcement Bulletin* 68 (Sept. 1999): 9–16.

94 shouted, "I'm crazy, I'm crazy!": William P. Heck, "The School Shooter: One Community's Experience," *FBI Law Enforcement Bulletin*, Sept. 2001; "Boy Shoots 5 Schoolmates in Oklahoma," *New York Times*, Dec. 7, 1999; "Shy, Sweet, and Nearly Deadly," *Boston Globe*, Dec. 14, 1999; "At 13, He Shot Five Fellow Students at Fort Gibson Middle School," *Tulsa World*, Mar. 30, 2005.

95 The FBI published a "four-pronged" model: "The School Shooter: A Threat Assessment Perspective," US Justice Department/FBI, Jan. 2000.

95 "leakage," whereby individuals reveal clues: Roger Depue, *Between Good and Evil* (Grand Central, 2005); and FBI "School Shooter" monograph. The FBI's Behavioral Science Unit was the predecessor to its Behavioral Analysis Unit.

97 the Safe School Initiative: My further account of the origin and development of the Safe School Initiative, its findings, and details from Evan Ramsey's and other school shooter cases is primarily from my interviews with Fein, Vossekuil, and Randazzo, and a multimedia presentation by Vossekuil. Other source materials include: "Safe School Initiative: An Interim Report," Oct. 2000; "The Final Report and Findings of the Safe School Initiative," July 2004; and media accounts, including: "Mind of the Assassin," *60 Minutes II*, Mar. 14, 2000; "Rage: A Look at a Teen Killer," *60 Minutes II*, Aug. 17, 1999; and an excellent series on the SSI by journalist Bill Dedman for the *Chicago Sun-Times*, published in October 2000.

98 White males would remain the most common: Data on nonwhite and female perpetrators from research by psychologist and school shootings expert Peter Langman.

100 no indications of psychopathy or psychosis: Peter Langman, "Rampage School Shooters: A Typology," *Aggression and Violent Behavior* 14, no. 1 (Feb. 2009): 79–86.

100 Ramsey had also left behind two notes: "Two Notes by Evan Ramsey," documented by Peter Langman on his site, SchoolShooters.info.

101 by definition, remorse can exist only *after* a shooting: "Evaluating Risk for Targeted Violence in Schools," *Psychology in the Schools* 38, no. 2 (Mar. 2001): 157–72.

102 "mainstream" social lives ... depression and suicidality: "The Final Report and Findings of the Safe School Initiative," US Secret Service and US Department of Education, July 2004.

103 "He said he could probably get away with it": Details of the Loukaitis case here are primarily from reporter Bill Dedman's Oct. 2000 series in the *Chicago Sun-Times*.

103 an attack at a Southern California high school: "Community Mourns Lives Lost in School Shooting," KGTV San Diego, Mar. 7, 2001; and "Rage: A Look at a Teen Killer."

104 "if kids snap, it lets us off the hook": "Examining the Psyche of an Adolescent Killer," *Chicago Sun-Times*, Oct. 15, 2000; and author interview with Vossekuil.

105   **"Connection through human relationships"**: "Threat Assessment in Schools: A Guide to Managing Threatening Situations and to Creating Safe School Climates," US Secret Service and US Department of Education, July 2004.

CHAPTER 6: THE PROGRAM

110   **"school shootings season"**: From my interviews with John Van Dreal and other threat assessment leaders; and my own related research on the copycat effect from "How Columbine Spawned Dozens of Copycats," *Mother Jones*, Oct. 5, 2015.

110   **the two took me up on my entreaties to shadow them**: Unless otherwise noted, my accounts in chapters 6 and 7 of the Salem-Keizer threat assessment system, from its history and development to operations observed in real time, are based on my extensive reporting trips to Salem in 2019; my series of interviews with Van Dreal, McCarthy, numerous of their STAT colleagues, and Salem-Keizer administrators; case files and other supporting documentation provided to me; and a book detailing the Salem-Keizer system: John Van Dreal, *Assessing Student Threats* (Rowman & Littlefield, 2017).

113   **55 cases each year . . . elevated to the STAT experts**: From my interviews with McCarthy and Van Dreal, and documentation they provided to me with data and analysis of three years' worth of cases, 2017–2020.

113   **a seventeen-year-old Northeast High School junior named Brandon**: Brandon is not the case subject's real name. As noted in the book's introduction, I have altered or omitted some identifying details to protect the privacy and legal rights of those involved.

114   **signs of personal deterioration, violent ideation, and attack planning**: Details on training for SROs serving on the STAT are from my interviews with Van Dreal and Clem Spenner, a former police officer on the team.

114   **"Maybe I'll just shoot up the school instead"**: This and other subjects' quotes throughout the narratives are from confidential threat-assessment case files.

116   **many school shooters used guns obtained from their homes**: There are various studies on this dating back to the time of the Safe School Initiative; recently reaffirmed in "Averting Targeted School Violence," a report from the US Secret Service's National Threat Assessment Center, Mar. 2021.

118   **the Menninger Triad**: Author interviews with Van Dreal and as detailed in his book, *Assessing Student Threats*.

121   **matters of school safety or relevant current events**: From my interviews with Van Dreal and McCarthy; also described in a 2018 internal summary document authored by Van Dreal: "Salem-Keizer School District's Threat Assessment System."

122   **Lowe had gone looking for the young man**: From reporting in the *Oregonian*, May 17, May 28, Nov. 8, and Nov. 9, 2019; publicly released school surveillance footage, via CBS/KOIN 6; and an interview with Granados-Diaz's defense attorney by the *Oregonian*, May 29, 2019.

122 **the thin line between suicidal and homicidal intent:** From my interviews with Fein, threat assessment and police psychology expert John Nicoletti, and a research presentation by stalking expert Lisa Warren.

123 **alongside rising suicide rates nationally:** "More Young People Are Dying by Suicide, and Experts Aren't Sure Why," *USAToday*, Sept. 11, 2020: "The rate of suicide among those aged 10 to 24 increased nearly 60% between 2007 and 2018, according to a report released Friday by the Centers for Disease Control and Prevention. The rise occurred in most states, with 42 experiencing significant increases." See also, the CDC report: "State Suicide Rates Among Adolescents and Young Adults Aged 10–24: United States, 2000–2018," from *National Vital Statistics Report* 69, no. 11 (Sept. 11, 2020).

123 **Oregon in particular was experiencing a rise in suicides:** Data from the Oregon Health Authority; "High School Student Takes Own Life on Campus; Suicide Up Dramatically Statewide," KATU News, Dec. 10, 2018; "Salem-Keizer Suffers Alarming Number of Suicides, Makes Preventative Changes," KATU News, Feb. 28, 2019; and "Parkrose High Student Who Brought Gun to School, Aimed at Self, Pulled the Trigger—but It Didn't Fire," *Oregonian*, Nov. 8, 2019.

125 **Lowe jumped into action and wrested it away:** Details from police reports and interviews in "Parkrose High Student Who Brought Gun to School," *Oregonian*, Nov. 8, 2019.

125 **mental health treatment and three years of probation:** "Former Parkrose High Student Who Brought Shotgun To School Pleads Guilty," Oregon Public Broadcasting, Oct. 10, 2019.

125 **According to his defense attorney's statements:** From the sentencing hearing on Oct. 10, 2019, as reported by Oregon Public Broadcasting: "The morning of May 17, he consumed alcohol. He decided he would kill himself at school so his family wouldn't find his body at home, [his attorney] Thayne said. Just before noon, Granados-Diaz entered Parkrose High School in Northeast Portland carrying a shotgun, according to police. Thayne said Granados-Diaz carried the gun into a classroom, intending to kill himself in a location where his body would be found quickly."

125 **"The last red pill, 5/17/19, just for me":** Oregon Public Broadcasting, Oct. 10, 2019; and *Oregonian*, Nov. 8, 2019.

126 **The subculture of sexually insecure and aggrieved men:** "'PUAhate' and 'ForeverAlone': Inside Elliot Rodger's Online Life," *Guardian*, May 30, 2014; and "Inside the 'Manosphere' That Inspired Santa Barbara Shooter Elliot Rodger," *Washington Post*, May 27, 2014.

126 **associated with . . . the virulent misogyny of incels:** "Armed and Misogynist: How Toxic Masculinity Fuels Mass Shootings," *Mother Jones*, May 2019.

126 **strangulation attempts correlate with increased danger:** From interviews with and various research presentations by threat assessment experts.

127 **widespread belief that the era of school shootings dawned with Columbine:** There are many examples of reporting and commentary framing the history of school shootings this way. A social media post from *CBS Evening*

News after a school shooting in May 2019, for example, referred to Columbine as "the site of the first mass school shooting 20 years ago" (author's files). See also a report on how Columbine permanently eclipsed a major school shooting that preceded it: "20 Years Later, Jonesboro Shooting Survivors Conflicted Over Parkland," National Public Radio, Mar. 23, 2018.

128 **Kipland Kinkel had gone into Thurston High School:** "8 Years Later: Thurston and Kinkel Revisited," *Daily Emerald*, Oct. 1, 2006; "Thurston 20 Years Later," *Oregonian*, May 20, 2018; and additional details from, "The Killer at Thurston High," *Frontline*, Jan. 18, 2000.

128 **a school shootings "epidemic":** From my interviews with Van Dreal; also described in Cullen's *Columbine* and other accounts of the late 1990s school shootings.

129 **a pair of middle school boys in Jonesboro, Arkansas:** Peter Langman, *School Shooters: Understanding High School, College, and Adult Perpetrators* (Rowman & Littlefield, 2015). Additional details on the Jonesboro case are from "20 Years Later, Jonesboro Shooting Survivors"; and an account from survivor Mary Hollis Inboden, "20 Years After the Shooting on the Playground," *New York Times*, Mar. 23, 2018.

129 **testified for the defense that he was psychotic:** "The Killer at Thurston High," and summary and excerpts of mental health experts' testimony, published online by *Frontline*.

129 **Hicks had met with Kinkel and his mother for therapy nine times:** These therapy sessions were between January and June of 1997, as reported in "The Killer at Thurston High."

130 **"God damn these VOICES inside my head":** "The Killer at Thurston High."

130 **so-called manifestos and other "legacy tokens":** From my interviews with FBI special agent Andre Simons and research authored by Simons and his colleagues in the Behavioral Analysis Unit.

130 **told two peers he thought the carnage was "cool":** From Joseph A. Lieberman, *School Shootings: What Every Parent and Educator Should Know* (Citadel Press, 2008); also cited by Peter Langman in *School Shooters*. Additional details here are from "The Killer at Thurston High" and related research published online.

130 **one instance when he pointed a gun at a peer:** From an investigative document I obtained regarding the Thurston case; the behavior's relevance, from my interviews with Russell Palarea and other threat assessment leaders.

131 **a problem of "information silos":** Author interviews with Gene Deisinger and other threat assessment leaders.

132 **The probability of a student homicide at a school:** Van Dreal, *Assessing Student Threats*.

132 **MacDonald Triad was marginally useful at best:** The insider joke was recounted to me by a veteran threat assessment practitioner; limitations of the tool are discussed in: "Not the Sum of Its Parts: A Critical Review of the MacDonald Triad," *Trauma, Violence, & Abuse*, April 2018.

134 **powerful emotional blind spot in parents:** Published accounts about and from Sue Klebold, and about Nancy Lanza, the mothers of Columbine and Sandy Hook perpetrators, respectively, are instructive on this point.

135 **state legislation about to pass in July 1999:** Oregon HB 3444, in effect from Oct. 1999.

135 **needed to build a more efficient approach:** Author interviews with Van Dreal.

136 **Keller remained connected in criminal justice circles:** Author interviews with Van Dreal.

CHAPTER 7: A ROAD LESS TRAVELED

139 **caseload . . . was as large and active as ever:** Author interviews with McCarthy and Van Dreal, and caseload data and analysis provided by McCarthy.

146 **the outfit worn two decades earlier by shooter Dylan Klebold:** Trevor's outfit as described to me by McCarthy and detailed in the case file; Klebold's 1999 attire detailed in *Columbine*, by Dave Cullen.

148 **"We had an arsonist working in the art department":** "How We Made One Flew Over the Cuckoo's Nest," *Guardian*, Apr. 11, 2017.

150 **"Most . . . on the spectrum of ASD are neither violent nor criminal":** Stephen G. White et al., "Autism Spectrum Disorder and Violence: Threat Assessment Issues," *Journal of Threat Assessment and Management* 4, no. 3 (Sept. 2017): 144–63. White, Meloy, Mohandie and Kienlen document research on ASD and violence, and examine how ASD may figure into complex comorbid afflictions and conditions in the case of Lanza, that of mass shooter Elliot Rodger, and others.

154 **Federal privacy laws would later loosen:** Author interviews with Van Dreal and Salem-Keizer general counsel Paul Dakopolos.

155 **Reform of the state's youth crime laws in 2019:** "Oregon Gov. Kate Brown Signs Major Juvenile Sentencing Reform Bill," Oregon Public Broadcasting, July 29, 2021.

155 **In response to a 2005 survey:** Summarized in a document provided to me by Van Dreal.

156 **What Modzeleski found:** From the audit report, provided to me by Van Dreal.

156 **Research from a similar behavioral threat assessment program:** "Racial/Ethnic Parity in Disciplinary Consequences Using Student Threat Assessment," *School Psychology Review*, volume 47, issue 2, 183–195 (June 2018).

158 **the STAT's history with a singular case:** The narrative account of the Erik Ayala case in this chapter further builds on my reporting that first appeared in "Inside the Race to Stop the Next Mass Shooter," *Mother Jones*, Oct. 2015.

161 **to establish "trip wires":** Author interviews with Russell Palarea, Mario Scalora, retired FBI special agent Eugene Rugala, and other threat assessment leaders.

162 **cranked up production and gave away high-capacity ammunition devices:** "Assault Weapons Ban Ends Quietly," *Los Angeles Times*, Sept. 10, 2004.

CHAPTER 8: VITAL CONNECTIONS

163 **Kristina Anderson felt a ripple of panic:** My account of Anderson's experience on April 16, 2007, draws on my extensive interviews with her and various
supporting documentation she provided to me, as well as from presentations of
her story she gave that I attended over a period of several years at conferences
and threat assessment trainings. Memory is well understood to be complicated for survivors of trauma, especially as an event fades further into the
past. To ensure accuracy, I also reviewed video of one of Anderson's earliest
presentations of her story, given by her the year after she graduated from Virginia Tech, in 2010. I also reviewed accounts from other survivors and eye-
witnesses and corroborated details using law enforcement reports, including a
non-public Virginia Tech PD post-case analysis, as well as the state-mandated
Virginia Tech Review Panel investigation published in August 2007, and various media reports.

165 **bloody footprints leading away from room 4040:** Crime scene photo from
Virginia Tech PD post-case analysis, obtained by author.

165 **Cho had no known connection to Hilscher:** "Mass Shootings at Virginia
Tech: Report of the Review Panel," Aug. 2007, p. 77.

165 **testing his resolve and ability to kill:** Author interview with Reid Meloy,
and research and presentations by him. The "novel aggression" theory is also
described in "Mass Shootings at Virginia Tech: Addendum to the Report of
the Review Panel," Nov. 2009, p. 86.

166 **warning that opening it would set off a bomb:** "Addendum to the Report,"
p. 100-A.

167 **Officers attempted to blast through an entrance:** From the Virginia Tech
PD post-case analysis obtained by author.

169 **Twenty-seven students and five faculty members:** Casualty and forensic details are from "Report of the Review Panel," pp. 89–100.

172 **fight-or-flight response in people varies:** Amanda Ripley, *The Unthinkable:
Who Survives When Disaster Strikes—and Why* (Crown, 2008).

174 **"No one knew all the information":** "Addendum to the Report," p. 2.

175 **the materials from Cho conveyed "a grandiose fantasy":** "Addendum to
the Report," p. 86. Additional forensic details and analysis are from "The
Concept of Identification in Threat Assessment," *Behavioral Sciences and the
Law* 33, no. 2–3 (Feb. 2015).

175 **details of his evaluation and treatment remained confidential:** "Addendum to the Report," pp. 2, 23–25.

176 **In the final weeks before the mass shooting:** From multiple sources, including the VTRP official report and addendum; "The Concept of Identification";
the Virginia Tech PD post-case analysis; and VTRP archival documents contained at the Library of Virginia in Richmond.

176 **key investigative evidence only in the final days:** Author interview with a
source knowledgeable about the Review Panel's process and work.

177 **"The Review Panel wanted to avoid obfuscating":** "Addendum to the Report," p. 5.

177 **program for the Graduate Student Assembly's . . . event:** Library of Virginia, VTRP report archives, box 10, folder 1.

178 **couldn't recall the poem or whether Cho had shown up to read it:** "Cho Poem Was Entry in 2006 Virginia Tech Event," *Roanoke Times*, Aug. 29, 2007.

179 **students were "very upset" by Cho's behavior:** Document contained in the Library of Virginia archives, faculty email correspondence with Virginia Tech PD, Box 10.

179 **"Everyone's afraid of him":** "Report of the Review Panel," p. 43; and Library of Virginia, VTRP archives, correspondence contained in Box 10.

180 **his character, named Bud:** The full document is contained in the Library of Virginia, in the VTRP archives. The contours of the story—which the VTRP only became aware of shortly before publishing its report—were disclosed by news media as the report was being finalized: "Paper by Cho Exhibits Disturbing Parallels to Shootings, Sources Say," *Washington Post*, Aug. 29, 2007.

181 **"you handle violence in interesting ways":** Library of Virginia, VTRP archives, Box 7, folder 3.

CHAPTER 9: THE NEW MINDHUNTERS

183 **BAU agents . . . gained an additional priority:** Author interviews with FBI supervisory special agent Andre Simons; "Campus Attacks: Targeted Violence Affecting Institutions of Higher Education," Department of Education, FBI, and Secret Service, Apr. 2010; and Eugene Deisinger and Andre Simons, "The Mass-Casualty Incident at Virginia Tech: Ten Years Later," *Journal of Threat Assessment and Management* 3, no. 3–4 (2016).

184 **mass shootings usually were investigated and prosecuted as state offenses:** "Mass-Casualty Incident at Virginia Tech."

184 **designed a team for standout agents and analysts:** Author interviews with Simons.

185 **a new generation of "mindhunters":** The recent history and workings of the BAU threat assessment team are from my series of interviews with BAU leaders Andre Simons, Karie Gibson, and John Wyman. Additional details are from my interviews with threat assessment experts and practitioners who have worked in partnership with the FBI team, and from research reports including "Campus Attacks" and "Mass-Casualty Incident at Virginia Tech."

187 **unsolved murders had sown fear in Tampa:** I was not aware of the case at the time; authorities had just apprehended the alleged "Seminole Heights serial killer."

190- **illuminating on multiple levels for Simons and his colleagues:** After the
191 Virginia Tech massacre, the FBI threat assessment specialists had increased their focus on advancing the underlying research; the NIU-DeKalb case in 2008 was the first major post-attack investigation of that period.

191 **fatally shot five students, wounded twenty-one:** Northern Illinois University, *Report of the February 14, 2008, Shootings at Northern Illinois University* (Mar. 2010).

191 **his relationships formed a starburst pattern:** Author interview with Simons.

191 **In the final three days:** Details here, including Kazmierczak's obtaining firearms throughout 2007, are from the NIU official report; and David Vann, "Portrait of the School Shooter as a Young Man," *Esquire*, Aug. 2008.

192 **shopped for ammunition . . . played loud techno:** Details on Loughner's "cocooning" and "energy burst" are from documents provided to me by a threat assessment expert knowledgeable about the case. Details on Holmes's drug use and techno music during his attack are from investigators who were involved in the case.

192 **understood that officers were quickly bearing down on him:** Further details of the case are from my interviews with Simons; the NIU official report, pp. 198–200; and Vann, "Portrait of the School Shooter."

194 **black backpack containing two magazines and a book:** Details on the items in the backpack are from the NIU official report and a confidential source knowledgeable about the investigation.

194 **Cho had brought along the hammer:** "The Concept of Identification."

195 **Kazmierczak, too, had identified with a violent antihero:** NIU, *Report of the February 14, 2008 Shootings*, pp. 20–47.

195 **a comparison of Kazmierczak and Cho:** NIU, *Report*, Appendix B, p. 19.

195 **"obviously planned it out well":** Vann, "Portrait of the School Shooter."

197 **evolving away from a long-held concern:** Author interviews with FBI's Simons, Wyman, and Gibson.

198 **documented a record high of thirty rampage shootings:** Andre Simons, James Silver, and Sarah Craun, *A Study of Pre-Attack Behaviors of Active Shooters in the United States Between 2000 and 2013* (FBI Behavioral Analysis Unit, June 2018).

200 **"Yeah, you think you got it":** "Bardo's Sister Sensed Trouble Before Actress Was Shot," *Oregonian*, Sept. 28, 1991.

200 **strongly echoed previous research elsewhere:** "Mass Shootings: Maybe What We Need Is a Better Mental-Health Policy," *Mother Jones*, Nov. 9, 2012.

201 **nearly half of all Americans are diagnosable:** "Lifetime Prevalence and Age-of-Onset Distributions of DSM-IV Disorders in the National Comorbidity Survey," *Archives of General Psychiatry* 62, no. 6 (June 2005): 593–602: "About half of Americans will meet the criteria for a DSM-IV disorder sometime in their life."

201 **"mental illness pulls the trigger":** President Donald Trump and the National Rifle Association highlighted this theme after a pair of mass shootings in Ohio and Texas in August 2019. "Trump Responds to El Paso, Dayton with the NRA's Favorite Talking Point," *Washington Post*, Aug. 5, 2019; and "NRA 'Welcomes' Trump's Response to El Paso, Dayton Shootings," *The Hill*, Aug. 5, 2019.

CHAPTER 10: EVOLUTIONS

203   **A popular satirical news story from *The Onion*:** After the Parkland mass shooting in February 2018, the Floridian behind the piece of satire, first published in 2014, commented on social media, "When I wrote this headline, I had no idea it would be applied to the high school a mile from my house." (Author's files.)

204   **searching online beforehand for tips on posting photos:** From a law enforcement source involved in the investigation. Where not otherwise attributed to public sources, further details on the Holmes investigation draw on documents and other information I obtained from law enforcement officials and threat assessment experts familiar with the case.

204   **the smiling face of James Holmes:** ABC News special report with Diane Sawyer, July 20, 2012. The midday special broadcast was one example, with Holmes's image on the screen for the better part of two minutes and Sawyer talking about "looking into his eyes" to try to understand who he was. (Video in author's files.)

204   **"We found nothing showing it had to do with Batman":** From a presentation on the case by Brauchler at a threat assessment conference that I attended. Similar comments from Brauchler debunking the Joker story also appeared in the *Denver Post* and *Vanity Fair*.

205   **the comic villain's hair was well known by fans to be green:** The character's origin story, from *Batmania*, Feb. 1967.

205   **based on tactical calculations and body count potential:** There were multiple screens showing the film that night at the cineplex. According to law enforcement sources familiar with the case, Holmes tried several times to get tickets to a specific theater, eventually giving up because it was sold out and settling on another one. In a notebook he had kept, Holmes had also considered tactical details of the cineplex location, including its distance from a nearby police station. Holmes also surveilled the cineplex in person prior to the attack, according to documents I obtained from the investigation.

205   **didn't concern themselves with correcting the record:** Brauchler presentation; and comments in the *Denver Post*. The Joker story was first debunked publicly by Brauchler interviewed in the *Denver Post* in mid-September 2015, about a month after Holmes was sentenced (August 24–26, 2015). Aurora police chief Dan Oates also later confirmed that the story was false, cited in the *Hollywood Reporter*, Sept. 2019.

205   **"They kind of turned me into a super villain":** "The James Holmes' 'Joker' Rumor," *Denver Post*, Sept. 18, 2015.

205   **including false claims about more than one attacker:** From various examples collected in author's files.

205   **a state of disbelief:** The accounts from Aurora echo Kristina Anderson's experience at Virginia Tech in 2007, and that of survivors of the NIU-DeKalb mass shooting in 2008: "Stunned, a few students at first thought it was a prank." Northern Illinois University, *Report of the February 14, 2008, Shoot-*

ings at Northern Illinois University (Mar. 2010). Victim disbelief in Aurora was also reported in the *New York Times*, July 20, 2012.

206   **head to toe in body armor and other tactical gear:** From case evidence and law enforcement officials knowledgeable about the investigation.

206   **Kelly did not respond to media inquiries:** "The Joker Didn't Inspire the Aurora Shooter, but the Rumor Won't Go Away," *Vanity Fair*, Oct. 3, 2019.

207   **finding emulation among far more plotters:** From my interviews with the FBI's Simons and other threat assessment experts.

207   **to trap his own victims in the NIU auditorium:** From a confidential source familiar with the case; echoed by Kazmierczak's "admiration" for Cho's use of chains as described by a friend of Kazmierczak's in "Portrait of the School Shooter."

207   **A mass shooter the following year in upstate New York:** "In a Killer's Own Words," CBS Evening News, Apr. 6, 2009. Perpetrator Jiverly Wong studied the Virginia Tech shooting ahead of murdering thirteen people at an immigration center in Binghamton, New York, on April 3, 2009, noting details including Cho's chaining of the doors; from my interviews with threat assessment experts knowledgeable about the case.

207   **"Cultural scripts are now spread globally within seconds":** "The Concept of Identification."

208   **first-ever "social media murder":** There was a wave of news coverage using and discussing the new term. From my contemporaneous notes (I was among journalists who watched the events develop that day online), and my reporting for "How the Media Inspires Mass Shooters," *Mother Jones*, Oct. 6, 2015.

208   **the initial few seconds of the killing no less than seven times:** The HollywoodLife.com video is no longer available online; retained in author's files. Snippets of the snuff footage also aired on CNN, MSNBC, and other outlets that day (author's contemporaneous notes).

208   **vast new opportunity for them to feed their pathological narcissism:** Author interviews with Meloy and Simons.

208   **at least two assailants went online in real time:** "The Orlando Mass Shooter Checked Facebook for News of His Attack As He Killed," *Mother Jones*, June 17, 2016; "California Bar Shooter Posted on Social Media Shortly Before and During Massacre," *Wall Street Journal*, Nov. 9, 2018; "Live-Streaming New Zealand Gunman Said He Aimed to Disrupt U.S. Politics," *Fast Company*, Mar. 15, 2019; and 4Chan post (posted Dec. 2017; screen cap in author's files).

209   **In a cluster of three separate attacks:** "Copycat Shooters Motivated by Columbine Keep Multiplying, Our Investigation Shows," *Mother Jones*, Apr. 17, 2019.

209   **the "Columbine effect," as I called the phenomenon:** All data and related case details on this subject are drawn from a database I created, my previous reporting for *Mother Jones*, and from additional research and interviews I conducted for the book. The database is not public, for self-explanatory purposes of caution; it is built primarily on news reports and other open-source material, but also includes case material I obtained or learned about from my interviews with various threat assessment professionals. I first used the term "Columbine effect" in reporting published in fall 2015: "Inside the Race to

Stop the Next Mass Shooter," *Mother Jones*, Oct. 5, 2015

210 **several different young women from out of state:** From my interviews with John McDonald; "The Columbine Shooters, the Girls Who Love Them, and Me," *VICE*, Jan. 31, 2016.

210 **a high schooler from Utah:** From my interviews with John McDonald; some details of the case also were reported publicly by the Associated Press and other news media.

212 **do not *cause* a person to commit violence:** *Media Violence and Aggression: Science and Ideology*, SAGE Publications, Sept. 2007; and "The Truth about Video Games and Gun Violence," *Mother Jones*, June 11, 2013. See also Reid Meloy and Kris Mohandie, "Investigating the Role of Screen Violence in Specific Homicide Cases," *Journal of Forensic Sciences* 46, no. 5 (Oct. 2001). The authors note that "screen violence appears to only account for a small proportion of the explainable variance in violence risk. Screen violence alone should never be used to predict risk, but is one of a number of static and dynamic variables that contribute to violent behavior."

213 **"Don't make me show you Kurt Cobain":** Sarah Goodrum and William Woodward, *Report on the Arapahoe High School Shooting*, Center for the Study and Prevention of Violence (Jan. 2016), pp. 125–26. The perpetrator bought the shotgun on December 6, a week before he struck: "Colorado's School Shooting—Over in 80 Seconds," CNN, Dec. 15, 2013. Notably, the perpetrator's behavior may have included emulation of another kind: Columbine perpetrator Eric Harris had named his shotgun Arlene after a *Doom* character, scratching that name into the barrel before the attack and referring to it in writings and videos.

213 **"aggression immersion":** "Investigating the Role of Screen Violence."

213 **The 2011 hit song "Pumped Up Kicks":** From voicemails shared with author by Jeffco's John McDonald; Parkland case as described by Cruz's brother in news accounts; and account of twelve year-old shooter at Sparks Middle School in Nevada from Sparks PD post-case analysis report, pp. 968–74, and *Reno Gazette-Journal* coverage.

213 **video games had served as a tool of psychological "rehearsal":** Author interviews with John Van Dreal and Lieutenant Dave Okada; also noted in Van Dreal's book, *Assessing Student Threats*, p. 38.

215 **the Hollywood blockbuster *Joker* was set to open:** "Landmark Theaters Bans Costumes at '*Joker*' Screenings to Ensure Customers Feel Comfortable," *Hollywood Reporter*, Sept. 26, 2019 (reporting ahead of film opening Oct. 4, 2019). Phillips and Phoenix pressed over the violence and copycat fears: "Joaquin Phoenix Couldn't Answer the Most Obvious Question About *Joker*'s Subject Matter," *Gizmodo*, Sept. 23, 2019; and "Joaquin Phoenix Explains He Felt 'Uncomfortable' about *Joker* Mass Shootings Debate," NME.com, Nov. 14, 2019.

216 **threatened to shoot up his high school graduation ceremony:** "Averting Targeted School Violence," a report from the US Secret Service's National Threat Assessment Center, Mar. 2021.

216 **erroneous blame of a young man of Chinese background:** "Inaccuracies Zoom Along Web's Strands," *Roanoke Times*, Apr. 19, 2007; and "Online Mob Seeking VT Killer Got the Wrong Guy," MTV.com, Apr. 17, 2007.

216 **"strategic silence":** "When You See Me on the News, You'll Know Who I Am," *NiemanReports*, July 30, 2019. I was interviewed by the writer of the article, which includes my comment suggesting the alternative term "strategic diminishment."

217 **"But he will, when I speak, be nameless":** Audio of Ardern's remarks from coverage of the New Zealand mass shooting and interview of author, *All Things Considered*, National Public Radio, Mar. 20, 2019.

218 **"the very girls who represent everything I hate":** Rodger's YouTube videos and "manifesto" posted online, "My Twisted World."

218 **had hired a prostitute in a motel room three weeks before he struck:** "The Concept of Identification."

218 **emergence of dangerous incels starting from 2014:** For further context, see "Mapping the Manosphere: A Social Network Analysis of the Manosphere on Reddit," a master's thesis in security studies by Kelly C. Fitzgerald, Naval Postgraduate School, Dec. 2020: "The manosphere network is a dispersed collection of online spaces that proliferate an anti-feminist ideology that in some cases has been associated with violence. . . . This research identified a unifying anti-feminist framework and found that informal social divisions within the network faded over time, which indicates that both moderate and extreme manosphere subgroups are now sharing common online spaces."

218 **translating their online grievances into real-world violence:** Source material includes: FBI affidavit from *United States of America v. Cole Carini*, Western District of Virginia, June 5, 2020; "Mapping the Manosphere"; "'Incel' Blows Own Hand Off With Bomb Meant for 'Hot Cheerleaders,' FBI Says," Cox Media Group, June 8, 2020; and "After Toronto Attack, Online Misogynists Praise Suspect as 'New Saint,'" NBC News, Apr. 24, 2018.

219 **extensively quoted and made available in full by media:** Examples include "Isla Vista Shooting: Read Elliot Rodger's Graphic, Elaborate Attack Plan," *Los Angeles Times*, May 24, 2014; and "What a Close Read of the Isla Vista Shooter's Horrific Manifesto, 'My Twisted World,' Says about His Values—and Ours," *Quartz*, May 26, 2014.

219 **targeted women in general, or had stalked and harassed specific women:** From a database I built and my reporting in *Mother Jones*, "Armed and Misogynist: How Toxic Masculinity Fuels Mass Shootings," May–June 2019.

219 **more racially diverse than is widely perceived:** "Online Poll Results Provide New Insights into Incel Community," Anti-Defamation League, Sept. 10, 2020; and "Online Hatred of Women in the Incels.me Forum: Linguistic Analysis and Automatic Detection," *Journal of Language Aggression and Conflict*, July 8, 2019.

220 **ten "attempted or completed mass murders":** "Mapping the Manosphere," p. 35.

220 **"target dispersion":** Author interviews with Meloy, Simons, and other threat assessment experts.

220 **attacks by far-right extremists increased sharply:** "White Supremacist Attacks Have Grown Deadlier During Trump's Presidency," *Mother Jones*, Aug. 8, 2019.

222 **speeches from a manosphere figure:** Author's research files (I'm declining to specify the videos so as not to help expand their reach).

222 **"extreme overvalued beliefs":** "Extreme Overvalued Belief and the Legacy of Carl Wernicke," *Journal of the American Academy of Psychiatry and the Law*, 47, no. 2 (June 2019); "Cognitive-Affective Drivers of Fixation in Threat Assessment," *Behavioral Sciences & the Law*, Aug. 2020; "DSM-V Cultural and Personality Assessment of Extreme Overvalued Beliefs," *Aggression and Violent Behavior*, Dec. 2020; and author interviews with Meloy.

222 **the lie spread by Trump:** "More Than a Dozen Accused Capitol Rioters Say Trump Incited Them," *Mother Jones*, Feb. 8, 2021; and "United by Disinformation, Trump's Supporters Share Dueling Accounts of Jan. 6 Insurrection," *Detroit Free Press*, Jan. 10, 2021.

222 **a convergence of extremist belief and misogyny:** From author's research on federal court filings, social media footage, and other data collected from January 6 criminal cases; a good resource for such data is the Capitol Hill Siege database from the George Washington University Program on Extremism.

CHAPTER 11: BUTTERFLY EFFECTS

225 **Gun sales soared:** "1st-Time Gun Buyers Help Push Record U.S. Gun Sales Amid String of Mass Shootings," National Public Radio, Apr. 26, 2021; and "Sales of Guns to First-Time Owners Rise Amid COVID-19 Pandemic," NPR, July 16, 2020.

225 **conspicuously quiet in terms of high-profile public massacres:** "Shootings Never Stopped During the Pandemic," *Washington Post*, Mar. 23, 2020; "The US Saw Significant Crime Rise Across Major Cities In 2020. And It's Not Letting Up," CNN, Apr. 3, 2021; and *Mother Jones* mass shootings database.

225 **that far fewer people simply were present:** As described by various commentators in the press, and per my interviews with threat assessment experts; and "In a Year of Pain, One Silver Lining: Fewer Mass Shootings," Associated Press, Dec. 29, 2020.

226 **motivated by far-right extremist views:** "Alleged Gunman in FedEx Shooting Browsed White Supremacist Websites, Police Say," ABC News, Apr. 20, 2021; and "FBI, IMPD final report on Indianapolis FedEx mass shooting reveals 'no racial bias,'" WTHR 13, Jul. 28, 2021.

227 **nearly four hundred million firearms in the United States:** From the global Small Arms Survey (data as of 2017): "Of the 857 million civilian-held firearms estimated in 2017, 393 million are in the United States—more than those held by civilians in the other top 25 countries combined. Even after adjusting for population, it is clear that the United States far outnumbers other

countries. The United States has 4% of the world's population, but its civilians hold almost 40% of the world's firearms." Notably, tens of millions more civilian firearms have been sold in the US since then, so the estimate is conservative. Source for gun ownership by approximately a third of Americans: "What Percentage of Americans Own Guns?" Gallup, Nov. 13, 2020.

227 **thirty-one shots in thirty seconds:** "Gunman in Giffords Shooting Sentenced to 7 Life Terms," *New York Times*, Nov. 8, 2012.

228 **a surge of interest in behavioral threat assessment:** Author interviews with Gene Deisinger, Marisa Randazzo, Russell Palarea, and other leaders in the field.

228 **at least six additional states:** "Preventing School Violence Through Threat Assessment," *Ed Note* blog, Aug. 19, 2019.

228 **pushback from civil liberties groups:** Author interviews and correspondence with Ron Schouten and Russell Palarea; "Oppose H.R. 838, the Threat Assessment, Prevention, and Safety Act of 2019 (TAPS Act)," Leadership Conference on Civil and Human Rights, Aug. 30, 2019.

229 **"I would argue that it's now the standard of care":** Author interview with Schouten.

229 **The strategy, as described by Aquil Basheer:** From a panel discussion, including author, on KQED *Forum*, Mar. 31, 2021.

230 **Modeled on domestic-violence restraining-order laws:** "Study: California's 'Red Flag' Law May Have Helped Reduce Mass Shootings," *San Jose Mercury News*, Aug. 19, 2019.

230 **Rodger's deadly rampage . . . "shy, timid, and polite":** "California sees record number of guns confiscated under 'red flag' law," *Los Angeles Times*, May 7, 2021; and "Elliot Rodger 'Welfare Check' Detailed by Sheriff's Department," *Santa Maria Times*, July 8, 2014.

230 **red flag laws spread . . . more than a third of the states:** "Boulder and Atlanta Shootings Rekindle Debate Over Red-Flag Gun Laws," *Washington Post*, Mar. 25, 2021; "Red Flag Laws: Where the Bills Stand in Each State," *The Trace*, Mar. 2018; and "Poll: Americans, Including Republicans and Gun Owners, Broadly Support Red Flag Laws," National Public Radio, Aug. 20, 2019.

230 **Preliminary research on twenty-one cases in California:** "Extreme Risk Protection Orders Intended to Prevent Mass Shootings," *Annals of Internal Medicine*, Nov. 5, 2019.

231 **rolled out model legislation in June 2021:** "Commentary for Extreme Risk Protection Order Model Legislation," US Department of Justice, June 7, 2021.

231 **an ethical code of conduct and a curriculum:** Author interviews with Palarea, Schouten, and Scalora; and documentation from ATAP.org.

232 **Virginia . . . law allows for but does not require oversight:** "Preventing School Violence Through Threat Assessment," *Ed Note* blog, Aug. 19, 2019; and Code of Virginia, title 22.1, ch. 7, §§22.1–79.4.

234 **"the club no one ever wants to join":** Various survivors have used this phrase in public talks and comments to the media, including Nicole Hockley, whose

six-year-old son, Dylan, was killed at Sandy Hook, and Sandy and Lonnie Phillips, whose daughter, Jessica Redfield Ghawi, was killed in the Aurora theater attack; author interviews with these and other survivors.

234 **At that point, Hockley made a decision:** The account of Hockley's experiences and work are from my interviews with her and a detailed presentation she gave about her work that I attended.

235 **his long pathway to mass murder:** Author interviews with multiple threat assessment leaders. Details about the perpetrator and his background can be found in *Shooting at Sandy Hook Elementary School*, a report from Connecticut's Office of the Child Advocate (Nov. 2014); and "Sandy Hook Elementary School Shooting," a collection of documentation available from the FBI's online Vault.

INDEX